RESPONSES TO RELIGION

Studies in the Social Psychology of Religious Belief

RESPONSES TO RELIGION

Studies in the Social Psychology of Religious Belief

by
Gary M. Maranell

THE UNIVERSITY PRESS OF KANSAS/LAWRENCE, MANHATTAN, WICHITA

Library of Congress Cataloging in Publication Data

Maranell, Gary Michael, 1932-
    Responses to religion.

    Bibliography: p.
    1. United States—Religious life and customs—Statistics. 2. Sociology, Christian—United States. 3. Christianity—Psychology. I. Title.
BR517.M37   200′.973   73-19860
ISBN 0-7006-0114-7

To Roberta

CONTENTS

LIST OF TABLES

LIST OF ILLUSTRATIONS

PART ONE

Responses to Religion: The Measurement of Religious Attitudes

1

INTRODUCTION AND OVERVIEW

What is religion? What are "responses to religion"? And why should behavorial scientists be concerned about either? The first question can be the most difficult if it is felt that we do not share a clear understanding of what is referred to by the concept "religion." I believe that the concept is sufficiently consensual to allow us to accept a somewhat general definition and proceed. I do not mean to suggest by this that there is simply one definition of religion. One could, with remarkably little effort, fill page after page with definitions which would make many gross and/or subtle differentiations. One could extend these pages with conceptual analyses of the nature, meaning, and implications of the different definitions. This is not the goal of this volume, however, so we will leave such work to others.

Any of a number of definitions of religion are acceptable. We can begin by defining it as Hoult did (1958: 9): "Religion is the belief in, and the attempt to relate favorably to (a) values thought to have some transcendental importance, and/or (b) ultimate power or powers thought responsible for all, or some significant aspect of the fundamental order of the universe." We might also begin with a definition provided by Glock and Stark (1965: 4) who synthesize several formulations into: "Religion, or what societies hold to be sacred, comprises an institutionalized system of symbols, beliefs, values, and practices focused on questions of ultimate meaning."

Another congenial definition is provided by Vernon (1962: 55–56): "Religion is that part of culture composed of shared beliefs and practices which not only identify or define the supernatural and the sacred and man's relationship thereto, but which also relate them to the known world in such a way that the group is provided with moral definitions as to what is good (in harmony with or approved by the supernatural) and what is bad (contrary to or out of harmony with the supernatural)." Such definitions are useful to identify the salient components of religion both within a single society and cross culturally.

In the same way that individuals respond differently to various situations and stimuli, they respond differently to religion. People differ in many ways and one of these ways is in the type, nature, and degree of religiousness. The members of a society occupy different roles and positions in social structure, accumulate different socialization experiences, have differing interests and life styles and therefore encounter variously and respond differentially to the sacred or supernatural, the transcendental values, the ultimate powers and the questions of ultimate meaning. The varieties of response produce different clusters and types of religious attitudes. These types of religious attitudes have been conceptualized in different ways by different researchers.

Glock and Stark (1965: 19–21), for example, identify five dimensions of religiosity: the experiential, the ritualistic, the ideological, the intellectual, and the consequential. The experiential dimension involves feelings, sensations, and perceptions that are experienced by an individual and are defined as involving communication with ultimate reality or God. The ideological dimension involves the expectation that a religious person will hold certain beliefs. The ritualistic dimension is concerned with practices expected of religious persons—worship, prayer, etc. The fourth dimension is the intellectual which involves the individual's knowledge of the basic tenets and sources of his faith. The consequential dimension involves the consequences or effects of religious belief, practice, experience, and knowledge on the person.

Putney and Middleton (1961a) described four somewhat different dimensions: (1) religious orthodoxy, (2) religious fanaticism, (3) the importance of religion, and (4) the consciousness of ambivalence concerning religious belief. Various factor analytic studies have also pointed up the importance of an analytic approach to religiosity (Allen and Hites 1961; Hadden 1963). The general analytic approach has seemed to offer an opportunity for increased understanding of the consequences and correlates of religious attitudes.

The present work suggests that the salient dimensions of religious attitudes are attitudes toward the major religious symbols, practices, and institutions. They involve attitudes toward God, the Bible, modes of worship, behaviors toward others, perception of powers in the universe, visionary principles, and religious groups and institutions. Attitudes toward God will be identified as theistic attitudes or theism; attitudes toward the Bible will be called fundamentalistic attitudes or fundamentalism; attitudes toward modes of worship will be labelled ritualistic attitudes and mystical attitudes, depending upon whether they are liturgical, collective, and institutionalized or individual, private, and idiosyncratic; attitudes toward behaviors toward others will be called altruistic attitudes; attitudes toward other powers in the universe will be identified as superstitious attitudes; attitudes toward visionary principles will be known as idealistic attitudes or idealism; and attitudes toward religious groups and institutions will be called church-oriented attitudes.

Given this classification of religious orientations, what are their accompanying characteristics? The research described in this book outlines the nature of these types of religiosities and attempts to document the importance of such world views in the behavior and beliefs of men and to identify some of the consequences and correlates of different types of religious attitudes. In other words, this book and the research it describes attempt to demonstrate among other things why behavorial scientists should be and are concerned with religion and the variety of responses to religion that are presented.

Religious belief and attitude has been measured or ascertained with indices derived from behavior, questions regarding membership and attendance, ad hoc questions of belief, standardized tests such as the Allport-Vernon scale of values, as well as belief and attitude scales of the Thurstone, Likert, and Guttman variety (Leuba 1916, 1950; Thurstone and Chave 1929; Kirkpatrick 1949; Gorer 1955; Liu 1961; Salisbury 1962; Putney and Middleton 1962; Wilson 1960; Brewer 1962; Brown 1962; Obenhaus and Schroeder 1963; and Glock and Stark 1965). These various studies have correlated religiosity with other psychological characteristics and sociological variables.

The present book follows the lead of those who have looked at "religiosity" in an analytic fashion and attempts to describe the differential impact of varieties or dimensions of religiosity, responses to religion, or religious attitudes. The chapters which follow describe the results of a "conceptual analysis" or "conceptual distillation" of religious attitudes and report the development of a set of scales designed to measure the distilled subvarieties of religiosity. This book also reports the results of a series of studies which have employed these scales. A major interest is the identification of the differential effect of the subvarieties of religious attitudes which are overlooked when unitary concepts and measures of religiosity are employed.

The book is divided into two main parts: the first dealing with the concepts and measurements, the second reporting the empirical studies. The second chapter in Part I describes the dimensions into which religiosity is conceptually distilled in this research. Eight dimensions of religiosity emerge: church orientation, ritualism, altruism, fundamentalism, theism, idealism, superstition, and mysticism. This particular chapter presents a detailed definition and description of the eight dimensions as well as an examination of their logical connections. Also included are the scales into which the dimensions have been translated. These scale items were derived from the definitions. The report of an analysis of these items allows for the identification of the most "sensitive" items in each scale as well as a general appraisal of the sensitivity of all the scale items. The mechanics of scoring the scales are also described.

Chapter three is concerned with questions and demonstrations of the validity and reliability of the scales. It reports the results of two independent examinations of test-retest reliability. In regard to validity the relevance of the research reported in Part II of the book is indicated and a validity-supporting anecdote is described. Various types of validity and reliability are also discussed.

The first chapter of Part II (chapter four) reports the results of a survey of the religious attitudes of a sample of clergymen of differing denominations. Clergymen of eleven denominations, in four regions of the nation, are studied. The survey investigates denominational, regional, and age differences in the eight dimensions of religious attitudes.

Chapter five is an investigation of the interrelationships of religiosity and political conservatism. This chapter begins with a conceptual analysis or "distillation" of political conservatism into fifteen separate attitude areas. An attitude scale is devised for each dimension and each scale is item analyzed. The results of the item analysis are included, as is a "known group" validity study of the fifteen scales of political conservatism. The intercorrelations of religiosity and political conservatism are ascertained in eight student populations. One half of the populations are rural; two of the eight are southern university student populations; two are midwestern university student populations; two are Catholic college student populations; and the remaining two populations are Mennonite college students. The pattern of correlation between religiosity and political conservatism is initially ascertained. Following this general analysis, correlation matrices of the eight populations are factor analyzed.

Chapter six presents the results of an investigation of the religious attitudes of college professors. Professors in northern and southern schools, state and denominational schools, larger and smaller schools, as well as professors of differing ranks and disciplines are examined. The layout selected for the analysis is a $3 \times 2 \times 2 \times 2 \times 2$ factorial analysis of variance. This allows us to examine all the influence of the five major variables as well as the various interactions.

Chapter seven presents the results of two surveys of socioeconomic status differences in religious attitudes in two communities. In the first, a small southern city was subjected to a stratification study. A sample from each stratum was drawn and interviews were conducted to further appraise socioeconomic status (with Warner's ISC) and ascertain religious attitudes. The study reports religiosity differences of the various strata as they are defined with the ISC, as well as religiosity differences of strata as they would be defined with the variables of education, dwelling area, occupation, and house type singly. The second study, a survey of a midwestern community, examines denominational, socioeconomic-status, and involvement differences in religious attitudes. By using a few denominations, the impact of involvement and socioeconomic status can be examined independent of denominational differences.

Chapter eight presents the results of three studies using situationally created variables: the first is an investigation of the influence of experimentally induced social derogation and arrogation upon religious attitudes. A population of students was randomly assigned to three groups: experimentally derogated, experimentally arrogated, and a control group. Two and one-half months after the premeasurement, the experimental variables were applied, and the differential impact of arrogation and derogation upon religious attitudes was noted. The second study reported in chapter eight is an investigation of the relationship between religious attitudes and suggestibility. This study involves a situational measurement of suggestibility which ascertains the extent to which individuals have been influenced by suggestions of others in a rather unstructured situation. Those more influenced are then compared with those less influenced in order to discover if they are higher or lower on the various measures of religiosity. The third study is an examination of the relationship between perceptual rigidity and religious attitudes. This study also employs situational measurement—this time of rigidity, which is measured by securing perceptions of changing stimuli presented with a tachistoscopic device. The religious attitudes of those retaining initial perceptions are compared with those perceiving and reporting change in the stimuli presented.

Chapter nine describes a study which investigates the correlation between scholastic aptitude and the dimensions of religiosity in both a midwestern and a southern student population. Scholastic aptitude is measured for this research with the ACE, SCAT, and the Cooperative English Test.

The next study (chapter ten) reports the correlation between personality adjustment and the dimensions of religiosity in both a midwestern and a southern student population. Personality adjustment is measured with some selected MMPI scales, including manifest anxiety, dependency, ego strength, general maladjustment, and social desirability.

The eleventh chapter describes the relationship or correlation between the eight dimensions of religiosity used here and another set of religious attitude scales. This study is also conducted in both a southern and a midwestern student population. The second set of scales were developed by Putney and Middleton (1961a) and include religious fanaticism, religious orthodoxy, and the importance of religion.

Chapter twelve describes the nature of the relationship between the dimensions of religious attitudes and alienation in a midwestern student population. Alienation is measured with Dean's scale of alienation which contains three subvarieties of alienation: powerlessness, normlessness, and social isolation.

Chapter thirteen is the report of a study of sex differences in the various dimensions of religiosity in a midwestern and a southern student population.

Chapter fourteen describes the factor analysis of the eight dimensions of religious attitudes in three populations of adults—a sample of clergymen from eleven denominations, a sample of college and university professors, and the members of two Methodist church congregations. The study reveals the varieties of clustering of belief in these different populations.

Finally, chapter fifteen presents a recapitulation and summary of the findings of the various studies and surveys. The recapitulation is by type of response to religion or attitude area and therefore provides a somewhat different perspective, one that cuts across the particular studies in order to ascertain the general operation of each particular dimension. It allows for the development of brief profiles of each dimension.

2

THE DIMENSIONS AND
THE SCALES

The dimensions of religiosity selected for investigation and the instrument employed for their measurement in the research reported in this book will be described in this chapter. The instrument is designed to measure eight dimensions of religious attitudes or eight types of religiosity: (1) church orientation, (2) ritualism, (3) altruism, (4) fundamentalism, (5) theism, (6) idealism, (7) superstition, and (8) mysticism.

The range of religious attitudes examined with these dimensions is not necessarily exhaustive and does not encompass the total spectrum of religious orientation; however, these dimensions do provide a description of an individual's attitudes toward and responses to most of the crucial aspects, symbols, and practices of religion. The attitudes studied include attitudes toward the church, the Bible, God, other forces in the universe, other people, moral principles, ways of relating to the deity and securing religious knowledge. Explicitly these become:

Theism—attitude toward God
Church orientation—attitude toward the church and its members
Fundamentalism—attitude toward the Bible
Altruism—attitude toward other people
Idealism—attitude toward visionary moral principles
Ritualism—attitude toward formal worship and one set of ways of relating to the deity

Mysticism—attitude toward informal worship, knowledge gained through mystical experience, and another set of ways of relating to the deity

Superstition—attitude toward luck, omens, charms, and other forces in the universe, generally involving a magical world view

These eight dimensions each involve a response on the part of an individual toward the identified aspects of religion.

Other researchers have examined additional and different aspects. Religiosity can thus be conceptualized in an infinite number of readily imaginable and independent ways or can be distilled into a nearly infinite number of variables.

After a discussion of the item analysis procedures used to secure sensitivity scores, the dimensions of religiosity employed in this book will be first defined and then described as clearly and as extensively as possible. Following the definitions will be a presentation of the items designed to measure each of the dimensions. Sensitivity scores will be presented with each item. These are the results of the item analysis. A description of the scoring techniques follows. Finally, the logical relationships between the scales and the varieties of combinations of response to religion will be examined.

The items constituting each scale are presented in this chapter. The final definition of an attitude scale is the content of the items of the scale. Therefore, the extent to which the formal definitions are reflected in the items should be open to immediate inspection. In this way the concept investigated can be clearly understood by all and even possibly redefined by some if necessary. The extent to which the items and definitions correspond is always open to argument. Regardless of what the definitions may imply in any research, the variable being investigated is the content of the scale and this content alone. It is, however, hoped that the correspondence between the definitions and the items or scales presented here will be sufficiently great that the following reports of the research will be useful.

ITEM ANALYSIS

The statements into which the dimensions were translated have been item analyzed in order to reject any insensitive or nondiscriminating items.* The technique used in this item analysis is that suggested and described by Edwards (1957b). The procedure is briefly summarized as follows:

1. A frequency distribution is prepared of the total scores of the subjects on the particular dimension being analyzed.

2. The 25% of the subjects with the highest scores in this total distribution and the 25% of the subjects with the lowest scores in this total distribution of the particular dimension are selected as criterion groups (X_H and X_L) with which to evaluate the individual items or statements of the dimension under analysis.

3. Each item or statement of the dimension in question is then subjected to the following procedure:

A. The mean score of the two criterion groups (X_H and X_L) is secured for the particular item being analyzed. The possible range in score is 0 to 4 (see section on scoring procedure).

B. The variance of each of the criterion groups' distribution of responses for the statement or item is secured (S_H^2 and S_L^2).

C. The number of subjects or judges in each of the criterion groups is noted (n_H and n_L).

D. Then the following computation is performed:

$$t = \frac{\bar{X}_H - \bar{X}_L}{\sqrt{(S_H^2/n_H + S_L^2/n_L)}}$$

The value of t is a measure of the extent to which a given statement has been responded to differently by the two criterion groups. The greater the difference between the mean responses of the two groups, the larger the t value. As a crude and approximate rule of thumb, Edwards (1957b) suggests that we regard any t value which is equal to or greater than 1.75 as indicating that the mean response of the high and low criterion groups to a statement differs significantly, if there are sufficient subjects in the two criterion groups. In our item analysis the criterion groups are sufficiently large to allow us to employ the 1.75 figure. An examination of the t values listed following the items of the various dimensions reveals that all the items are sufficiently sensitive or discriminating. The items of the

---

* Prof. Rex Enoch contributed significantly to the conceptual analysis and the construction and testing of items.

various scales are listed with t values in descending order. This allows for the easy identification of the most sensitive items of each scale. The item analysis reported here was conducted in a relatively homogeneous population of university students.

THE DIMENSIONS AND SCALES

Church Orientation

This dimension concerns an individual's attitudes or orientation toward the church, for example, his involvement in the church, his respect or disrespect for the church, his evaluation of the position of the church in society and community, his feelings of satisfaction or dissatisfaction with the church, his appraisal of the historical position and importance of the church, his estimate of the utility, social and psychological, of affiliation with or favorable orientation toward the church, and so on.

The crucial elements in the concept are: (1) the definitional elements regarding church, and (2) the definitional elements regarding orientation. Looking first at the definitional elements regarding church, we might ask what this word means in the church orientation scale. It is felt that any, or indeed all, of the usual meanings would be appropriate in any particular statement if the statement or scale item made sense or could be understood with that meaning. Meaningful interpretations of the items are thus assumed. Most of the usual understandings of the concept "church" are appropriate; we can see that when the word is used in the scale statement and the statements are examined, the church is viewed as an organization or association of members, a historic institution, the body of believers, or a place of worship involving the association of others. Crucially and primarily it can be seen as the body or organization or association of religious believers. The referent may or may not be divided on a denominational basis. That is, for Catholics the "church" could mean the Catholic church, for Methodists it could mean the Methodist church, or both denominations might use it to refer to the Christian church.

If we examine the definitions of "orientation," we find that this examination further aids us in the identification of this particular dimension. Orientation involves the determination of one's bearings, the choice or adjustment of associations, connections, or dispositions, which in this case we apply to religious bodies or associations, i.e., the church. This, then, is identified as the dimension of church orientation.

The church-oriented individual is devoted to realizing a type of life which conforms to associationally determined ideas. This individual enjoys the mutual support and common purpose which he finds in the church. The church provides him with ways of believing and ease for his conscience if this is necessary. The religious community is one of his important social groups or reference groups or categories. It provides him with patterns to which he can conform. Church association is a useful and valuable affiliation which he feels increases his and others' usefulness. Through the church he can become a part of a larger historical institution. He feels that church affiliation and involvement (orientation) is and should be an important part of social status and positioning. It should and does give prestige and status to the individual and determines the nature and type of one's religious experience.

Church Orientation Items

	Items	t value
*1.	I don't believe church-going will do anyone any harm.	6.65
*2.	I believe in the church and its teachings because I have been accustomed to them since I was a child.	5.41
3.	The church is important as it helps in deciding one's role in the community.	5.03
*4.	I believe that membership in a good church increases one's self-respect.	4.88
5.	The history of the church qualifies it as a lasting institution of which one would want to be a part.	4.88
*6.	I believe that membership in a good church increases one's usefulness to society.	4.88
7.	The church affords an atmosphere favorable to the furthering of the ideals of the good life.	4.83
8.	Church members are especially good people to associate with.	4.72
9.	Church attendance helps me to rid myself of any guilt feelings for not living up to the proposed ideals of the church.	4.00
10.	Church is a good place for one to win social approval.	2.73

11. When one fails to live up to certain ideals of the good life, he finds a way to make restitution for these failures through the church.   2.54
12. Few important members of our society maintain any degree of religious affiliation. (This item is scored backwards to help prevent a response set.)   2.17

* From Thurston and Chave (1929).

Ritualism

Another response to religion focuses upon the ceremony of worship. The various aspects of this dimension include such things as aesthetic sensitivity, liturgical appreciation, and a devotion to prescribed and ritual forms and standards in religious worship.

The person with ritualistic attitudes is impressed with the orderliness, precision, beauty, and the formality of religious ritual. He has a predisposition to be inspired by these active ritualistic aspects, the more ritualistic the better. He enjoys a service in which there is much *formal* congregational participation. He enjoys the appeals made to his eyes and ears by the vestments he prefers the minister and choir to wear and the litanies he feels should be sung. He enjoys, even relishes, the standardization of the religious service.

For the ritualist not the sermon but the service of worship is the important thing. It is the ceremony and not the ideas that he finds awe inspiring. He enjoys the emotional effect, not intellectual instruction, in religion (Boisen 1955: 218).

Ritualism Items	t value

1. The ritual of worship is a very important part of religion.   9.17
2. One of the most important aspects of religion is the religious service itself.   7.71
3. The precision and orderliness with which religious ceremonies are performed is important to me.   7.51
4. The more a religious service is ritualized the more it has meaning for me.   7.23
5. Religion is most real to me during my attendance at public church or religious services.   7.07
6. I think that the placement and treatment of the various articles of worship is very important in a worship service.   7.00

7. When I recall my experiences with religion I most readily remember the impressive formal rites and rituals.   6.74

8. I like to think that people all over are going through nearly the same ritual in their religious worship.   6.67

9. A religious service must be beautiful to be really meaningful to me.   6.02

10. It is important to me that religious service be standardized.   4.96

11. I do not think that the sequence of prayers, songs, etc., is very important in religious services. (This item is scored backwards to help prevent a response set.)   4.76

12. Prayers in religious services are better if they are formalized—as litanies, that is, with responses.   4.73

Altruism (Christian)

Another type of religiousness can be referred to as altruism. This response involves an unselfish concern for the welfare of others, focusing upon the relation to others demanded by religion. This, of course, includes a regard for or a devotion to others and the interests of others, often in accordance with ethical principles. The source of the ethical principles will vary with the individual, and each could have a separate or idiosyncratic source for his own attitude. Altruism does not necessarily imply Christianity or any other particular theological position or indeed theological positions in general. The focus in this case allows only for a centering of attention upon the prevailing religious beliefs of the communities to be studied. This is not necessarily required or desirable, but is only a recognition of the actual dimension measured.

Included in this dimension are ideas of helpfulness, understanding, cooperation, respect for others, justice, sympathy, the brotherhood of man, and a dislike for hypocrisy. All of these elements are subscribed to by the altruist.

Altruism Items   t value

*1. The paternal and benevolent attitude of the church is quite distasteful to me. (This item is scored backwards of help prevent a response set.)   9.76

2. The church is helping me to develop the social attitudes of understanding, sympathy, and cooperation. 8.28
*3. I believe the church is absolutely needed to over-
come the tendency to individualism and selfishness,
for it seeks to practice the golden rule. 8.14
4. We should be concerned with our own private welfare and stop trying to help others by butting into
their private lives. (This item is scored backwards
to help prevent a response set.) 6.44
*5. I am interested in the church because of its work for
moral and social reform in which I desire to share. 5.96
6. Unselfish love is the prerequisite for any real knowledge of religion. 5.23
7. Tender concern for others is a means of finding joy
in one's religion. 5.06
8. Religion causes one to love his enemies. 3.72
9. Brotherly love was the heart of the teaching of Jesus. 3.72
10. "Do-gooders" usually do much more harm than
good. (This item is scored backwards to help prevent a response set.) 3.29
*11. I believe that church is attempting to correlate sci-
ence and religion for the good of humanity. 2.45
12. Our world is in need of a more positive emphasis on
life. 1.93

* From Thurston and Chave (1929).

Fundamentalism

The response to religion identified as fundamentalism is a very
familiar set of beliefs in American society. The concept, as it is employed here, refers to a somewhat restricted definition of fundamentalism, a definition which is, however, generally accepted and which
better isolates the central or core issue in the fundamentalist-modern-
ist debate. Although the more inclusive usage of the concept involves
beliefs beyond that concerning the accuracy of the Bible, these beliefs
derive directly from this central notion. Commonly seen to be a part
of fundamentalism are beliefs in the imminent and physical second
coming of Christ, physical resurrection, substitutionary atonement,
and the virgin birth (*Webster's Third New International Dictionary
of the English Language*). Here belief in the literal acceptance of the
absolute authority of the Scripture is taken as the central indicator

of fundamentalism. This notion of the infallibility and ineffability of the Bible is the core of this dimension (Hoult 1958: 85–88).

The fundamentalist therefore expects, and indeed demands, adherence to a set of what is seen to him to be unchanging dogma, dogma which he feels has been once and for all inscribed in a particular sacred book. This book is viewed, in turn, as the infallible guide for all men, regardless of whatever social and economic changes they may encounter. Fundamentalism strongly opposes teachings which in any way differ from those "inscribed" or "revealed" in the Bible. Thus, for example, a particularly common enemy has been the doctrine of evolution. Science, after all, is also contained in the Good Book, or at least science should not call religion into question.

Fundamentalism, in summary, concerns an insistence upon the literal interpretation of the Bible, which is believed to be everlastingly true.

Fundamentalism Items	t value
1. The Bible is completely and everlastingly true.	12.15
2. The Bible is the Word of God.	12.00
3. The Bible is His message to me as His son or daughter.	11.44
4. The Bible is the book upon which I should try to base my living.	9.53
5. The Bible is too illogical. (This item is scored backwards to help prevent a response set.)	8.50
6. The Bible is an instrument which brings me closer to God.	6.79
7. The Bible is only a group of myths. (This item is scored backwards to help prevent a response set.)	5.89
8. The Bible is one of the best history books ever written.	5.76
9. The Bible should not be taken seriously. (This item is scored backwards to help prevent a response set.)	5.50
10. The Bible contains the teaching given by God to His disciples and other peoples.	5.12
11. Any scholar can see that the Bible just isn't true. (This item is scored backwards to help prevent a response set.)	3.12
12. The Bible is a book in which the moral values of the world in general can be found.	2.84

Theism

The fifth dimension of religiosity is referred to as theism. This attitude area involves principally the belief in the existence of a God or gods. This God is viewed as transcendent, all-powerful, all-knowing, and attentive. The scale or dimension is not concerned with an examination of the great variety of deity ideas which may exist in the mind of any particular believer. Therefore the notions of the exact nature of deity believed in may range from an anthropomorphic father to a more sophisticated "spirit." The dimension is perhaps best expressed as "theism as opposed to atheism."

	Theism Items	t value
1.	God is always watching over us.	10.62
2.	I do not feel that a belief in God is necessary. (This item is scored backwards to help prevent a response set.)	10.19
3.	God is my Father.	9.74
4.	God is a divine spirit guiding my life.	9.67
5.	There is no proof for the existence of God. (This item is scored backwards to help prevent a response set.)	9.57
6.	God is not a certainty. (This item is scored backwards to help prevent a response set.)	7.87
7.	God is hard to visualize as really existing. (This item is scored backwards to help prevent a response set.)	6.92
8.	God is all-powerful and all-knowing.	6.87
9.	God is an all-pervading spirit.	6.79
10.	God's voice keeps me on the straight and narrow path.	6.00
11.	I personally feel that the notion of God is inappropriate in this world of science. (This item is scored backwards to help prevent a response set.)	5.78
12.	God is nothing. (This item is scored backwards to help prevent a response set.)	4.63

Idealism

Another response to religion is idealism. This dimension is not necessarily supernaturally oriented; it recognizes that dedication to upright principle is an aspect of a theistic or a nontheistic religiousness. This dimension does not necessarily require a dedication to Christian beliefs or supernatural deities but simply involves a dedication to visionary ideals and principles. The person who is idealistic, as the term is used here, is a visionary, a person of integrity, of principles. The individual subscribes to a self-imposed rule of right conduct. His behavior is based, he feels, upon a conception of things as they should be or as one would wish them to be. The idealist strives to achieve moral standards of conduct.

The idealist, in addition to subscribing to lofty principles and ideals, feels that such dedication is important for its own sake. He places great value upon the presence of dedication to principle in others as well as himself. The idealist has a clear notion of personal honor and conscience. He feels that men must find the important causes of mankind and serve them. The fact that he is a visionary leads him to be optimistic, to believe in justice, freedom, brotherhood, equality, peace, and honesty among other things. This leads him to be, in short, a man of honor who will right wrongs or feels that such activity is necessary and who will not be willing to accept compromise.

Idealism Items

		t value
*1.	In the end justice will prevail.	5.43
2.	Great causes must be supported.	4.53
3.	Brotherhood, freedom, and equality are workable concepts for man.	4.46
**4.	The best way to handle people is to tell them what they want to hear. (This item is scored backwards to help prevent a response set.)	4.23
5.	Men will never learn to live peacefully with one another. (This item is scored backwards to help prevent a response set.)	4.06
6.	If individuals would act in accord with their consciences, the world would be a lot better off.	3.94
7.	An individual without principles is an individual without honor.	3.90
8.	We must behave as if men were completely honest.	3.56
9.	Identification with a "cause" is an important part of life.	3.35

**10. It is better to compromise with existing evils than to
go out on a limb in attacking them. (This item is
scored backwards to help prevent a response set.)   3.10
**11. When you come right down to it, it's human nature
never to do anything without an eye to one's own
advantage. (This item is scored backwards to help
prevent a response set.)   2.90
12. The people who get ahead in the world are individuals who are willing to compromise with their
principles. (This item is scored backwards to help
prevent a response set.)   2.77

* From Goldman-Eisler (1953).
** From Christie and Geis (1970).

Superstition

The seventh response is superstition. This is a belief or attitude
that is inconsistent with the known laws of science or with what is
generally considered in society to be true and rational. It involves a
fear of the unknown, an aggrandizement of the unknown, and a trust
in magic, charms, and chance. Of particular importance is the irra-
tionally abject attitude of mind toward the unknown, natural and
supernatural. The attitude is also marked by fears, bad-luck notions,
beliefs in enchantments, in charms, and in ghosts. Particular beliefs
involve a sympathetic orientation to and an appreciation of astrology,
divination, clairvoyance and other such phenomena. It involves the
positing of explanations, generally threatening, and a fixity upon the
irrational which is stoutly maintained even in the face of evidence to
the contrary.

Superstition Items	t value

1. One should never step on or walk across a grave.   8.56
2. To be perfectly honest, I am bothered by a black cat
crossing my path.   5.15
3. It is silly to believe that people are born under certain stars or planets which influence their futures.
(This item is scored backwards to help prevent a response set.)   5.05
4. Failure to live up to the laws of God will result in
hard times for an individual.   4.29

5. One should never treat a Bible disrespectfully or tear it.   4.00

*6. Every person should have a deep faith in some supernatural force higher than himself.   3.50

7. It is conceivable that there are spirits and spiritual beings in our world today.   3.00

8. Only fools and extremely gullible individuals believe in extrasensory perception, that is, such things as telepathy and clairvoyance. (This item is scored backwards to help prevent a response set.)   2.77

9. Sickness is a result of present or past sins on the part of an individual or some of his relatives.   2.75

*10. It is entirely possible that this series of wars and conflicts will be ended once and for all by a world-destroying earthquake, flood, or other catastrophe.   2.69

*11. Although many people may scoff, it may yet be shown that astrology can explain a lot of things.   2.42

*12. Sciences like chemistry, physics, and medicine have carried men very far, but there are many important things that can never possibly be understood by the human mind.   1.83

* From Adorno et al. (1950).

Mysticism

The eighth and last response is mysticism. These are attitudes which maintain that it is possible to achieve communion with God and attain knowledge of spiritual truths through contemplation, insight, illumination, and intuition acquired by fixed meditation without the medium of human reason or ordinary sense perception. William James (1902) has suggested that mysticism has four necessary qualities or characteristics: (1) *Ineffability* or inexpressibility—that is, a mystic state is a result of feeling rather than intellect and thus no adequate report of the contents of the feeling can be given in words. The experience cannot be transmitted or imparted to others and can't be discussed intelligently between individuals. (2) *Noetic quality*—that is, mystical states seem to be states of knowledge and that which is acquired in them is experienced knowledge. This involves notions that states of insight are found in a superconscious or transcendent state. (3) *Transiency*—mystical states are generally of very short duration; and when they have faded they can only be imperfectly recalled, but when they recur they are recognized. They are experienced during periods of meditation but a certain amount of knowledge of the experience remains. (4) *Passivity*—that is, the mystic feels as if his will is in abeyance or is subjected to some greater force or grasped and held by a superior power. The mystic views religious experience as involving these general characteristics as well as other more explicit aspects, such as the necessity of silence.

Mysticism Items   *t* value

		t value
1.	The true seeker will eventually reach his goal of union with God.	8.54
2.	The final authority in religion is the inner light or the testimony of the Holy Spirit.	6.36
3.	True religious experience occurs in periods of profound silence.	5.81
4.	Communion with God is a result of the complete loss of one's will (or the subjection of it), giving way to a superior power.	5.30
5.	The visible manifestations of life are a partial manifestation of the spiritual.	5.27
6.	Real worship involves a perfect union between man and God.	5.12
7.	Religion finds its working expression in intellectual speculation and not in prayer. (This item is scored backwards to help prevent a response set.)	3.94
8.	Man must endeavor with the human mind to grasp the divine essence or the ultimate reality of things, and to enjoy the blessedness of actual communion with the highest.	3.62
9.	The mind has a higher state of existence beyond reason and in this super-conscious state, knowledge beyond reasoning comes.	3.33
10.	Meditation is the most important phase of one's religious experience.	2.42
11.	Purely intellectual life does not have a mystical state.	2.41
12.	Our verbal language isn't adequate to express or communicate real religious experience.	2.01

RESPONSE CATEGORIES, SCORING AND ARRANGEMENT

The foregoing items, which make up eight Likert scales, have been arranged in a questionnaire. The arrangement could be either random or systematic; however, a random arrangement has been used in all the research reported in this book. One must recognize that it is possible to begin the resulting questionnaire with items of differential ability in soliciting rapport. For example, an item that is strongly worded and nontheistic could if it occurs first in the series of items damage rapport, whereas after rapport is established the item can be viewed and responded to in a more congenial context. This suggests that certain reasoned deviations from completely random arrangements are sometimes advisable.

The subjects to whom the questionnaire was administered were given the opportunity to respond to the various items by employing any of a given set of response categories provided. They were asked to describe the nature of their agreement or disagreement with each statement or item by checking one of the following response categories which are provided with each statement:

—Strongly Agree,
—Agree,
—Undecided,
—Disagree,
—Strongly Disagree.

In scoring these categories the method suggested by Likert was used (Likert 1932; Edwards 1957b). By attending to the direction of the item content, the appropriate weights were secured. For example, if "agreement" is the fundamentalistic or mystical or idealistic, etc., response, the following scoring is used.

Strongly Agree = 4
Agree = 3
Undecided = 2
Disagree = 1
Strongly Disagree = 0

It is, however, necessary that some items be reversed or stated negatively in order to prevent the development of a "response set" (Robinson et al. 1968:11–14). In these cases "disagreement" is the fundamentalistic or mystical or idealistic, etc., response. In these cases the scoring is reversed, and we employ the following weights.

Strongly Agree = 0
Agree = 1
Undecided = 2
Disagree = 3
Strongly Disagree = 4

All statements or items which use this reversed weighting are noted in the foregoing lists of items. Fewer items have been reversed here than would be desired generally. In the case of the particular content of these scales, it is found that too large a number of reversed items gives the questionnaire a strongly negative tone, which in turn lessens rapport with typical American research populations.

The scoring of each subject on each scale is secured by simply summing the weights of the response categories the subject has selected for each item of the scale. Each dimension or scale contains twelve items; and since the maximum score possible for each item is 4, the maximum score possible for each scale is 48 with a minimum of 0.

In some instances it is advisable to convert the scores obtained in the previously described manner to standard scores in order to put the dimensions on a common scale and also to allow other useful comparisons to be made.

In view of the fact that the research in which this religiosity instrument has been used thus far has been for the most part survey, correlational, and experimental, there has been little or no interest in the development of norms for the various scales. This may be viewed as regrettable by many, but those who are particularly interested in this area of the research will find some means, standard deviations, and standard scores reported in the various studies in Part II of this book as well as in the appendixes.

The form of the questionnaire is also variable. In some cases the response categories have been provided immediately below each statement. In other cases the statements have been presented in a booklet with a standardized response sheet provided. The employment of a response sheet allows for the use of coding templates which greatly simplify the scoring procedures.

LOGICAL RELATIONSHIPS BETWEEN DIMENSIONS AND VARIETIES OF RESPONSE

The eight dimensions stand, in American society at least, in a logical relationship to each other. If we begin to examine the possible combinations of these religious-attitude dimensions, we find a large, rich, and complex structure. By identifying an individual with a high score on each scale as: (1) church oriented, (2) ritualistic, (3) altruistic, (4) fundamentalist, (5) theist, (6) idealistic, (7) superstitious, and (8) mystic, we can then examine both the pure and the mixed types of response to religion.

The eight dimensions of attitude each identify a pure variety in isolation when an individual has only one high score. These pure types can be identified by the eight labels listed above. In practice, however, we would not expect to find a fundamentalist who is not also a theist, although we may well find a theist who is not a fundamentalist. To be a fundamentalist demands a belief in God, which creates a high theistic attitude score. Furthermore, we would expect to find that most mystics are theists as well; but we might find theists who are not mystics. Finally, we would expect that superstitious individuals are also theist but that not all theists are superstitious. Therefore we must recognize that the eight varieties of responses are not fully independent of each other.

In addition to the eight pure or single types, there are twenty-eight logically possible combinations of two characteristics; for example, church-oriented–idealist, ritualistic–theist, fundamentalist–theist, church-oriented–ritualist, etc. However, certain types would not be expected to occur; for example, a fundamentalist–idealist would also be a theist and thus would not exist as a pure diad or two-characteristic variety. The superstitious–fundamentalist would also be theist and thus would not occur as a diad.

There are fifty-six possible triadic combinations (persons having three high religious-attitude scores), such as ritualistic–fundamentalist–theist, etc. And there are seventy combinations of four high religious-attitude scores. There are also fifty-six combinations with five high scores. These can be seen as simply the reverse of the fifty-six combinations with three high scores. Finally there are twenty-eight combinations with two low scores (or alternatively six high scores); and eight types with one low score (alternatively seven high

TABLE 2-1. VARIETIES OF RESPONSES TO RELIGION, PURE AND MIXED TYPES

	NON-THEIST								THEIST							
	NON-FUNDAMENTALIST				**FUNDAMENTALIST**				**NON-FUNDAMENTALIST**				**FUNDAMENTALIST**			
	Non-mystical		Mystical		Non-mystical		Mystical		Non-mystical		Mystical		Non-mystical		Mystical	
	Non-ritualist	Ritualist	Non-ritualist	Ritualist	Non-ritualist	Ritualist	Non-ritualist	Ritualist	Non-ritualist	Ritualist	Non-ritualist	Ritualist	Non-ritualist	Ritualist	Non-ritualist	Ritualist
Non-superstitious																
Non-church oriented																
Non-altruist																
Non-idealist	None	R	M	RM	F	RF	*FM*	*RFM*	T	RT	TM	RTM	FT	RFT	*FTM*	*RFTM*
Idealist	I	RI	IM	RIM	FI	RFI	*FIM*	*RFIM*	TI	RTI	TIM	RTIM	FTI	RFTI	*FTIM*	*RFTIM*
Altruist																
Non-idealist	A	RA	AM	RAM	AF	RAF	*AFM*	*RAFM*	AT	RAT	ATM	RATM	AFT	RAFT	*AFTM*	*RAFTM*
Idealist	AI	RAI	AIM	RAIM	AFI	RAFI	*AFIM*	*RAFIM*	ATI	RATI	ATIM	RATIM	AFTI	RAFTI	*AFTIM*	*RAFTIM*
Church oriented																
Non-altruist																
Non-idealist	C	CR	CM	CRM	CF	CRF	*CFM*	*CRFM*	CT	CRT	CTM	CRTM	CFT	CRFT	*CFTM*	*CRFTM*
Idealist	CI	CRI	CIM	CRIM	CFI	CRFI	*CFIM*	*CRFIM*	CTI	CRTI	CTIM	CRTIM	CFTI	CRFTI	*CFTIM*	*CRFTIM*
Altruist																
Non-idealist	CA	CRA	CAM	CRAM	CAF	CRAF	*CAFM*	*CRAFM*	CAT	CRAT	CATM	CRATM	CAFT	CRAFT	*CAFTM*	*CRAFTM*
Idealist	CAI	CRAI	CAIM	CRAIM	CAFI	CRAFI	*CAFIM*	*CRAFIM*	CATI	CRATI	CATIM	CRATIM	CAFTI	CRAFTI	*CAFTIM*	*CRAFTIM*
Superstitious																
Non-church oriented																
Non-altruist																
Non-idealist	S	RS	SM	RSM	FS	RFS	*FSM*	*RFSM*	TS	RTS	TSM	RTSM	FTS	RFTS	*FTSM*	*RFTSM*
Idealist	IS	RIS	ISM	RISM	FIS	RFIS	*FISM*	*RFISM*	TIS	RTIS	TISM	RTISM	FTIS	RFTIS	*FTISM*	*RFTISM*
Altruist																
Non-idealist	AS	RAS	ASM	RASM	AFS	RAFS	*AFSM*	*RAFSM*	ATS	RATS	ATSM	RATSM	AFTS	RAFTS	*AFTSM*	*RAFTSM*
Idealist	AIS	RAIS	AISM	RAISM	AFIS	RAFIS	*AFISM*	*RAFISM*	ATIS	RATIS	ATISM	RATISM	AFTIS	RAFTIS	*AFTISM*	*RAFTISM*
Church-oriented																
Non-altruist																
Non-idealist	CS	CRS	CSM	CRSM	CFS	CRFS	*CFSM*	*CRFSM*	CTS	CRTS	CTSM	CRTSM	CFTS	CRFTS	*CFTSM*	*CRFTSM*
Idealist	CIS	CRIS	CISM	CRISM	CFIS	CRFIS	*CFISM*	*CRFISM*	CTIS	CRTIS	CTISM	CRTISM	CFTIS	CRFTIS	*CFTISM*	*CRFTISM*
Altruist																
Non-idealist	CAS	CRAS	CASM	CRASM	CAFS	CRAFS	*CAFSM*	*CRAFSM*	CATS	CRATS	CATSM	CRATSM	CAFTS	CRAFTS	*CAFTSM*	*CRAFTSM*
Idealist	CAIS	CRAIS	CAISM	CRAISM	CAFIS	CRAFIS	*CAFISM*	*CRAFISM*	CATIS	CRATIS	CATISM	CRATISM	CAFTIS	CRAFTIS	*CAFTISM*	All

NOTE: Italicized combinations are not expected to occur.

scores); as well as the two polar varieties, one with no high scores and one with no low scores. The combinations and frequencies are

no scores high—eight scores low   1
one score high—seven scores low   8
two scores high—six scores low   28
three scores high—five scores low 56
four scores high—four scores low 70
five scores high—three scores low 56
six scores high—two scores low   28
seven scores high—one score low   8
eight scores high—no scores low   1

The various combinations can be found in table 2-1. In this classification table the letters indicate which scores are high. The letters identify the eight dimensions: C is church-orientation, R is ritualism, A is altruism, F is fundamentalism, T is theism, I is idealism, S is superstition, and M is mysticism. Therefore RT is a ritualistic–theist, and CI is a church-oriented–idealist, and I is a pure idealist. The cells that contain letters which are italicized are combinations that we do not logically expect to find, e.g. F, a fundamentalist who is not theistic. The cell labelled "none" designates individuals who are low on all scales or dimensions—where nothing is high; and the cell labelled "all" designates those high on all eight dimensions.

The table is carried through combinations of four. The five high-three low, six high-two low, and seven high-one low combinations have been left blank. However the table is symmetrical, and the cell immediately above the "all" cell is that containing the seven high and only idealism low combination, which is the obverse of the cell below the "none" cell which contains the pure, single characteristic, idealistic type. The cell to the left of the "all" cell contains the combination which has seven high scores with ritualism alone low, and this balances the cell to the right of the "none" cell which is the variety which has a single high score, in this case ritualism.

Table 2-1 is designed to illustrate the complexity and variety of types of response to religion. The research which follows does not employ the full range of this complex variety but rather examines group differences in the eight basic scales and the correlations of these basic variables with other sociological and psychological variables.

3
VALIDITY AND RELIABILITY

Following the development of the aforementioned scales of religiosity, our attention must necessarily turn to a consideration of the reliability and validity of the eight scales.

RELIABILITY

There are various types of relationships referred to collectively as reliability. They include such factors as "temporal stability," "homogeneity of items," "scorer reliability," and "adequacy of item sampling" (Anastasi 1954; Selltiz et al. 1959; Cronbach 1960; Robinson et al. 1968). These can be reduced for our purposes to "problems of stability," "problems of scoring," and "problems of items."

Problems of Stability

This problem area concerns the consistency of scores or measurements in repeated applications through time. The smaller the observed degree of change, the greater the stability of the measurements. Changes in scores are often attributed to change in subject instead of instability. This is certainly a possible explanation in some instances; however, when one is attempting to examine the stability of measures, one simply cannot attribute all observed change in score to change in subjects instead of instability of measures. Similarly, one cannot judge the degree to which either of these factors has operated;

in view of this it is perhaps best not to attempt to "explain" any of a measure's lack of stability by conjuring images of subject change.

Problems of stability are best investigated through test-retest methods. In view of this, a group of students was administered the religiosity scales and after a week had passed was rechecked on the same scales. Recall, attempts to remain unchanged, attempts to appear different, etc., all no doubt had their effects. However, in view of the fact that the questionnaire contained ninety-six similar items, anything beyond a limited recall would be quite difficult to accomplish. The test-retest coefficients of correlation of this first examination can be found in table 3-1 below. In general the coefficients are respectably high, averaging .87.

TABLE 3-1. TEST-RETEST RELIABILITY FOR THE EIGHT RELIGIOSITY SCALES,
FIRST EXAMINATION
(df = 66)

Scales	Correlation Coefficients
Church orientation	+.945
Ritualism	+.89
Altruism	+.88
Fundamentalism	+.90
Theism	+.99
Idealism	+.68
Superstition	+.83
Mysticism	+.81
Total religiosity score	+.92
Mean correlation coefficient	+.87

Some months following the first test of stability, a second was conducted. The investigation this time employed a different and somewhat larger population of students and a slightly longer time lapse—one and one-half weeks. These test-retest coefficients of correlations can be found in table 3-2 below.

It is interesting to note the great similarity between these two stability checks, particularly the fact that in both cases the mean correlation coefficient of all eight scales was .87 (if rounded). Also the theism scale was the most stable in both checks. Thus there is some evidence that the scales are relatively stable. (See the comparison provided in table 3-3.)

We thus observe a high consistency of relative stability or a consistent ordering of the relative stability of certain kinds of religious

TABLE 3-2. TEST-RETEST RELIABILITY FOR THE EIGHT RELIGIOSITY SCALES,
SECOND EXAMINATION
(df = 84)

Scales	Correlation Coefficients
Church orientation	+.87
Ritualism	+.87
Altruism	+.855
Fundamentalism	+.94
Theism	+.95
Idealism	+.82
Superstition	+.86
Mysticism	+.79
Total religiosity score	+.96
Mean correlation coefficient	+.869

TABLE 3-3. RANKINGS OF ORDERED STABILITY OF THE EIGHT SCALES IN TWO STABILITY
EXAMINATIONS
(From greatest to least stability)

	First Examination	Second Examination
Theism	1	1
Church orientation	2	3
Fundamentalism	3	2
Ritualism	4	4
Altruism	5	6
Superstition	6	5
Mysticism	7	8
Idealism	8	7

attitudes. The Spearman rank correlation between these two orderings is +.89 which is significant at the .01 level.

Problems of Homogeneity of Items

Frequently in cases where test-retest studies cannot be made, a
split-half test is substituted, although the information secured in a
split-half test is not the same as that secured in a test-retest. There
are situations in which the type of information secured from the split-
half study is more appropriate than the test-retest; but it is more
relevant to problems of homogeneity of item. In this research this
type of information has been provided through the item analysis
reported in the previous chapter. Therefore, only a test-retest study
was used to examine stability.

Problems of Scoring

In view of the nature of the scales and the fact that they were for the most part scored with standardized templates, scoring was not seen to be a serious problem.

VALIDITY

In one sense this entire book is a demonstration of the validity of the scales—at least a demonstration of a particular type of validity. However, we might pause to examine a variety of forms of validity.

Content Validity

Content validity concerns the extent to which the content area being tested is covered by the test items. In this area we can best demonstrate content validity by ascertaining if in each case the items of the scales are concerned with the dimensions as they are defined. An examination of the relationship between the defined dimensions and the items in the scales will demonstrate the extent to which this particular variety of validity is present in the scales.

But perhaps more crucially we might suggest, to cite an example, that the person who agrees with statements which maintain or even insist that the Bible is completely and everlastingly true and who disagrees with items that question the truth and value of the Bible is a fundamentalist as this has been defined. If this person is not what has been defined as a fundamentalist, who is? The person who agrees with items that question the value of the Bible and who disagrees with those items that value the Bible is a nonfundamentalist or is "low" on fundamentalism.

The person who agrees with items favorable to the church and who disagrees with those items unfavorable to the church is church-oriented. In addition, the person who subscribes to statements reinstating ideals and who disagrees with nonidealistic statements is idealistic. And further the person who subscribes to statements supporting the existence of mystical experience and reflecting the experiencing of such states is a mystic. And is not his crucial difference from those who derogate and deny such experience this very mysticism?

In view of these and all the other obvious examples suggested regarding the various dimensions of religiosity, I respectfully submit that the previously described scales have that which has been referred to as "content validity."

Face Validity

This type of validity concerns itself with the question of whether the test looks as if it measures what it is supposed to measure. The researcher suggests that the relevancy of the items to the dimensions of religiosity is sufficiently great to suggest that the scales possess face validity. It is, however, possible for an otherwise valid test to lack face validity, but for the most part it is a desirable aspect of a test.

Construct Validity

The research in this book can be seen as a demonstration of the construct validity of the scales, for all, or nearly all, of the investigations demonstrate that the measures or scales behave in such a way as to suggest a close relationship to the construct from which they were derived. We might also note the utility of the constructs to account for the total empirical performances which follow in the remainder of this book.

Known-Group Validity

This type of validity is demonstrated in the first study reported, which examines denominational differences in religious attitudes. The discovery of such differences as, for example, that Catholic and Episcopal groups score highest on the ritualism dimension reinforces our confidence in the validity of these scales. We would be much less confident in the validity of the scales if, for example, Baptists scored higher than Catholics on a ritualism scale. Other instances of known-group validity can be found in the first study, and, of course, elsewhere in the book.

Some social scientists would prefer a series of anecdotes to the previous discussion. They would find a discussion of personal experiences and insights gained from such experiences more satisfying than demonstrations and discussions. For these individuals, and for others who might be interested, I would like to describe a particularly enlightening series of related experiences which I believe bear on the question of validity. The following situations encountered by the researcher might be seen as constituting a general, and perhaps less impressive, demonstration of validity.

Early in the research program described in this book, I administered questionnaires to students in various denominational groups on a university campus. The research was primarily concerned with the investigation of student denominational differences in religious attitudes (Maranell 1962). After the data were gathered and analyzed, the researcher was asked to "return the favor" by the cooperating student groups and was called upon to report to one denominational group after another on the nature of the research and the findings of the study they had participated in. All the groups that made this request turned the "report" into a regular program for their group.

The first group I was called upon to speak to was the Unitarian-Universalist student group. The evening was what you would expect; the students were intellectually interested in the research and probed well regarding methods, presuppositions, etc. But crucially their response to my descriptions of the various denominations was just what I expected, for they were very pleased to have scored as low as they had on fundamentalism, mysticism, theism, church orientation, etc., and they were frankly amused at the high scores received by the Methodist, Baptist, Episcopal, Catholic, etc., students. At some points they even broke into bursts of laughter. Yet I knew this group very well and was not at all surprised or irritated by their behavior.

The second group I visited regarding the research was the Methodist student group. I was a little less certain of their response since I was less familiar with the particular group. Because of my uncertainty, I treated the presentation much more cautiously or tentatively. At one point in the presentation I was describing to them how they had scored on fundamentalism; and I was attempting, as I saw it, to "put the findings tactfully," explaining or actually apologizing somewhat to them for their somewhat high scores on this dimension. They seemed to become puzzled. When I perceived that they were puzzled by my approach and by my apologetic attitude, I became more apologetic and attempted to make myself more clear. They appeared to become even more confused. Finally and thankfully, an explanation in the form of an alternative perception occurred to me. I realized that they didn't know why I was apologizing or what I was apologizing about. Seeing this, I then altered my approach and described "bluntly" how they had scored in comparison to the other groups. I was amazed to discover that they were pleased. They were similarly pleased to discover how they had scored on each of the other scales also. They laughed often, loud and long at the scores of the

Lutheran, Baptist, and Catholic students, and most of all at the scores of the Unitarian-Universalist students. I was shocked.

At this point I came to realize that persons are no doubt somewhat disinclined to lie or falsify their responses to religiously oriented statements. This would also apply to other attitude or belief areas about which people feel strongly. This is the case because they are not in any way ashamed of their beliefs, especially of their religious beliefs. In view of this, falsification would seem to them to be a serious business. Who would disagree with statements supporting the existence of God when he actually believes devoutly in God; and who would agree with statements challenging the validity of the Bible if he feels it is literally true? To falsify or misrepresent one's position about such things is serious indeed. Also, what agnostic would agree with highly devout statements in view of his serious commitment to an antithetical position?

Following this delayed discovery, the subsequent speaking engagements served as small, informal, unscientific but very successfully predicted personal "experiments." I discovered, for example, that the Episcopal students laughed at the Catholic, Methodist, and Unitarian-Universalist students as they had, in turn, been laughed at by these groups.

Each group visited, without exception, was highly satisfied with their own scores and found differing scores and scores of differing groups laughable and even unbelievable. They seemed to respect only those groups whose scores were very similar to their own. Their pride in their own scores and their contempt for the scores of others was truly astonishing.

I realize that "for example is not proof" but this series of experiences was too impressive for me to ignore or to overlook at this point. The insight I gained from them was most valuable even if it was perhaps somewhat belated.

PART TWO

Responses to Religion: Studies of Religious Attitudes

4

CLERGYMAN SURVEY

This chapter reports the results of a mail question-naire survey of the religious attitudes of metro-politan clergymen. The religious attitudes are measured with the scales described in the foregoing part of this book. An examination of the denominational, regional, and age differences in clergymen's religious attitudes is, of course, a basic way in which the utility of the scales can be demonstrated. It can also serve as a preliminary demonstration of the validity of the instrument. That is, if denominational differences are not identified with the scales, the utility and validity of the scales must be seen as somewhat limited. In spite of this, however, it is possible that sig-nificant religious attitude differences are not related to denomination, region, and age differences of clergymen. It is also possible that clergymen are too homogeneous a group for religious attitude differ-ences to occur—they may all simply be highly religious in all ways possible.

The general hypotheses of this survey are that (1) there are sig-nificant differences in the religious attitudes of metropolitan clergy-men of various denominations; (2) there are significant differences in the religious attitudes of metropolitan clergymen in various regions of the nation; (3) there are significant differences in the religious attitudes of metropolitan clergymen of various ages.

The population sampled in this study is made up of clergymen serving churches in standard metropolitan areas in four different regions of this country. Standard metropolitan areas are used because it is recognized that rural-urban differences in religious attitude might well be significant. Realizing this, the survey was limited to examining denominational differences in either rural or urban areas. This restriction was made necessary by the projected size of this study. It was decided to examine attitude differences only in urban areas. This decision was based upon many considerations, including the fact that rural areas presented greater problems of comparability and of varying numbers of available respondents. Certain denominations, Unitarian-Universalist and Episcopalian for example, have very few clergymen in rural areas. Since only urban clergymen were to be studied, it was felt that the use of standard metropolitan areas provided for some comparability of urban populations. Recognizing that rural-urban differences are obviously very important, the researcher simply excluded them from consideration in this particular survey. The region differences which will be examined might well be greater in rural than in urban areas, for we can quite easily imagine that regional differences of clergymen's attitudes in standard metropolitan areas will be less great than the regional differences of clergymen's attitudes in rural areas. In view of this we could very well be examining our regional hypothesis in the least promising sector of the rural-urban continuum.

THE VARIABLES

Religiosity

The religious attitudes are measured by the scales previously described. These scales measure eight dimensions of religious attitudes: (1) church orientation, (2) ritualism, (3) altruism, (4) fundamentalism, (5) theism, (6) idealism, (7) superstition, and (8) mysticism. In this particular survey a summary score was also used; however, the meaning of such a summary measure is unclear, and its major use will be to order the denominations in terms of "general religiousness." It will not be used in subsequent research.

Region

A task similar to that of deciding between rural and urban areas was involved in the selection of the appropriate regions for investigation. Once again the major problem was one of meaningfully limiting the universe to be surveyed. An examination of the literature regarding regions and regionalism suggested some solutions. Regionalists have identified certain areas which can be used as starting points in the selection of the regions for analysis.

In view of the limited nature of this study, it was felt that restrictions were needed. Thus "relatively homogeneous" regions were required. This dictated the exclusion of certain states whose regional nature was in some doubt (i.e., border states, etc.). Thus the necessary limitations coupled with the desire for more clearly homogeneous regions led to the selection of four different regions to be studied in this survey.

The included or sampled regions are:

(1) The New England states (Maine, New Hampshire, Vermont, Massachusetts, Connecticut, Rhode Island);

(2) The southern states (Virginia, North Carolina, South Carolina, Georgia, Florida, Alabama, Mississippi, Tennessee, Kentucky, Arkansas, Louisiana, and Texas);

(3) The midwestern states (Iowa, Minnesota, Wisconsin, Nebraska, North Dakota, South Dakota, and the upper part of Illinois);

(4) The Pacific Coast states (California, Oregon, and Washington).

The degree of homogeneity of these regions is relative and varies considerably; however, given the necessity of selecting regions, it was felt that the foregoing qualified as somewhat "homogeneous regions."

The size of the regions was determined by two considerations: the number of clergymen available in the standard metropolitan areas and the need to restrict the region to as small and homogeneous an area as possible. The first of these led to larger areas, the second to smaller. The final regional decisions involve attention to both factors.

In view of these considerations Texas was added to the southern state region in order to add more clergymen to the sampling frame, and this in turn allowed for the study of additional denominations. This addition was made even though the state of Texas may best be described as a southwestern rather than a southern state. In many ways Texas shares a great number of characteristic southern state factors, such as its political climate (recall that V. O. Key, Jr., included it in *Southern Politics*), its racial picture, or even its apparent attitude to crime and violence (Key 1949). Oklahoma, on the other hand, was not included because it had many non-southern characteristics and also appeared to be more of a border state. In general, questionable states were excluded rather than included. In this same manner, northern Illinois was added to the midwestern region. The whole of Illinois was not included in this category because of the obvious border or even southern aspects of the downstate region. However, what metropolitan area is more midwestern than Chicago or the other northern Illinois areas? The states of Michigan, Indiana, and Ohio were excluded because their regional orientation may be more "eastern midwestern" (whatever that means) than central midwestern. Missouri and Kansas were excluded in view of their "marginal" border-state natures. The Pacific Coast area is certainly less than homogeneous; however, it was felt that the region provided a contrast with the other regions involved in the study and in turn should be distinguished from the mountain states. However, even the state of California has extreme regional variation within its borders.

The general importance of the regional variable may be somewhat questionable, although previous research has suggested great regional variation in the effect and nature of certain aspects of religiosity (Maranell 1968). This regional influence may be diminished by the selection and use of a metropolitan sample.

Denomination

Eleven denominations were chosen for investigation in this study on the basis of their distribution in the regions sampled, their accessibility or the registration of clergymen (do they publish a directory from which one can draw a sample?), and their use of clergymen (obviously a church like the Church of Christ, Scientist, which has no clergymen, could not be included in a clergyman survey). Thus the denominations sampled in this study are those with both sufficient national distributions and adequate clergyman registration for sampling on a national level.

The eleven denominations included in the survey are (1) Catholic, (2) Episcopal, (3) Lutheran (Missouri Synod), (4) Presbyterian (both the southern and the northern branch), (5) Methodist, (6)

Seventh-Day Adventist, (7) Baptist (both the southern and northern groups), (8) Church of Christ, (9) Disciples of Christ, (10) United Church of Christ (this body is the result of a merger of the Congregational-Christian Church and the Evangelical and Reformed Church), and (11) Unitarian-Universalist.

The Missouri Synod Lutheran Church was selected over the other available Lutheran churches because it has a more general national distribution than the others—it is difficult to find other Lutheran synods in the South, for example—and because it is also the Lutheran church with the greatest number of clergymen (*World Almanac* 1971).

The Presbyterian denomination includes both the Presbyterian Church in the U.S. and the United Presbyterian Church in the U.S.A. Similarly the Baptist denomination is made up of the Southern Baptist Convention and a Northern Baptist Convention. The other denominations have national distributions sufficiently large to permit regional sampling, with the exception of the Disciples of Christ and the Church of Christ, which were used in this survey despite exceedingly small numbers of registered clergymen in the metropolitan areas of the New England states. The cooperativeness of both of these denominations more than compensated for the smaller samples.

Age

Distribution of the age variable obviously could not be determined until the returned questionnaires were examined, since clergyman age is not included in denominational directories. Therefore a separate analysis of this variable was necessary, since it could not be added to the denomination-by-region analysis without seriously reducing cell size, sometimes to zero. Consequently a separate age-by-denomination analysis was undertaken which reveals age differences in religious attitudes and allows for the examination of age-by-denomination interactions. The trichotomy of the age variable was accomplished by inspection after the questionnaires were returned and was undertaken in such a way as to divide the population into as nearly equal age groups as possible—simultaneously observing as meaningful a division of age as possible. The resulting division is as follows:

(1) Ages up to and including 38   N = 168
(2) Ages 39 to and including 49   N = 164
(3) Ages 50 and over   N = 173

SAMPLING

The clergymen were drawn into a stratified random sample on the basis of denomination and region in the following manner.

First, a sampling frame of clergymen serving in the standard metropolitan areas of each region was prepared from the denominational directories. Second, a random sample of twenty-five clergymen from each denomination in each region was selected from this list, or sampling frame, and a mail questionnaire was sent to each.

After the first nine denominations were selected, it was discovered that this had exhausted the number of denominations with a sufficient number of clergymen in each region's standard metropolitan areas for sampling. Two additional denominations were selected which had nearly adequate regional distributions; these were the Disciples of Christ and the Church of Christ. A sample of twelve or thirteen (randomly determined) clergymen from each denomination in the standard metropolitan areas of each region was selected. Happily, both of these denominations were sufficiently cooperative, i.e. had high enough rates of return, to be included in the analysis. The total analyzed sample was 543. Table 4-1 gives the rates of questionnaire return for each region and denomination.

TABLE 4-1. PERCENTAGE OF CLERGYMEN PARTICIPATING
(By denomination and region)

	New England	South	Midwest	Pacific Coast	Total
Catholic	.18	.36	.40	.25	.285
United Church of Christ	.42	.56	.63	.44	.51
Presbyterian	.60	.48	.56	.52	.54
Episcopal	.48	.54	.64	.56	.55
Seventh-Day Adventist	.56	.52	.52	.64	.56
Methodist	.68	.36	.57	.68	.57
Lutheran (Missouri synod)	.68	.56	.40	.64	.57
Unitarian-Universalist	.56	.60	.52	.64	.58
Baptist	.40	.68	.75	.62	.61
Church of Christ	.60	.67	.50	.77	.64
Disciples of Christ	.91	.85	.67	.91	.83
Total	.52	.54	.56	.58	.55

NOTE: In view of the need to round the percentage of each subsample, the total percentage cooperating in each denomination or region may not equal the mean of the columns or rows of percentages.

This general rate of return should be considered to be quite good when one considers the usual rates of mail questionnaire returns coupled with the fact that this questionnaire was quite lengthy, containing ninety-six attitude statements. Some interesting systematic rates of cooperation can be noted in table 4-1.

These sampling procedures provided us with roughly comparable numbers of clergymen in each cell—region, age, and denomination—and corrected for the different sizes of the denominations in the various areas as well as in the nation as a whole. The resulting stratified random sample thus allowed for examination of the differences in religious attitudes by denomination, region, and age, and necessarily ignored other differences, such as the fact that there are nearly as many Unitarian-Universalist clergymen in Massachusetts as in the rest of the nation combined or that the Lutheran population is largely concentrated in the midwestern region or that both the Church of Christ and the Disciples of Christ are concentrated largely in the southern states. Such data as these are readily available in religious censuses and other sources (Rosten 1955; Gaustad 1962; *World Almanac* 1971).

It seems that clergymen prefer to answer questionnaires of a more concrete nature and would prefer not to respond to attitude scale items. I am led to this perception by the thirty or thirty-five somewhat assaultive letters I received. These letters objected to the investigation of anything as sacred and important as religious beliefs with a procedure as unfamiliar to the respondents as a structured attitude questionnaire. They did not like nor did they approve of a questionnaire which asked them to agree or disagree with statements about religion, God, the Bible, the church, etc., and which did not allow them to tell what they believe regarding such things as the virgin birth and baptism.

RESULTS

The general hypotheses can be examined in two series of analyses of variance. Two separate analyses are necessary since the simultaneous examination of all three factors—denomination, region, and age—reduces the cell size significantly. The analysis of variance summary tables are presented in Appendix A. The various F ratios and significance levels will be presented as each scale of religious attitude is examined. It is recognized that the use of two analyses creates a certain redundancy which, however, is necessary in order to identify the significant interactions of the two sets of variables; and the examination of the three-level interactions will, of course, not be possible since the analysis is divided into two 2 × 2 analyses of variances. The three general hypotheses will be examined simultaneously.

In this survey there will be nine tests of each hypothesis, one involving each of the eight scaled dimensions of religiosity and one involving the total religiosity score, which is a sum of all of the scale scores. The analysis demands the use of a correction for the disproportionality of the data. The differences in total N observed in the two analyses are due to the fact that several of the clergymen did not answer the age question; they are, of course, omitted from the age-by-denomination analysis.

In the description of the differences between the means, we will present a chart diagramming the means of all the cells only where we find significant interactions. For example, if we observe a significant age-by-denomination interaction, we will chart and examine the means of all the cells. Where there are no significant interaction effects, we will present only charts or graphs of the significant main effects.

Total Religiosity

We will first turn our attention to a consideration of the three general hypotheses in regard to the total religiosity score. Table A-1 in Appendix A summarizes the results of the analysis of this variable. The analysis reveals that there are significant differences in the total religiosity scores between denominations ($F = 43.605$, $P < .01$), and between the three age groups ($F = 21.609$, $P < .01$). Since there are no significant interactions we will not concern ourselves with the cell means but will rather examine only the main effects.

Figure 4-1 describes the denomination differences in total religiosity which were found to be statistically significant. An examination of this chart shows that the total religiosity scores are highest for the Catholics, followed closely by the Seventh-Day Adventists, Methodists, Baptists, Church of Christ, Lutherans, United Church of Christ, Episcopalians, Disciples of Christ, and Presbyterians. We

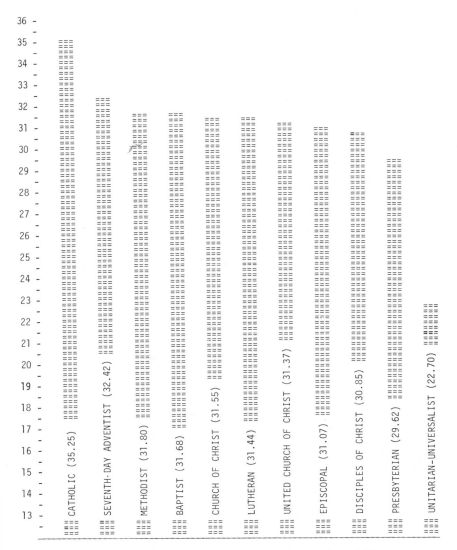

Figure 4-1. Denomination scores on the total religiosity variable

note also that Unitarian-Universalist clergymen are inclined to score
much lower than the other denominations. We should keep in mind
that this total religiosity score is being used only as a device to order
the denominations initially. Observing this regular progression of
denominations in regard to the total (or mean) religiosity score, subsequent deviations of denominations from this initial denominational

order will be more apparent, for we shall maintain it in subsequent charts so that when the means vacillate greatly their deviation from the initial order can be easily noted.

In addition to the statistically significant denominational differences we observed in the preceding chart, the analysis reveals that the clergymen differed significantly in total religiosity score in regard to age (table A-1, Appendix A). The means of the three age groups were:

Ages up to and including 38   29.34
Ages 39 to and including 49   31.03
Ages 50 and over   31.72

Thus we observe that total religiosity increases regularly and significantly with age of clergymen. Again we should keep this regular age progression in mind in order to contrast subsequent findings with it if necessary.

Church Orientation

The analysis of church orientation, which is reported in table A-2, Appendix A, reveals that clergymen of the various denominations differ significantly in their orientation to church ($F = 7.249$, $P < .01$). The analysis also discloses the fact that clergymen of the various regions of the country sampled are also significantly different in church orientation ($F = 3.675$, $P < .05$) and that clergymen of various age categories are significantly different in this dimension of religiosity ($F = 21.979$, $P < .01$).

Figure 4-2 describes the mean scores of the various denominations on this dimension. The denomination with the highest scale score is the Methodist, followed closely by the Catholic and Disciples of Christ. The Unitarian-Universalist clergymen have the lowest church-orientation scores with the Presbyterian second lowest.

The initial analysis also reveals significant regional differences in church-orientation attitudes. The mean scores of the various regions are:

Southern region   31.23
Pacific Coast region   29.98
New England region   29.41
Midwestern region   29.34

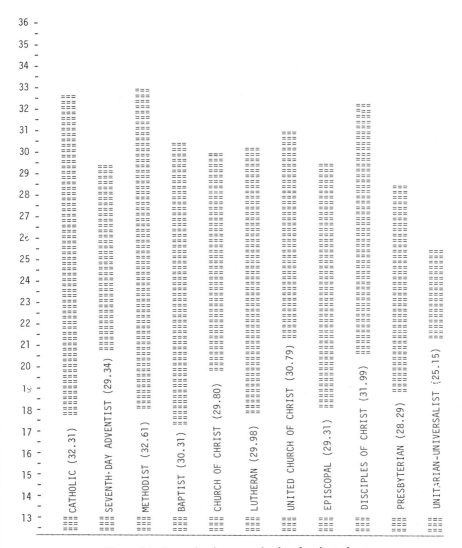

Figure 4-2. Denomination scores in church orientation

Thus we find that the southern clergymen are more church oriented than others. New England clergymen and midwestern clergymen are least church oriented and are not greatly different.

The analysis of variance also indicates that there are statistically significant age differences in clergymen's church-orientation attitudes. This difference takes the following form:

Ages up to and including 38   27.60
Ages 39 to and including 49   30.39
Ages 50 and over   31.50

The significant age differences reveal a pattern in which church orientation increases with age; that is, the older clergymen are more inclined to be church oriented.

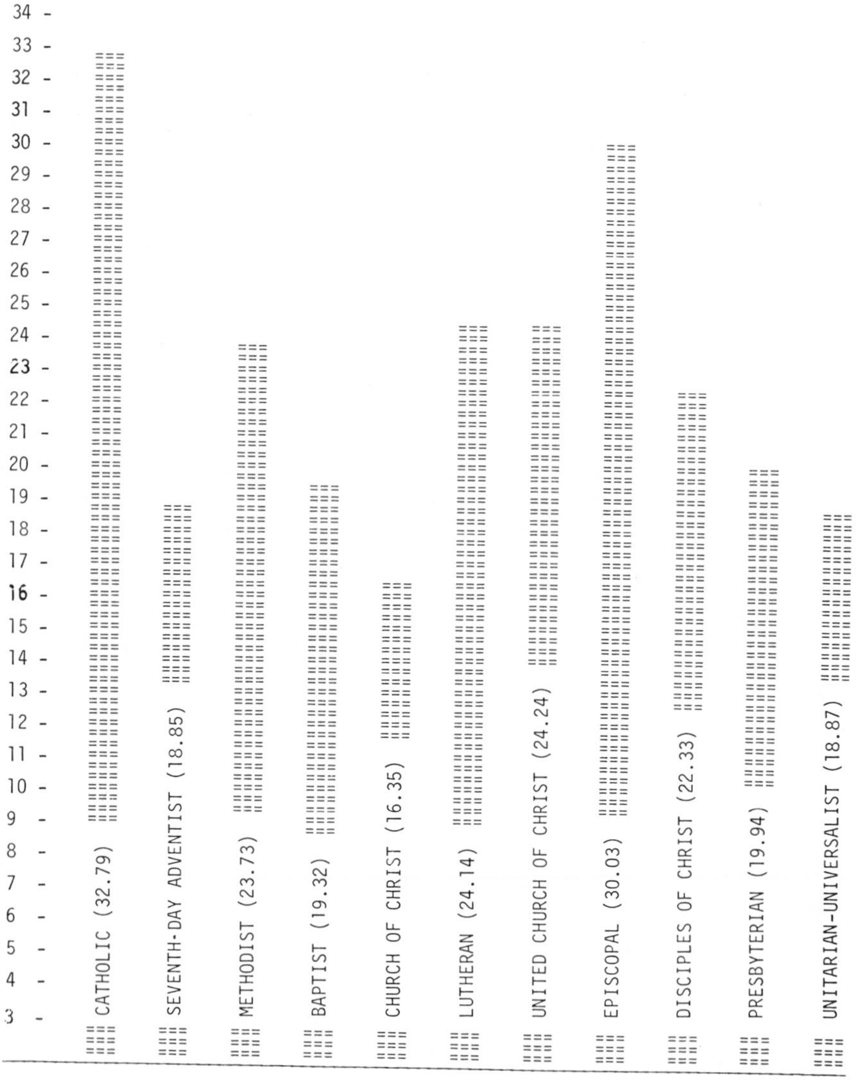

34 -
33 -
32 -
31 -
30 -
29 -
28 -
27 -
26 -
25 -
24 -
23 -
22 -
21 -
20 -
19 -
18 -
17 -
16 -
15 -
14 -
13 -
12 -
11 -
10 -
9 -
8 -
7 -
6 -
5 -
4 -
3 -

CATHOLIC (32.79) SEVENTH-DAY ADVENTIST (18.85) METHODIST (23.73) BAPTIST (19.32) CHURCH OF CHRIST (16.35) LUTHERAN (24.14) UNITED CHURCH OF CHRIST (24.24) EPISCOPAL (30.03) DISCIPLES OF CHRIST (22.33) PRESBYTERIAN (19.94) UNITARIAN-UNIVERSALIST (18.87)

Figure 4-3. Denomination scores in ritualism

Ritualism

The analysis of ritualism, which is reported in table A-3, Appendix A, reveals that there are no significant region or age differences in this dimension but that a highly significant denomination difference does exist (F = 30.148, P < .01). An examination of figure 4-3 reveals that the most highly ritualistic denominations are the Catholic and Episcopal. This is, of course, no startling disclosure; but it does reinforce our confidence in the ritualistic scale. The other denominations above the total group mean on ritualism are the United Church of Christ, Lutheran, and Methodist. Below the total group mean, we find the more antiritualistic denominations, such as Baptist, Disciples of Christ, Seventh-Day Adventist, and Church of Christ. We also find that Unitarian-Universalist and Presbyterian clergymen score low on this dimension, but that the typically low Unitarian-Universalists are not the lowest denomination on this dimension. This might be seen to reflect a slight liturgical aspect in metropolitan Unitarian-Universalist churches.

Altruism

The analysis of altruism (table A-4, Appendix A) reveals that we have statistically significant denominational differences (F = 8.823, P < .01), statistically significant age differences (F = 25.348, P < .01) as well as a statistically significant age-by-denomination interaction (F = 2.033, P < .01). An examination of figure 4-4 discloses that, in regard to denomination differences, the Lutheran and Episcopal are the least altruistic denominations. The exclusiveness and nationality orientation of the Lutheran denomination is easily recognized as relevant, as is the class position of the Episcopal church. The class analysis seems to follow, for we see that the Presbyterians and Unitarian-Universalists, both upper-class oriented churches, are also rather low in this dimension. With the possible exception of the United Church of Christ, most of those denominations scoring high in this dimension come from the lower parts of the class structure; see, for example, the scores of the Catholics, Seventh-Day Adventists, Church of Christ, Methodists, and Baptists.

The analysis indicated that the clergyman age category was relevant, for there were statistically significant age differences in al-

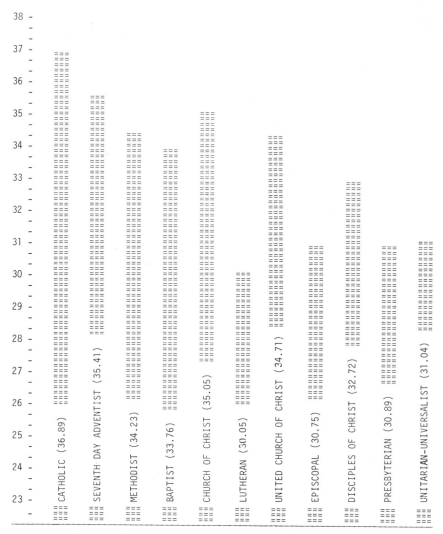

Figure 4-4. Denomination scores in altruism

truism. In regard to age, we observe the following arrangement of means:

Ages up to and including 38   31.04
Ages 39 to and including 49   33.17
Ages 50 and over   34.93

Thus we find that the older clergymen are more altruistic than the middle-aged clergymen, who are in turn significantly more altruistic than the younger clergymen.

We note also that there is a statistically significant age-by-denomination interaction in regard to altruism. This interaction is diagrammed in figure 4-5. An examination of this chart reveals some interesting phenomena. In spite of the general increase in altruism with age, we note two reversals, middle-aged Seventh-Day Adventist and Baptist clergymen are less altruistic than youthful clergymen of these denominations. We might note also the relatively great differences between youthful and middle-aged Catholic, United Church of Christ, Lutheran, and Presbyterian clergymen compared with smaller differences between middle-aged and older clergymen of these denominations. There are, in general, greater differences between the youthful and the middle-aged than between the middle-aged and the older clergymen.

Fundamentalism

The results of our analysis of fundamentalism (table A-5, Appendix A) indicate that there are statistically significant differences in the fundamentalistic attitudes of clergymen of different denominations (F = 131.475, P < .01), regions (F = 2.737, P < .05), and ages (F = 7.174, P < .01). There is also a statistically significant region-by-denomination interaction (F = 1.606, P < .05). By examining denominational differences in figure 4-6, we note that clergymen of the Seventh-Day Adventist, Lutheran, Catholic, Church of Christ, and Baptist denominations score high on this dimension and that Presbyterian, Disciples of Christ, Episcopalian, Methodist and United Church of Christ clergymen score medially, and that Unitarian-Universalist clergymen score very low. We can recognize that this variable has divided the conservative-orthodox denominations from the liberal-orthodox to a fairly great extent and has completely isolated the very liberal Unitarian-Universalists.

Our analysis also has revealed statistically significant region differences in regard to fundamentalistic attitudes. The nature of this difference can be discovered by inspecting the following regional mean scores:

Southern region   38.89
Pacific Coast region   38.21

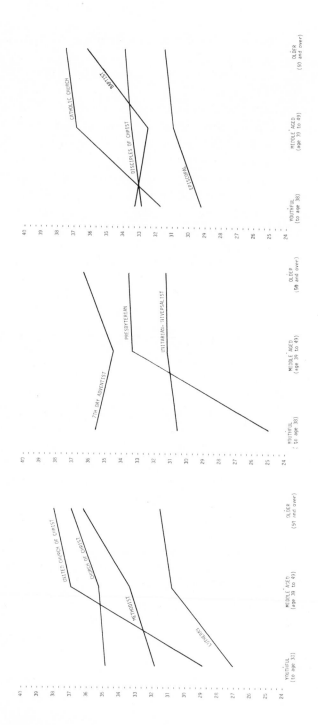

Figure 4-5. Age differences in the altruism scores of clergymen by denomination

<pre>   New England region   38.14
            Midwestern region   37.21
</pre>

The southern scores are the highest on fundamentalism, and this
certainly corresponds with expectations regarding the South. And
once again we find the midwestern region to be the most liberal in
religiosity.

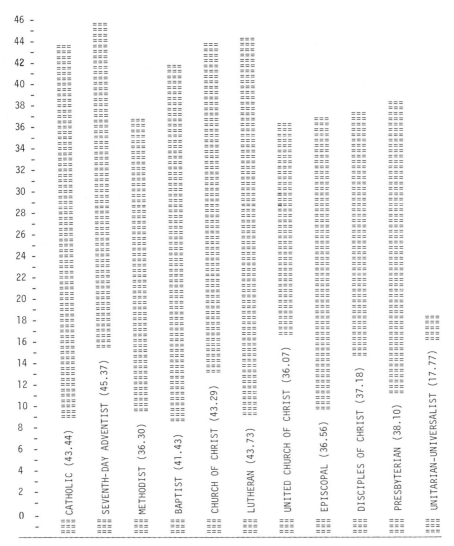

Figure 4-6. Denomination scores in fundamentalism

The analysis of variance also indicated that statistically significant age differences exist in the clergymen's fundamentalistic attitudes. The nature of this difference is described in the following means:

Ages up to and including 38   36.77
Ages 39 to and including 49   38.17
Ages 50 and over   38.13

Thus we discover that the crucial difference is between the youthful, on one hand, and the middle-aged and older clergymen on the other, with the youthful being less fundamentalistic than older clergymen.

In regard to the region-by-denomination interaction in this analysis, we find a number of interesting facts by examining figure 4-7. We can note at once the markedly high fundamentalism score among the eastern Unitarian-Universalist clergymen in comparison to those in the other sampled regions. Also of note is the higher fundamentalism scores of Methodist and United Church of Christ clergymen in the South. Thus we find that the commonly suspected New England orthodoxy within Unitarian-Universalism is confirmed, as well as the general effect of the fundamentalistic South upon the less fundamentalistic Methodist church and the United Church of Christ.

Theism

In the analysis of theism (table A-6, Appendix A), we note statistically significant differences in denomination ($F = 137.233$, $P < .01$), region ($F = 5.110$, $P < .01$), and age ($F = 7.453$, $P < .01$), as well as a statistically significant region-by-denomination interaction ($F = 1.896$, $P < .01$).

The theism scores of the various denominations can be compared by using figure 4-8. In this figure we are immediately struck by the low theism score of the Unitarian-Universalist clergymen. Beyond this we once again observe an orthodox-conservative and an orthodox-liberal division in the denominations with the Catholic, Seventh-Day Adventist, Lutheran, Church of Christ, and Baptist clergymen scoring quite high or conservatively and the Methodist, Episcopal, Presbyterian, Disciples of Christ, and United Church of Christ clergymen scoring less high or more liberally.

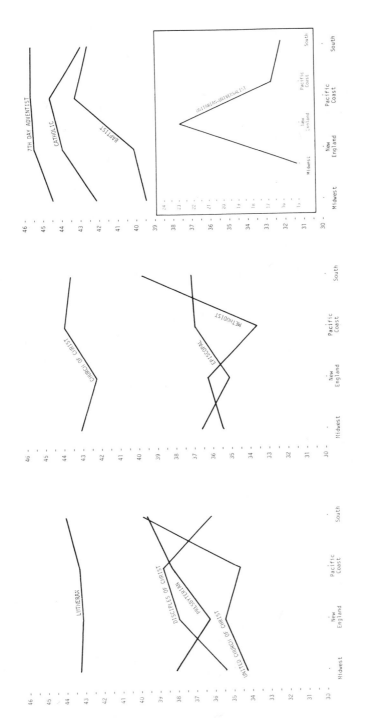

Figure 4-7. Regional differences in fundamentalism scores of clergymen

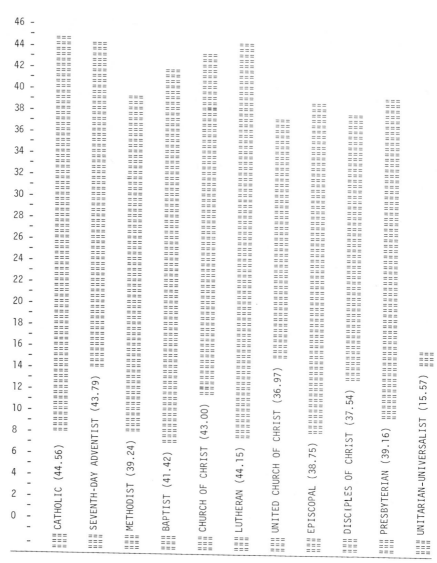

Figure 4-8. Denomination scores in theism

In regard to region we find the following arrangement of means:

Southern region	39.36
New England region	39.21
Pacific Coast region	38.60
Midwestern region	36.99

Once again we find the midwestern clergymen are significantly more liberal in religiosity, this time theism.

An examination of the statistically significant age differences in theism reveals the following arrangement:

Ages up to and including 38   37.04
Ages 39 to and including 49   38.57
Ages 50 and over   38.80

As we have observed before, we again find that religiosity, this time theism, increases regularly with age.

An examination of the interaction (figure 4-9) reveals once again a much higher religiosity score, in theism, among New England Unitarian-Universalist clergymen than is found among Unitarian-Universalist clergymen elsewhere in the regions sampled. Another factor to note is the high theism scores found among the Pacific Coast Disciples of Christ clergymen, which are higher than those found within the denomination in the southern region, an area that is generally considered to be much more religious.

Idealism

The analysis of idealism reveals statistically significant differences between denominations $(F = 7.697, P < .01)$ and age categories $(F = 11.037, P < .01)$ in our samples of metropolitan clergymen (table A-7, Appendix A). First, in regard to denominational differences, we find by examining figure 4-10 that the denominations high in idealism are the Catholic, Methodist, Church of Christ, United Church of Christ, and Disciples of Christ. We should note that Unitarian-Universalist clergymen score above the total group mean on this scale. This is the only time they are above the mean; since it is on this scale, it tends to reinforce the idealistic, high principled, and yet unorthodox nature of this denomination. We find Lutheran, Presbyterian, Episcopalian, and Seventh-Day Adventist clergymen low on this dimension. A combination of cultural ethnocentrism and favored class position may enter into this placement.

An examination of the age differences in idealism reveals:

Ages up to and including 38   32.74
Ages 39 to and including 49   34.29
Ages 50 and over   34.93

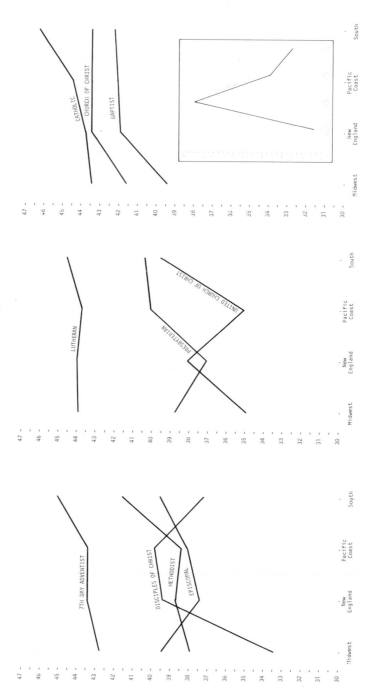

Figure 4-9. Regional differences in the theism scores of clergymen

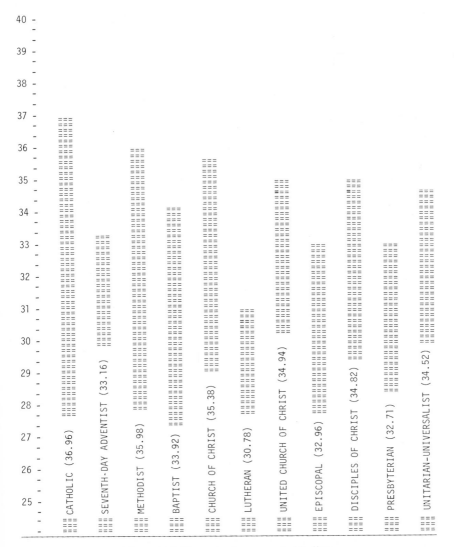

Figure 4-10. Denomination scores in idealism

We discover that idealism increases with age. We might well have expected the more youthful clergymen to be the most idealistic and the older clergymen a bit more cynical. This is not the case, however; and it raises some interesting issues for speculation. Is there no disenchantment in the clergy, or does it occur so soon or so early that the younger clergymen are closer to it and consequently more cynical and less idealistic? Perhaps, on the other hand, the resignation of the older clergyman has as an important aspect an idealistic rationalization. It is also possible that highly idealistic young clergymen tend to drop out of the ministry.

Superstition

For the dimension of superstition, the analysis of variance disclosed two areas of statistically significant difference (table A-8, Appendix A). One of these is the denominational difference (F = 16.251, P < .01), and the second is the age category difference (F = 4.052, P < .05).

When we examine the diagrams of denominational means in figure 4-11, we find that Catholic and Baptist as well as Seventh-Day Adventist clergymen have the highest superstition scores. We recognize that these are the less empirically articulated denominations. The least superstitious denomination is the Unitarian-Universalist, which has as one of its most important goals the complete acceptance of science and scientific orientations to life.

In regard to age and superstition we find the following means:

Ages up to and including 38   20.92
Ages 39 to and including 49   21.11
Ages 50 and over   22.17

Once again we observe that a religiosity variable, this time superstition, is related to age and is greatest among the older clergymen.

Mysticism

The final dimension of religiosity that has been examined is mysticism. The analysis of variance (table A-9, Appendix A) indicates that there are statistically significant mysticism score differences between denominations (F = 10.041, P < .01), and between age categories (F = 6.008, P < .01), and that there is a statistically significant region-by-denomination interaction (F = 1.759, P < .01). The denominational differences can be interpreted with figure 4-12. We find that the most mystical denominations are the Methodist, United Church of Christ, Catholic, and Seventh-Day Adventist; and the least mystical denominations are the Unitarian-Universalist, the Lutheran, and the Presbyterian.

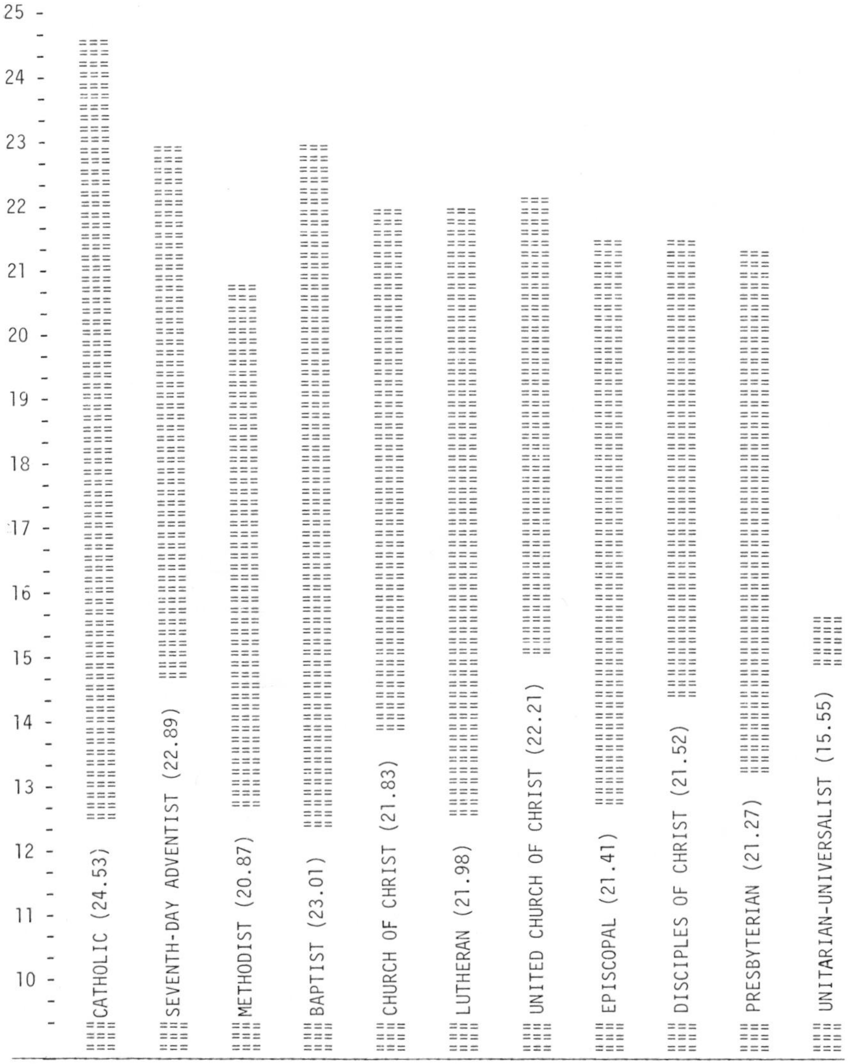
25
24
23
22
21
20
19
18
17
16
15
14
13
12
11
10
CATHOLIC (24.53)
SEVENTH-DAY ADVENTIST (22.89)
METHODIST (20.87)
BAPTIST (23.01)
CHURCH OF CHRIST (21.83)
LUTHERAN (21.98)
UNITED CHURCH OF CHRIST (22.21)
EPISCOPAL (21.41)
DISCIPLES OF CHRIST (21.52)
PRESBYTERIAN (21.27)
UNITARIAN-UNIVERSALIST (15.55)

Figure 4-11. Denomination scores in superstition

An examination of the age differences in mysticism scores leads to the following arrangement:

Ages up to and including 38	27.15
Ages 39 to and including 49	28.57
Ages 50 and over	29.31

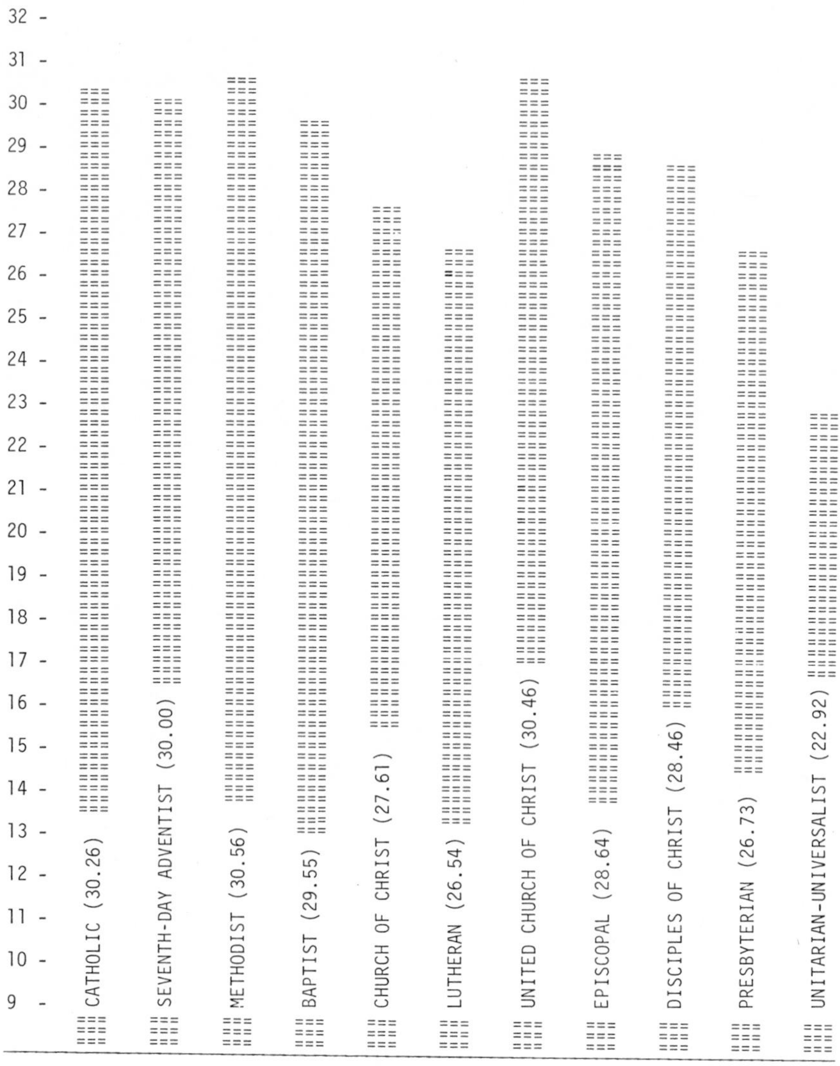

32 -
31 -
30 -
29 -
28 -
27 -
26 -
25 -
24 -
23 -
22 -
21 -
20 -
19 -
18 -
17 -
16 -
15 -
14 -
13 -
12 -
11 -
10 -
9 -

CATHOLIC (30.26)
SEVENTH-DAY ADVENTIST (30.00)
METHODIST (30.56)
BAPTIST (29.55)
CHURCH OF CHRIST (27.61)
LUTHERAN (26.54)
UNITED CHURCH OF CHRIST (30.46)
EPISCOPAL (28.64)
DISCIPLES OF CHRIST (28.46)
PRESBYTERIAN (26.73)
UNITARIAN-UNIVERSALIST (22.92)

Figure 4-12. Denomination scores in mysticism

We find that the final dimension of religiosity also is higher in the older age groups. Older clergymen are most mystical; the middle aged are, in turn, more mystical than the youthful clergymen.

The nature of the statistically significant interaction can be appraised with figure 4-13. An examination of this chart reveals that again New England Unitarian-Universalists are more religious, in

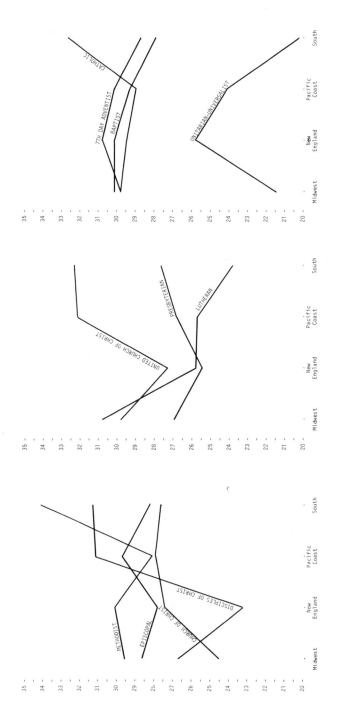

Figure 4-13. Regional differences in the mysticism scores of clergymen

particular more mystical, than those in the three other sampled regions. We can note also the interesting drop in mysticism among Lutheran clergymen in the southern region. Other variations are also apparent; for example, southern Catholics and Methodists score higher on mysticism than Catholics and Methodists in other parts of the nation, while Baptists and Seventh-Day Adventists are less mystical in the southern region.

A CLUSTER-ORIENTATED ANALYSIS OF THE DENOMINATIONS

The presence of highly significant denominational differences in each of the dimensions of religious attitudes suggests that a comparative examination of denominations in terms of all eight religious attitude variables might be fruitful. In view of this we can prepare denominational profiles of religiosity. Recognizing that the various scales are not standardized scores suggests that the profiles would be more easily compared if the obtained scores were converted to standard or z scores.* This is easily accomplished by finding the mean of the scores on each dimension, subtracting this mean from each denomination's score, and dividing this difference by the standard deviation of the scores on the particular dimension. When the z scores of each denomination on each of the eight dimensions are diagrammed, we have a denominational profile.

These denominational profiles are directly comparable since they are all in standard scores expressed as standard units above and below the mean. When these eleven denominational profiles are compared, we find that they can be clustered into subsets of highly similar profiles. This, in turn, indicates certain denominational similarities in religious attitude. The presence of these subsets also can facilitate the presentation of the profiles, since they can be diagrammed together in clusters of similar denominations.

The denominations are found to divide roughly into three fairly clear clusters. In addition to these three clusters, we find three denominations which are somewhat unique. The first cluster can be found diagrammed in figure 4-14. This cluster is made up of clergy-

---

* Standard scores have the advantage of having a mean equal to zero and a standard deviation of one.

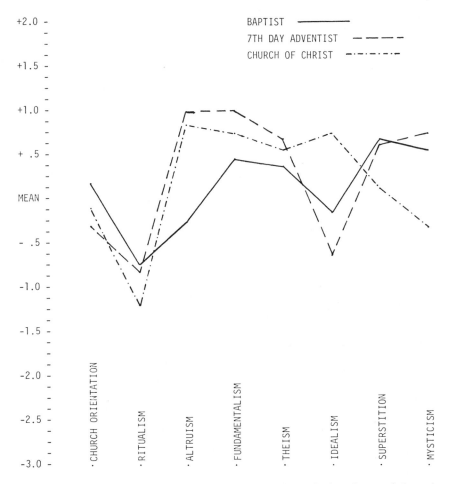

+2.0 —

+1.5 —

+1.0 —

+ .5 —

MEAN —

- .5 —

-1.0 —

-1.5 —

-2.0 —

-2.5 —

-3.0 —

BAPTIST ————————

7TH DAY ADVENTIST — — — —

CHURCH OF CHRIST —··—··—··—

·CHURCH ORIENTATION ·RITUALISM ·ALTRUISM ·FUNDAMENTALISM ·THEISM ·IDEALISM ·SUPERSTITION ·MYSTICISM

Figure 4-14. The lower-socioeconomic-status conservative-orthodox cluster of denominations

men of three denominations: Seventh-Day Adventist, Church of Christ, and Baptist. These three denominations certainly do not have identical attitude profiles; however, examination reveals that on all but three dimensions they are roughly comparable, and in the case of these deviate dimensions two of the denominations are in each case very similar. An examination of the deviations is also revealing, for one of them involves the altruism dimension and we find Baptist clergymen less altruistic than their other two cluster mates. The second deviation involves the idealism dimension, and we find the

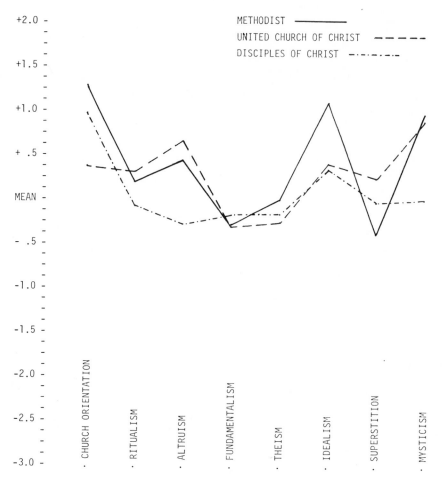

Figure 4-15. The middle-class liberal-orthodox cluster of denominations

Church of Christ more idealistic than its cluster mates. The third deviation occurs in the mysticism dimension, and here we find the Church of Christ to be less mystical than the other denominations of the cluster.

This particular cluster of denominations can be recognized as a "conservative-orthodox" cluster of Protestant denominations. We should also note that these three denominations have been found in the past to attract persons of lower socioeconomic status (Hoult 1958; Yinger 1957; Demerath 1965). Thus perhaps we should make this class element explicit in the cluster's label and refer to this total grouping of denominations as a "lower-socioeconomic-class conservative-orthodox" cluster.

The cluster is described by above average scores in fundamentalism, theism, superstition, and a strong inclination to be above average in altruism and mysticism as well. The cluster is found to be below average or below the mean in ritualism and idealism. These two variables are joined by church orientation, which is below the mean for two of the three groups. We would expect higher church-orientation scores in middle-class denominations.

The second cluster includes the Methodist, United Church of Christ, and the Disciples of Christ denominations (figure 4-15). This cluster is found to be above average in church orientation, idealism, and mysticism in all three cases and below the mean in fundamentalism. The cluster is inclined to be below the mean in theism, very close to the mean in superstition, and above the mean in altruism and ritualism. Although this cluster is not greatly different from the first cluster, it is nonetheless perceptibly different. Where we found the first cluster to be fundamentalistic, this one is not; whereas the first cluster is not idealistic, this cluster is. This cluster is also more church oriented.

The consensually perceived similarity of the denominations in this cluster combine to aid in the interpretation of the cluster. The scores of the three denominations included in this cluster are closely grouped on all of the dimensions.

When we turn our hand toward the identification of this cluster we must take two elements suggested by the previous analysis into account. The first of these is socioeconomic position, and the other is the appraisal of the liberalness of the religious position to the cluster which is provided by the data. In the case of this second cluster we find that the religious positions are slightly more liberal than those of the first cluster; they are, however, clearly orthodox. Certain differences, such as the differences in church orientation, ritualism, idealism, and superstition, tend to reflect identification with different aspects of religious experience. The members of the denominations involved in this cluster are also typically from a slightly higher socioeconomic position than those of the previous cluster. They tend to be more middle class, whereas members of denominations in the first cluster were generally found to be lower class (Hoult 1958). In view

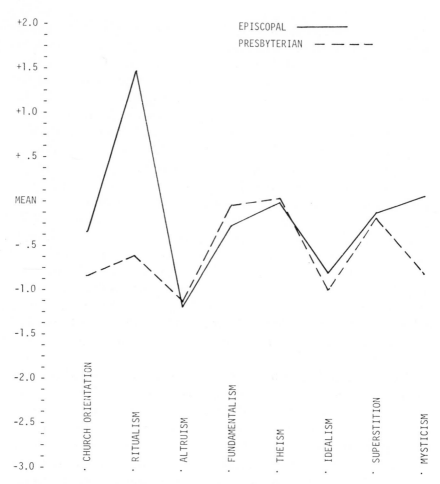

Figure 4-16. The upper-middle-class liberal-orthodox cluster of denominations

of these two aspects, we may identify this second cluster as a "middle-class liberal-orthodox" cluster of denominations.

In the third cluster, two denominations show a striking similarity on all but one dimension (figure 4-16). The dimension in which the crucial difference occurs tends to isolate a major distinction that can apparently be drawn between the two denominations in view of the great similarity of the denominations in all the other dimensions of religiosity. The Presbyterian and Episcopalian religious attitude profiles are almost identical except for the ritualism dimension on which Presbyterians score below average and Episcopalians score well above average. This exception shows a crucial ritualistic proclivity among Episcopal clergymen which differentiates the two otherwise nearly identical denominations.

The denominations in this cluster are commonly identified as upper class (Hoult 1958; Yinger 1957; Vernon 1962) and are generally more liberal than the middle-class liberal-orthodox cluster, with the exception of the fundamentalism and theism dimensions and the very high Episcopal ritualism score. In view of this, perhaps we can identify this cluster of two denominations as the "upper-middle-class liberal-orthodox" cluster. And we might note again the startling similarity of the two upper-class Protestant denominations.

In addition to these three clusters of denominations, we find three denominations that do not fit into any of the previous clusters and do not in any way resemble each other (figure 4-17). These three denominations are the Catholic, Lutheran, and Unitarian-Universalist. First, in regard to the Catholics, we find that the Catholic clergymen score well above the total mean on each dimension. These typically high scores suggest a concept for further research which is borrowed from the area of social class, the concept of "crystallization," which in this case becomes attitude crystallization. Crystallization refers to the extent to which there is agreement among the various aspects of the concept or dimensions of religiosity in this case. If such a concept were to be used by employing, for example, the standard deviation or range of normalized scores, we would find Catholics to be highly crystallized in religious attitude. Other denominations would also score high on the crystallization dimension; and others, such as the Unitarian-Universalists and Lutherans would be found to be somewhat lower in crystallization.

In passing we should note that any measure of religious attitude upon which Catholic clergymen did not score high should be carefully reexamined. The high Catholic scores, especially in ritualism, are validity reinforcing.

The second of the unique denominational profiles is that of the Lutherans. The clergymen of this denomination score high on only two dimensions, fundamentalism and theism. They score especially low on the altruism and idealism dimensions. The profile of this denomination tends to reinforce the notion of subcultural nationalism, or even ethnocentric exclusiveness in this denomination.

The last of the unique denominations is the Unitarian-Univer-

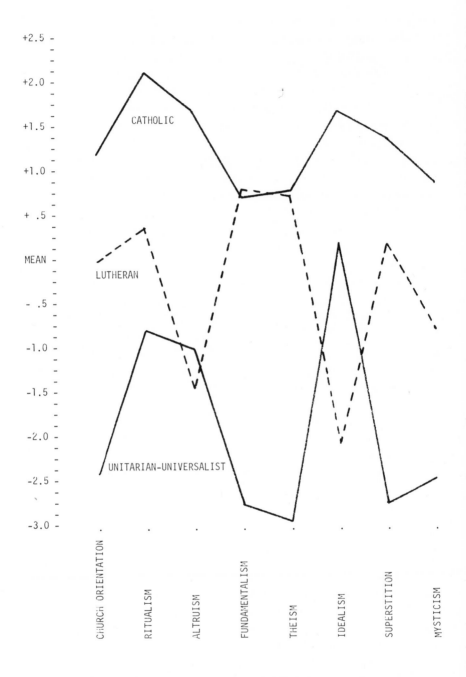

Figure 4-17. The denominations not found in the main clusters

Responses to Religion

salists. This denomination is found to score low on everything, but it scores even lower than usual on the more typically Christian dimensions of church orientation, fundamentalism, theism, superstition, and mysticism and higher on the "good-will" dimensions of idealism and altruism. The Unitarian-Universalists also scored slightly higher on the liturgically oriented ritualism dimension, which involves an appreciation of beauty in ritual ceremony.

In summary we have examined the religious attitudes of a sample of metropolitan clergymen of eleven denominations in four regions of the country. We have attempted to identify denomination, region, and age differences in the religious attitudes of these clergymen. Scores were obtained on eight dimensions of religious attitudes from this sample of 543 clergymen from the sampled regions.

Analysis revealed the existence of the significant differences described in table 4-2. In addition there was a statistically significant

TABLE 4-2. SUMMARY OF DENOMINATION, REGION, AND AGE DIFFERENCES IN THE RELIGIOUS ATTITUDES OF CLERGYMEN
(Probabilities of result being due to chance listed)

	Denomination	Region	Age
Total religiosity	.01	NS*	.01
Church orientation	.01	.05	.01
Ritualism	.01	NS	NS
Altruism	.01	NS	.01
Fundamentalism	.01	.05	.01
Theism	.01	.01	.01
Idealism	.01	NS	.01
Superstition	.01	NS	.05
Mysticism	.01	NS	.01

* NS = not significant

age-by-denomination interaction in regard to altruism and a statistically significant region-by-denomination interaction in fundamentalism, theism, and mysticism.

The denominational differences reveal relatively complex variations in the religious attitudes of clergymen of the various denominations which are best summarized in the charts following each analysis. In general, however, the liberalism of the Unitarian-Universalists is underscored, as is the uniquely Protestant antiritualistic attitudes of Baptists, and the relatively great church orientation of the Methodists and Catholics.

The regional differences generally reveal that the southern region is the most religiously orthodox and that the midwestern region is the most religiously liberal. We can also note that generally Unitarian-Universalist religiosity scores in the New England region are higher than they are elsewhere. The age differences disclose a general increase in religiosity with age; that is, where significant differences occur, the older clergymen score higher than the middle-aged clergymen, who in turn score higher than the youngest clergymen.

Secondly, a cluster analysis of the denominations was undertaken. It was found that the denominations clustered into three roughly homogeneous groups on the basis of their scores on the eight dimensions of religiosity: (1) The lower-socioeconomic-class conservative-orthodox cluster, including Baptists, Seventh-Day Adventists, and Church of Christ; (2) the middle-class liberal-orthodox cluster, made up of Methodist, Disciples of Christ, and the United Church of Christ denominations; (3) the upper-middle-class liberal-orthodox cluster, made up of Presbyterians and Episcopalians. Three denominations did not fit with any of these clusters. They were Catholics, who were generally high on all variables; Lutherans, who were low on altruism and idealism and high on fundamentalism and theism; and Unitarian-Universalists who were low on all variables except idealism.

5

RELIGIOSITY AND
POLITICAL ATTITUDES

This study involves the joint examination of religiosity and political conservatism and will undertake two separate analyses and approaches to the problem. The first of these approaches will examine the interrelations of religiosity and political conservatism as two separate pools of attitudes. The second approach will examine the joint correlations of all the dimensions and will extract the common factors in the numerous attitude dimensions employed in this study.

The general area of religiosity and political conservatism has been the subject of a number of investigations. Religious people have generally been found to be more politically conservative than the nonreligious (Eysenck 1954). Protestants have been found to be more conservative than Catholics, and Jews more liberal than Protestants or Catholics (Argyle 1958). Richard Centers (1949) discovered a correlation of .36 between Republican (conservative) voting and Protestantism. Johnson found religiously conservative ministers more likely to prefer the Republican party than religiously liberal ministers (Johnson 1962, 1964, 1966, 1967). There is also evidence that religious people are less interested in politics than are the nonreligious (Ringer and Glock 1954–55).

Little or no investigation has been attempted which examines either religiosity or political conservatism in an analytic manner. In order to be consistent, we will attempt to "distill" political conservatism into its component dimensions much as we have previously distilled religiosity. Having done this, we will examine the inter-relations of the component dimensions of each attitude area.

A conceptual analysis of political attitudes can, of course, follow many possible lines of division. It would be possible to distill the concept along lines of liberalism-conservatism as has been suggested by Clinton Rossiter in his analysis of conservatism (1962:6–15). Another approach might be to ascertain to what extent individuals approximated any of various aspects of either political liberalism or conservatism (Rossiter 1962:64–66).

The area of political attitude can also be meaningfully divided in another way. For example, we can determine individuals' attitudes toward social welfare and distinguish those who are in favor of it from those who are opposed to it. The same thing can be done with many other aspects of the American political scene. A consideration of the possible divisions of political attitude, coupled with an examination of political literature, leads to the following divisions of political attitudes: (A.) Domestic politics; (B.) International politics; (C.) Pure economic politics; (D.) Nationalism or "image" politics; (E.) Responses to threat; (F.) Issues of individualism; (G.) Issues of bigotry. This does not encompass the entire range of issues in the political arena; however, these are areas in which we can determine individual attitudes.

These seven areas of concern in American politics can be further divided into subareas. Each of these subareas will be subsequently translated into an attitude scale. Again it should be noted that these areas and subareas are identified through the conceptual analysis of the phenomena of political attitude and an examination of political literature. The subdivisions are as follows:

A. Domestic politics
  1. Attitudes toward the welfare state
  2. Attitudes concerning the issue of states' rights
  3. Attitudes revolving around the idea of return to a previous and preferred political arrangement or era; attitudes involving ideas of restoration
B. International politics
  4. Attitudes toward foreign aid
  5. Attitudes toward the issue of isolationism
C. Pure economic politics

6. Attitudes toward business and businessmen
7. Attitudes involving classical "laissez-faire" economic policies
D. Nationalism or "image" politics
   8. Attitudes concerned with the general area of patriotism
   9. Attitudes favoring strong leaders and obedient followers
E. Response to threat
   10. Attitudes regarding warfare and a garrison state (external response)
   11. Attitudes regarding civil liberties (internal response)
F. Issues of individualism
   12. Attitudes regarding individual manipulation
   13. Attitudes regarding government control and guidance
G. Issues of bigotry
   14. Attitudes toward the major racial minority (Blacks)
   15. Attitudes toward the major ethnic minority (Jews)

These fifteen attitude areas can then be carefully defined; or more correctly, the issue that has led to its identification must be clearly specified. One should not presume that these dimensions encompass all aspects of political attitude; neither are they entirely independent of one another. On the following pages I will identify and define each of these political attitude dimensions and will present the attitude scale items which are used to measure an individual's orientation in each dimension. Each dimension or area is translated into a summated rating scale or Likert scale.* The items of each scale have been analyzed in a student population to test their sensitivity. The item analysis used is a *t* test, which tests the significance of the difference between the means of a criterion high and a criterion low group. A *t* of over 1.75 is indicative of significant sensitivity (Edwards 1957b). The higher the *t* score, the more sensitive the item. The *t* scores will be found with each item; this will allow the reader to identify the most sensitive items in each scale and to appraise the general sensitivity of the total scale. A more detailed description of item analysis procedures can be found in chapter 2 of this book.

The scale items are constructed in such a way that a high score indicates what is typically recognized as a conservative political posi-

---

* The scales designed to measure the dimensions of political attitudes were devised largely by Prof. G. Simmons, when we were jointly engaged in a conceptual analysis of conservatism and the measurement of its components.

tion, and a low score indicates a liberal position in regard to the dimensions concerned. The subjects can respond to each statement with one of the following responses: strongly agree, agree, undecided, disagree, and strongly disagree. These responses were weighted in such a way that agreement or strong agreement with a conservative statement or disagreement or strong disagreement with a liberal statement increased the total score, thus making the higher scores the more conservative positions. The scoring weights are: 4 for the most conservative response, 3 for the next most conservative response, 2 for undecided, 1 for a liberal response, and 0 for the most liberal response for any particular item. In view of this direction in the scoring system, the scales will be renamed and identified by their high score ends: they are, in effect, scales of conservatism with low scores indicating liberalism. Although each scale was developed from political literature, I will not attempt to include anything approaching a sampling of this literature. It is believed that such literature is sufficiently well known and the areas employed are sufficiently well understood to require only a brief introduction to each area or dimension (Robinson et al. 1968; Maranell 1974).

THE ATTITUDE SCALES

Anti-Welfare State Attitudes

Attitudes toward the welfare state are the first area to be scaled. In view of the direction employed in the scaling of this dimension, it is more appropriate to refer to it as "anti-welfare state attitudes." These are attitudes in opposition to any welfare program sponsored or started by either the state and/or the national government. Examples of such welfare programs would be Social Security and Medicare. Such welfare programs are attempts on the part of the government to assist persons through social services using money secured through taxes. Opponents fear freeloading, welfare chiseling, and, as it is often put, "the destruction of initiative," apparently feeling that anyone with real initiative would get busy and earn some money. The items used to measure this aspect of domestic politics are:

Anti-Welfare State Items	t values
1. Welfare assistance contributes to lack of individual initiative.	16.50

2. Welfare assistance usually contributes to individual laxity. 12.92
3. Welfare programs take money from the pockets of the thrifty and put it into the pockets of the shiftless. 12.13
4. Once a family accepts welfare assistance they tend to become a ward of the government. 8.80
5. Welfare programs are not needed because jobs are always available to those who seek them. 7.80
6. Social Security payments undermine the initiative of any individual receiving such benefits. 7.13
7. A medical health program sponsored by a government would not result in improved health conditions. 5.53
8. Social reforms are best undertaken by individuals rather than by a governmental agency. 5.50
9. The people should support the government but the government should not support or contribute to the support of the people. 5.07
10. We need welfare programs to establish minimum standards of health, education, and security. (This statement is scored backwards since it is a liberal statement, i.e., "strongly disagree" is scored 4.) 3.47

States' Rights Attitudes

Attitudes concerning the issue of states' rights or the championship of states' rights in opposition to the power of the federal government are the second domestic issue to be examined. Attitudes within this area include support of constitutional amendments designed to curb the power of the federal government, opposition to Supreme Court rulings that increase federal power and diminish state control, opposition to federal handling of apportionment cases, and so on. The following items measure attitudes in this dimension:

States' Rights Items t values

1. A court, composed of justices of each State Supreme Court, is needed to check and balance decisions of the United States Supreme Court. 10.41
2. The state governments should have more of the total governmental power than they have at present. 10.12

3. In the United States, state governments should have more of the total governmental power.   9.31
4. The states should have complete power over civil rights.   8.82
5. The national government has entirely too much power.   8.06
6. The states, and not the national government, should regulate voting qualifications.   7.71
7. The greatest enemy of man is, and always has been, national government.   6.36
8. Tax money had best be kept at home with state governments so as to receive full value.   6.21
9. State governments ought to relinquish some of their power to the national government. (This item was scored backwards to help discourage a response set.)   4.79
10. Any type of national government planning will result in duplication of effort and inefficiency.   4.38

Restorationist Attitudes

The third area of political attitude to be considered is that which involves notions in favor of restoring the government to some past condition. Individuals with these notions prefer some rearrangement of government which will return some "better" condition. They cling to ideas which maintain that most government changes have been errors and would like to abolish such things as income tax, extension of voting privileges, etc. They cannot bear to forsake "the good old days." The items used to measure this dimension follow:

Restorationist Items   t values

1. The Supreme Court should have power only as specifically indicated in the Constitution.   7.44
2. The right to vote should be restricted to those who have property or special qualifications to do so.   6.74
3. Presidential electors should be selected by state legislatures as in the past.   6.72
4. The powers exercised by the United States Supreme Court are not what the Founding Fathers envisaged.   5.56
5. Some congressional officials, perhaps Senators, should be elected by state legislatures.   5.35

6. The Liberty Amendment to abolish the income tax would be good for America.   5.18

7. The Founding Fathers never intended for voting rights to be extended so as to include practically everyone.   5.16

8. The income tax should be done away with.   5.08

9. We should return to constitutional government as specifically stated by the Founding Fathers.   4.25

10. We would do better to accept changes in our governmental system and try to give these changes constructive expression. (This item was scored backwards to help prevent a response set.)   2.81

Anti-Foreign Aid Attitudes

Since the high scores on this foreign aid scale are conservative and the lower scores liberal, we will refer to this dimension in terms of the high scores, which are anti-foreign aid. These attitudes oppose the foreign aid programs of our government, which are considered a waste of money, a "give-away policy," and of no real value. The following statements are seen to measure anti-foreign aid attitudes:

Anti-Foreign Aid Items	t values
1. Foreign aid is really nothing but a give-away policy.	12.07
2. Foreign aid is a waste of time, money, and effort.	11.86
3. We should stop foreign aid programs because they are wasteful.	11.71
4. We ought to keep our money at home and not waste it on foreign aid.	10.88
5. We can't win allies abroad with foreign aid money.	10.80
6. America's rush to ruin is being augmented by foreign aid programs.	10.00
7. Aid to foreign nations is undermining our solvency.	9.44
8. Foreign aid programs have been formulated by do-gooders.	8.31
9. Foreign aid is actually a plot to weaken Uncle Sam financially.	8.09
10. You can't buy friends with money, so foreign aid is a useless endeavor.	3.85

Isolationist Attitudes

The fifth dimension of political attitudes involves attitudes which oppose the government's international cooperation with other nations. The isolationist also opposes our participation in the United Nations and our observance of international law. Our nation, it is believed, could get along better if it would not become involved in international or foreign disputes. The isolationist does not willingly observe United Nations Day. The items which are seen to measure isolationist attitudes are:

Isolationist Items	t values
1. Let's get the United Nations out of the United States, and the United States out of the United Nations.	11.25
2. We should never give up any of our nation's sovereignty to an international body such as the United Nations.	10.33
3. We shouldn't put much faith in the United Nations to solve problems, but should have more faith in ourselves to solve our own problems.	10.00
4. If our nation would concern itself less about other people in other countries, we would be more likely to achieve peace.	7.35
5. We would be better off to concentrate on internal problems than get involved in foreign disputes.	7.29
6. We should be willing to give up some of our national sovereignty to make international cooperation possible. (This item was scored backwards to help prevent a response set.)	7.00
7. International law is of no validity as the United States is a sovereign nation.	6.73
8. America can get along without the help of foreign nations.	6.67
9. Our best chance for the survival of our way of life is to continue negotiation in world-wide conflicts. (This item was scored backwards to help prevent a response set.)	4.61
10. We should do all we can to support international languages, which will in turn promote international cooperation. (This item was scored backwards to help prevent a response set.)	2.83

Probusiness Attitudes

This attitude dimension includes attitudes that are highly favorable to businessmen and the business community. It also involves an appreciation of positive free enterprise. A low score on this scale may involve a prolabor orientation as well as others, but it is definitely not probusiness. The items in this scale are:

Probusiness Items	t values
1. The free enterprise system is the only economic system that preserves individual freedom.	10.53
2. Without the free enterprise system, men would not be free.	10.33
3. Anyone against the profit system represents anti-freedom forces.	8.93
4. I would trust a businessman more than a union official.	7.56
5. Free enterprise and democracy are, for all practical purposes, the same thing.	6.61
6. Businessmen make better school board members than the average citizen.	6.23
7. Men should be willing to work longer hours for less pay to strengthen our free enterprise system.	5.31
8. A businessman automatically deserves more respect than a workingman.	5.29
9. The business of government is business.	4.79
10. What's good for General Motors is good for the United States.	3.57

Classical "Laissez-Faire" Attitudes

This dimension of political attitude concerns basically the economic theories of Adam Smith and David Ricardo. The theories involve notions that a free economy operates according to "natural law." In such a situation government action is seen as governmental interference, in this case interference with natural law, and in effect government action works to sustain temporarily the weak and to disrupt the process of evolutionary sequence. That is, governmental action can only work to prevent the evolutionary process of enterprises destined to collapse or survive. The items used to measure this aspect of economic political attitudes are:

Classical Laissez-faire Items | t values

1. A free market determines prices and should not be tampered with by the government. | 12.08
2. Prices of goods should always be determined by a free market and not by governmental control. | 11.47
3. There is no need for governmental control of prices because legitimate profit is always determined by the skill of different managers. | 10.33
4. Government should let people alone, allowing each man to seek his own highest economic interest. | 9.93
5. The government's activity in economic affairs should be kept at an absolute minimum. | 8.80
6. Business should be allowed to do what it considers best for its own welfare without government interference. | 8.50
7. The law of supply and demand operates best in an economy free of government control or regulation. | 7.42
8. Government intervention into business conditions is nearly always harmful. | 5.13
9. Business will always be fair to its customers, thus the government does not need laws to protect the consumer. | 4.69
10. The best good of society can be achieved if industry is free from any regulation by law. | 4.07

Superpatriotic Attitudes

These are attitudes which involve a conscious, intense concern for national loyalty. They are termed "superpatriotic" because of the implied superiority they hold for the person manifesting them. For this group, if one is not a "superpatriot," his loyalty is questioned. The items included in this dimension are:

Superpatriotic Items | t values

1. One should always be a 100%, "red-white-and-blue" American. | 13.50
2. To serve one's country is an honor above all others. | 12.77
3. Americanism is the only "ism" for me. | 11.56
4. Loyalty to your country is a 24-hour-a-day, 365-day-a-year obligation. | 11.29

5. Each individual should think his nation is due his highest and final loyalty.   10.80
6. To be absolutely sound in Americanism is an important qualification for any candidate for public office.   8.81
7. To be an American, one should be loyal to Americanism at all times.   8.47
8. A nation deserves its citizens' loyalty at all times.   7.17
9. One should always subscribe to the philosophy of "My country, right or wrong."   7.12
10. Only those Americans willing to die for their country are fit to live in it.   6.74

Authoritarian Attitudes

Authoritarian attitudes are those which favor obedience to power or authority. The authoritarian is rigid in his beliefs and makes frequent use of stereotypes in his perceptions and judgments. He is sympathetic with the use of violence against his enemies and makes extremely sharp distinctions between in-groups and out-groups. He admires strong men and successful, manly men who have no tender sides (Shils 1954:29). The items that measure authoritarian attitudes were derived from T. W. Adorno et al., *The Authoritarian Personality* (1950:235–36):

Authoritarian Items	*t* values

1. What young people need most is strict discipline, rugged determination, and the will to work and fight for family and country.   10.88
2. Great men are made to lead, the people to follow.   10.57
3. Obedience and respect for authority are the most important virtues children should learn.   9.76
4. A child should never be allowed to talk back to his parents, or else he will lose respect for them.   9.44
5. What this country needs most, more than laws and political programs, is a few courageous, tireless, devoted leaders in whom the people can put their faith.   7.56
6. Most people really don't know what's good for them, thus they need someone to lead them.   7.41
7. Great men are always tough, determined, and never waver from a course of action.   7.06

8. Any good leader should be strict with people under him in order to gain their respect.   6.88
9. The course of history has always been determined by a few individuals.   6.78
10. People can be divided into two distinct classes: the weak and the strong.   5.22

Pro-Warfare State Attitudes

This attitude dimension maintains that a continuous and extensive armament program is necessary and desirable. The position is described in the phrase—"more and better bombs." Adherents to the position oppose civilian control of the military. The dimension also involves attitudes which stress the heroic aspects of war. War is seen as a challenge, a glorious challenge. Individuals that subscribe to this position are unaware of, or at least unconcerned about, the havoc of war. The victory sought by the persons who subscribe to this position is the victory of war, not the victory of peace or survival. The items in this scale are as follows:

Pro-Warfare State Items	t values
1. That wars are often gloriously and justly waged is proven historically by our own gallant victories.	9.43
2. To expect World War III is simply being realistic.	8.38
3. Thermonuclear weapons are our best instruments of peace.	7.69
4. Military forces in the United States should be free of civilian control.	7.33
5. Decisions on the use of weapons systems should be made by uniformed military personnel rather than by a civilian Secretary of Defense.	7.00
6. If we stay strong, we can have a peace based on force.	6.61
7. Disarmament talks are a waste of time because peace is not possible.	6.31
8. The military forces of our nation should be given more power to deal with our aggressive enemies.	6.00
9. Preventive wars are sometimes necessary.	5.63
10. Marginal risks in war must be accepted if we can thus eliminate vastly greater risks.	4.56

Anti-Civil Liberty Attitudes

The dimension involves attitudes which favor the restriction of individual civil liberties. The Bill of Rights is systematically ignored by the subscribers to this attitude. They feel that our civil liberties are inconvenient restrictions in our response to a dangerous threat. This attitude dimension involves the expansion of the powers of the state. This element is a suspicious, loyalty-oriented attitude, which favors the establishment of norms which are then to be preserved against violations. This is an intolerant dimension as well as a harsh one. The items in this scale are:

Anti-Civil Liberty Items   t values

1. A man should not be allowed to receive subversive propaganda through the mail.   10.00
2. If one's religious beliefs are wrong, they should be outlawed.   9.00
3. When a man refuses to tell a congressional committee whether or not he has committed acts of subversion, he should be thrown in jail.   8.53
4. A loyalty oath to the American form of government is the best way to determine a teacher's Americanism.   8.31
5. Foreign broadcasts should not be permitted to enter our country because of the danger of spreading false propaganda.   8.06
6. Persons accused of suspected subversion should be dealt with harshly without recourse to due process of law.   7.07
7. There are times when freedom of speech should be limited.   5.88
8. An American who spies for a foreign nation should have his citizenship taken away.   4.64
9. A man whose loyalty has been questioned before a congressional committee, but who swears under oath he is loyal, is still suspect.   4.60
10. The government should recognize some specific denomination as the national church.   4.08

Machiavellian Attitudes

This attitude dimension involves the belief that the end always justifies the means. They are attitudes which involve political cunning. They are in many instances unscrupulous. This attitude scale was derived from a longer scale devised by Christie and Geis (1970). The dimension is most relevant to the current right-wing activity which advocates the infiltration of parent-teacher associations and other community organizations and the use of these organizations for the aims of reaction. The items of this scale are:

Machiavellian Items	t values
1. A white lie is often a good thing.	15.54
2. It is hard to get ahead without cutting corners here and there.	10.80
3. When you come right down to it, it's human nature never to do anything without an eye to one's own advantage. (This item also appears on the Idealism scale—unfortunately.)	9.83
4. The best way to handle people is to tell them what they want to hear.	8.94
5. One should take action only when it is morally right. (This item is scored backwards to help prevent a response set.)	6.95
6. The man to be admired is one who pushes ahead regardless of the fact that he may hurt others in so doing.	6.92
7. A clever, shrewd individual always wins out in the end.	6.67
8. Humility is not only of no service but actually harmful.	6.07
9. Friends should be chosen with an eye toward what they might be able to do for you.	4.94
10. If one is morally right, compromise is out of the question.	1.47

Anarchistic Attitudes

This dimension involves attitudes which are antigovernment. Government is felt to be an enemy of individual freedom and liberty, as well as inefficient and nonproductive. The items of this scale are as follows:

Anarchistic Items	t values
1. All governments are inefficient.	7.75

2. Governments are not to be trusted.   7.62
3. Government is always an enemy of freedom.   7.55
4. The best government is the one that governs least.   7.11
5. Government often operates in an atmosphere of plunder and blunder.   6.53
6. Government is inherently evil and dishonest.   6.18
7. Government is a nonproductive enterprise.   5.88
8. When government programs seem benevolent, we should be on our guard.   5.59
9. We should have less government and more individual responsibility.   5.55
10. Government should be watched by the people so that it does not acquire too much power.   3.53

Anti-Black Attitudes

This dimension involves attitudes hostile to Blacks. The nature and origin of anti-Black feeling and of prejudicial beliefs in general is the topic of a great deal of sociological writing and research. It is a well-known, familiar attitude area and has clear political aspects serving as an integrated part of much political action and belief. The items in this scale are:

Anti-Black Items   t values

*1. Black people have their rights, but it is best to keep them in their own districts and schools and to prevent too much contact with whites.   19.69
*2. Most Blacks would become overbearing if not kept in their place.   15.60
*3. It would be a mistake ever to have Blacks for foremen and leaders over whites.   14.07
*4. There may be a few exceptions, but in general Black people are pretty much alike.   13.44
*5. The people who raise all the talk about putting Blacks on the same level as whites are mostly radical agitators trying to stir up conflict.   13.24
6. Black people will always have lower morals than whites.   13.07
*7. To end prejudice against Blacks, the first step is for

the Blacks to try sincerely to get rid of their harmful
and irritating ways.   11.13

8. Blacks are biologically inferior to white men.   9.56

*9. There is something different and strange about
Blacks; it's hard to tell what they are thinking and
planning and what makes them tick.   9.25

10. There is nothing really wrong with segregated Black
and White housing.   8.64

* Derived from Adorno et al. 1950 :142.

Anti-Semitic Attitudes

This, the final dimension, involves attitudes of prejudice against
the Jews. It is also a well-investigated dimension in sociology and
psychology. The political aspects of this dimension are similar to
those in anti-Black attitudes; however, the target group is in this case
ethnic and not racial. The items of this scale are:

Anti-Semitic Items t values

1. Jews can never be good citizens because they owe
allegiance to foreign ideologies.   21.90

2. The Jews are always interested only in making
money.   12.73

3. Jews are different and strange and somewhat repul-
sive to me.   12.55

4. Jews are overbearing and disagreeable and should be
kept in their place.   11.55

5. Jews should be excluded from some social organizations such as the local country club.   11.50

*6. I can hardly imagine myself marrying a Jew.   11.12

*7. One trouble with Jewish businessmen is that they
stick together and prevent other people from having
a fair chance in competition.   10.20

8. A Jewish businessman will cheat you if you don't
watch out.   7.56

9. You can always tell a Jew by his looks.   7.43

10. The Jews control most of the financial interests in
the world.   4.69

* Derived from Adorno et al. 1950: 142.

A VALIDITY CHECK OF THE POLITICAL
ATTITUDE SCALES*

In view of the fact that the political attitude scales will not be as completely described, analyzed, and employed as the religiosity scales, it was deemed necessary to secure some evidence regarding their validity. They have not been used long enough to establish construct validity. Thus some attempt should be made to demonstrate their validity by examining the results obtained with them from two different "politically known" groups.

The task is to discover two groups, one a criterion liberal group and the second a recognized conservative group. Two groups which met these requirements were located in the student body of a midwestern university. The first group of twenty students were members of a left-oriented or liberal action campus committee, plus a few other active students who had recently participated in various demonstrations on campus. These individuals are the recognized leftist-liberals in the student culture.

An ideal conservative or right-oriented group would have been a YAF (Young Americans for Freedom) group; however, the campus studied did not have a YAF group at the time of this study. Thus a fairly serious problem appeared—where could we find a group of student conservatives? Even though this was in a conservative state, it was not felt appropriate to accost students on the street and assume that they would all be conservatives, although many may feel that the number of errors would probably not be great using this procedure in the state studied. A feasible solution involved securing the cooperation of a group of fraternity members who considered themselves to be "conservative" and "Republicans." Thus we now had a group of students (all male) who considered themselves to be liberal and were so considered by others (N = 20) and another group of students (all male) who considered themselves to be conservative Republicans and were so considered by others (N = 14).

Given these two groups and the set of fifteen political attitude scales previously described, we felt that we might examine the scoring of the two groups on the various scales. The scales will be con-

---

* The data presented in this section were gathered for the author by Christopher Ruhe.

sidered somewhat valid if, granting the content or face validity, we find the criterion or known groups differing from one another in the appropriate direction to a significant extent. In table 5-1 we find the mean scores secured by the criterion groups.

TABLE 5-1. MEAN SCORES OF THE TWO CRITERION GROUPS ON THE VARIOUS POLITICAL ATTITUDE SCALES

	Mean Scores		
	Liberals	Conservatives	t scores
Anti-welfare state attitudes	7.50	23.00	7.35**
States' rights attitudes	5.45	20.79	6.94**
Restorationist attitudes	6.75	20.43	7.28**
Anti-foreign aid attitudes	4.90	20.36	6.96**
Isolationist attitudes	3.90	17.64	6.90**
Probusiness attitudes	5.15	19.86	8.50**
Laissez-faire attitudes	4.70	19.71	6.53**
Superpatriotic attitudes	4.10	24.07	10.14**
Authoritarian attitudes	7.65	19.36	7.10**
Pro-warfare state attitudes	4.80	19.50	9.67**
Anti-civil liberty attitudes	4.90	15.07	6.60**
Machiavellian attitudes	11.60	19.64	3.79**
Anarchistic attitudes	10.90	21.07	4.67**
Anti-Black attitudes	2.80	15.50	7.02**
Anti-Semitic attitudes	3.05	13.43	6.65**

** $P < .005$ if t is 2.739 or larger (thus all are highly significant).

We observe that all the t scores are highly significant statistically. Therefore the differences observed between the two groups on all of the fifteen scales of political conservatism are significant. An examination reveals that occasionally the two distributions, left-oriented and right-oriented, do not even touch, much less overlap. Thus we have some evidence, though it is admittedly limited, that the scales discriminate, as they should, in a known-group situation.

These fifteen scaled dimensions of political conservatism and the eight scaled dimensions of religiosity described earlier in this book were administered in eight different student populations, or more correctly, in four populations each of which has been partialled in regard to the rural-urban variable. In this study, following census classification, we shall consider towns with populations over 2,500 to be urban. This arbitrary distinction is used to separate farm-rural students from nonfarm (urban) students. Even this distinction allows for only rather small urban samples of Mennonite students. The samples used in this study are:

A. State university populations—these samples include freshmen, sophomores, juniors, and seniors.
   1. Southern university students from urban areas (N = 137)
   2. Southern university students from rural areas (N = 45)
   3. Midwestern university students from urban areas (N = 140)
   4. Midwestern university students from rural areas (N = 37)
B. Denominational college populations—these samples include only freshmen.*
   1. Catholic college students from urban areas (N = 198)—this includes students from a male and a female Catholic college.
   2. Catholic college students from rural areas (N = 82)—this includes students from both a male and a female Catholic college.
   3. Mennonite college students from urban areas (N = 38)—this includes students from three Mennonite colleges.
   4. Mennonite college students from rural areas (N = 237)—this includes students from three Mennonite colleges.

In view of the differences in the eight samples, our analysis will examine each population independently and will then attempt an integration of the findings.

The general characteristics of the eight populations can be found in table 5-2. The university samples were drawn from the

TABLE 5-2. GENERAL CHARACTERISTICS OF THE EIGHT POPULATIONS

		Sex		Year in School			
	N	M	F	Fr	So	Jr	Sr
Southern university							
urban	137	67	70	15	70	41	11
rural	45	24	21	6	21	10	8
Midwestern university							
urban	140	58	82	55	48	31	6
rural	37	16	21	13	16	7	1
Catholic college							
urban	199	113	86	199			
rural	82	45	37	82			
Mennonite college							
urban	38	18	20	38			
rural	237	104	133	237			

* The denominational samples were gathered by Prof. Paul Wiebe.

general undergraduate introductory sociology classes. The Catholic and Mennonite samples included all freshmen students in the colleges involved. The general comparability of the data is contingent upon the sample differences described in table 5-2.

The first analysis of this data on political and religious attitudes will have as a focus of attention the interrelationship between these two pools of attitude scales. This analysis follows the major line of development of this book, analyzing, as it were, the effects and correlates of religiosity. A second and later analysis will concentrate on a factor analysis of the intercorrelations of all twenty-three variables.

First, however, let us examine the relationship between religious attitudes and political attitudes as such. The total intercorrelations among the twenty-three variables were found in each of the eight populations. These correlation matrixes can be found in Appendix B. In view of our basic interest at this point in the correlation of the various political attitude dimensions to the dimensions of religiosity, these intercorrelations were graphed in line graphs which recorded the correlation of each political attitude variable with each religious dimension in each population. This permitted the construction of 120 such graphs. An example or specimen graph can be found in figure 5-1. The turning points of the graphs are the intercorrelations found in Appendix B. In the graph (figure 5-1) we find the following correlations (an asterisk indicates statistically significant correlations which are in this case positive):

Church orientation and anti-civil liberties attitudes	$r = +.26*$
Ritualism and anti-civil liberties attitudes	$r = +.35*$
Altruism and anti-civil liberties attitudes	$r = +.15$
Fundamentalism and anti-civil liberties attitudes	$r = +.20*$
Theism and anti-civil liberties attitudes	$r = +.10$
Idealism and anti-civil liberties attitudes	$r = +.03$
Superstition and anti-civil liberties attitudes	$r = +.30*$
Mysticism and anti-civil liberties attitudes	$r = +.22*$

A preliminary analysis concentrated upon identifying typical graph or chart types and clustering the political variables in the various populations together on the basis of the form the graph assumed. It soon became clear that there was a rather limited set of such graph forms. Further inspection revealed that the variable which deter-

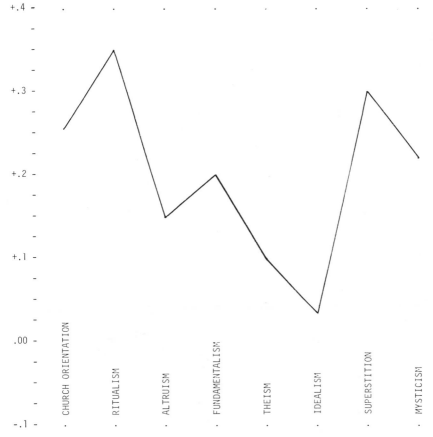

a correlation of .21 is significant at the .01 level with a sample of this size
a correlation of .16 is significant at the .05 level with a sample of this size

Figure 5-1. Diagram of the correlations between scales of religious attitudes and anti-civil liberties attitudes among midwestern university students from urban areas.

mined to an overwhelming extent the form of the graphs was the pattern, number and type, of significant correlations. For example, the graphs which clustered together were graphs which described and identified political variables which had the same significant correlations, both positive and negative, with the various dimensions of religiosity. Thus a cluster would be made up of those political attitude variables that were, for example, significantly and positively correlated with superstition and no other religiosity variable. Given then the fact that similar charts are those having the same positive and negative correlations with religiosity, it was discovered that these line graphs could be reduced to a series of pluses (for significant positive correlations), zeros (for nonsignificant correlations), and minuses (for significant negative correlation). This step permits the further summarizing of the line graphs. For example, the graph presented in figure 5-1 can be reduced and summarized by the following series of symbols: + + 0 + 0 0 + + keeping the variables in a constant order. This allows for the simplified handing of the 120 line graphs.

By examining these summaries one can note which dimensions of political conservatism have the greater number of significant positive and negative correlations with each dimension of religiosity in each of the samples. This permits the construction of a summary table (table 5-3) describing the number of significant correlations with each religiosity dimension.

TABLE 5-3. NUMBER OF SIGNIFICANT POSITIVE AND NEGATIVE CORRELATIONS BETWEEN RELIGIOSITY AND POLITICAL CONSERVATISM IN THE EIGHT POPULATIONS

	SUPER-STITION + −	RITUAL-ISM + −	CHURCH ORIEN-TATION + −	MYSTI-CISM + −	FUNDA-MENTAL-ISM + −	THEISM + −	ALTRU-ISM + −	IDEAL-ISM + −	TOTAL
Superpatriotic attitudes	6–0	8–0	6–0	5–0	5–0	3–0	4–0	1–1	38–1
Authoritarian attitudes	7–0	7–0	7–0	6–0	4–0	2–0	4–0	0–2	37–2
Anti-civil liberty attitudes	6–0	6–0	5–0	3–0	5–0	2–0	2–0	0–2	29–2
States' rights attitudes	4–0	4–0	3–0	4–0	3–0	3–0	1–0	0–1	22–1
Probusiness attitudes	4–0	5–0	5–0	3–0	2–0	1–1	1–1	1–1	22–3
Pro-warfare state attitudes	5–0	4–0	3–0	2–0	2–0	2–2	0–2	0–4	18–8
Anti-Black attitudes	6–0	4–0	4–0	1–0	2–1	1–3	0–3	0–5	18–12
Restorationist attitudes	5–0	4–0	3–0	3–0	2–0	0–2	0–0	0–2	17–4
Anti-Semitic attitudes	5–0	4–0	3–0	1–0	2–2	1–2	1–2	0–3	17–9
Machiavellian attitudes	4–0	5–0	5–0	0–0	0–4	0–3	0–1	0–6	14–14
Anti-foreign aid attitudes	2–0	4–1	3–0	1–0	0–1	1–2	0–4	0–3	11–11
Isolationist attitudes	4–0	1–1	1–0	1–0	2–2	1–2	0–3	0–4	10–12
Anarchistic attitudes	1–0	0–0	2–0	2–0	0–2	0–1	1–1	1–2	7–6
Laissez-faire attitudes	1–0	1–0	1–0	1–0	1–1	0–2	0–1	0–1	5–5
Anti-welfare attitudes	0–0	0–2	1–0	0–0	0–1	0–2	0–4	0–0	1–9
Totals	60–0	57–4	52–0	33–0	30–14	17–22	14–22	3–37	266–99

At this point it was noted that the significant correlations of political conservatism and religiosity formed a definite pattern and could with a little rearrangement of item order be formed into a small cumulative or "Guttman-like" scale (Maranell 1974). Thus, not only are certain political variables more often correlated with religiosity and with certain particular dimensions of religiosity, as noted in table 5-3, but there exists a definite pattern to these correlations in each population as is indicated by the presence of the eight cumulative scale patterns. These cumulative scales can be found in tables 5-5 to 5-12. If we examine the coefficients of reproducibility of these eight scale patterns, we observe that they are all acceptably, even impressively, high. In view of the extreme marginal frequencies, Menzel's coefficient of scalability and a measure of statistical significance were also computed with highly satisfactory results (Menzel 1953; Schuessler 1961; Chilton 1969). It should, of course, be noted that these are in some ways very different from regular Guttman scales. In this particular case we are scaling not items which are endorsed but rather the presence of significant correlations. Also we must note that a number of scale criteria are not satisfied, such as number of items, range of marginal proportions, etc. However, I decided to calculate the coefficients of reproducibility in spite of this. Noting that certain items do not have acceptable marginal proportions (are more extreme than 20/80) we can omit them from the calculations. In spite of the small number of "items," etc., we find the coefficients of reproducibility and coefficients of scalability and probabilities reported in table 5-4, which indicate the presence of a cumulative, or Guttman, pattern. Furthermore, the pattern and size of the various coefficients are not influenced by the number of items, etc.

TABLE 5-4. COEFFICIENTS OF REPRODUCIBILITY AND SCALABILITY OF PATTERN OF SIGNIFICANT CORRELATIONS IN THE EIGHT POPULATIONS

| | Coefficients of Reproducibility | | | |
	Items with Marginal Proportions More Extreme Than 20/80 Omitted	All Items	Menzel's Coefficient of Scalability	Probability of Arrangement Occurring by Chance
Southern				
rural	.93	.95	.76	P< .001
urban	.95	.96	.75	P< .001
Catholic				
rural	.97	.98	.87	P< .001
urban	.98	.99	.96	P< .001
Midwestern				
rural	.96	.96	.81	P< .001
urban	.95	.96	.82	P< .001
Mennonite				
rural	.93	.97	.79	P< .05
urban	.91	.96	.69	P> .05

	Fundamentalism	Theism	Superstition	Church Orientation	Ritualism	Altruism	Mysticism	Idealism
Authoritarian attitudes	+	+	+	+	+	+	+	0
Probusiness attitudes	+	+	+	+	+	0	+	0
Superpatriotic attitudes	+	+	+	+	+	+	0	0
States' rights attitudes	+	+	+	0	+	0	0	0
Pro-warfare state attitudes	+	+	+	+	0	0	0	0
Isolationist attitudes	+	+	+	0	0	0	0	0
Anti-civil liberty attitudes	+	+	0	0	0	+	0	0
Restorationist attitudes	+	0	+	0	0	0	0	0
Anti-Black attitudes	+	0	0	0	0	0	0	0
Anti-Semitic attitudes	+	0	0	0	0	0	0	0
Machiavellian attitudes	0	0	0	+	+	0	0	0
Anarchistic attitudes	0	0	0	0	0	0	0	0
Anti-foreign aid attitudes	0	0	0	0	0	0	0	0
Laissez-faire attitudes	0	0	0	0	0	0	0	0
Anti-welfare state attitudes	0	0	0	0	0	0	0	0
Guttman scale errors	(0)	(0)	(1)	(2)	(1)	(2)	(0)	(0)

NOTE: Guttman's coefficient of reproducibility = .93 (.95 in all items).
Minimum reproducibility = .72.
Menzel's coefficient of scalability = .76.
Probability of arrangement occurring by chance < .001.

Overlooking the obvious difficulties, such as sample size and number of items, an examination of the foregoing tables suggests a definite cumulative scale pattern in seven of the eight populations. This indicates that there may exist an underlying unidimensionality in these relationships for each population and perhaps for the populations as a whole.

These cumulative scales of correlations are, first of all, serendipitous findings. Not only are certain variables of political conservatism differentially correlated with the religiosity dimensions, but in addition there is a definite pattern to these correlations. In each population we find that the incidence of significant correlation increases systematically. Therefore, if a dimension of conservatism is correlated significantly with five dimensions of religiosity, they are a predictable five dimensions; if there are four significant correlations, they are a predictable four dimensions, and so on. With the exception of the Catholic rural population, only positive correlations are scaled. In this single case negative correlations are scaled because there are so few significant positive correlations. We might also note that when positive correlations are scaled, the negative correlations are also very nearly scaled simultaneously.

The existence of a cumulative scale in seven populations suggests the presence of unidimensionality. What, we might ask, is the unidimensional variable? If we recognize that any answer to this ques-

TABLE 5-6. SIGNIFICANT CORRELATIONS BETWEEN RELIGIOSITY AND POLITICAL ATTITUDES IN THE SOUTHERN URBAN UNIVERSITY STUDENT POPULATION (N = 137)

	Church Orientation	Superstition	Fundamentalism	Mysticism	Ritualism	Theism	Altruism	Idealism
Superpatriotic attitudes	+	+	+	0	+	+	+	+
Probusiness attitudes	+	0	+	+	+	0	+	+
Authoritarian attitudes	+	+	+	+	+	+	+	0
Anti-civil liberty attitudes	+	+	+	+	+	+	+	0
Anti-Semitic attitudes	+	+	+	+	+	+	+	0
States' rights attitudes	+	+	+	+	+	+	+	0
Anti-Black attitudes	+	+	+	+	+	+	0	0
Pro-warfare state attitudes	+	+	+	+	+	+	0	0
Restorationist attitudes	+	+	+	+	0	0	0	0
Machiavellian attitudes	+	0	0	0	+	0	0	—
Anti-foreign aid attitudes	+	0	0	0	0	0	0	0
Isolationist attitudes	+	0	0	0	0	0	0	0
Anarchistic attitudes	0	0	0	+	0	0	0	0
Laissez-faire attitudes	0	0	0	0	0	0	0	0
Anti-welfare state attitudes	0	0	0	0	0	0	0	0
Guttman scale errors	(0)	(1)	(0)	(2)	(1)	(1)	(0)	(0)

NOTE: Guttman's coefficient of reproducibility = .95 (.96 in all items).
　　　Minimum reproducibility = .64.
　　　Menzel's coefficient of scalability = .75.
　　　Probability of arrangement occurring by chance < .001.

	Superstition	Mysticism	Church Orientation	Ritualism	Fundamentalism	Altruism	Theism	Idealism
Superpatriotic attitudes	0	0	0	+	0	0	0	0
Authoritarian attitudes	0	0	+	0	0	0	0	0
Probusiness attitudes	0	0	0	0	0	0	−	0
Anti-civil liberty attitudes	+	0	0	0	0	0	0	−
Anarchistic attitudes	0	0	0	0	0	0	0	−
Anti-Semitic attitudes	0	0	0	0	0	0	0	−
States' rights attitudes	0	+	0	0	0	0	0	−
Pro-warfare state attitudes	0	0	0	0	0	0	−	−
Anti-welfare state attitudes	0	0	0	−	0	0	−	0
Restorationist attitudes	0	0	0	0	0	0	−	−
Anti-Black attitudes	+	0	0	0	−	−	−	−
Machiavellian attitudes	+	0	0	0	−	−	−	−
Laissez-faire attitudes	0	0	0	0	−	−	−	−
Anti-foreign aid attitudes	+	0	0	−	−	−	−	−
Isolationist attitudes	0	0	−	−	−	−	−	−
Guttman scale errors	(0)	(0)	(0)	(1)	(0)	(0)	(1)	(1)

NOTE: Guttman's coefficient of reproducibility = .97 (.98 in all items).
Minimum reproducibility = .80.
Menzel's coefficient of scalability = .87.
Probability of arrangement occurring by chance < .001.

tion is an extrapolation, we might make a guess. One answer might be that there is a variable which could be termed "integration of conservatism" underlying the scaled correlations. This integration of conservatism is then described by the systematic scaling of religious and political conservatism.

In each population the particular ordering of the two sets of variables and their joint systematic arrangement describes the nature of something we refer to as the integration of conservatism. By this we mean that the pattern discovered reveals the make-up or system of connections or integration of conservative attitudes (religious and political) in the particular populations. The interpopulation simi- larities in the orderings of the variables and the scale patterns can

TABLE 5-8. SIGNIFICANT CORRELATIONS BETWEEN RELIGIOSITY AND POLITICAL ATTITUDES IN THE CATHOLIC URBAN COLLEGE STUDENT POPULATION (N = 199)

	Ritualism	Superstition	Church Orientation	Fundamentalism	Mysticism	Altruism	Theism	Idealism
Authoritarian attitudes	+	+	+	+	+	+	0	−
Superpatriotic attitudes	+	+	+	+	+	0	0	−
Anti-civil liberty attitudes	+	+	+	+	0	0	0	−
Probusiness attitudes	+	+	+	0	0	0	0	0
Pro-warfare state attitudes	+	+	+	0	0	0	0	−
Machiavellian attitudes	+	+	+	−	0	0	−	−
Anti-Semitic attitudes	+	+	+	−	0	−	−	−
Anti-Black attitudes	0	+	+	0	0	−	−	−
Restorationist attitudes	+	0	0	0	0	0	−	0
States' rights attitudes	+	0	0	0	0	0	0	0
Anarchistic attitudes	0	0	0	0	0	0	0	0
Laissez-faire attitudes	0	0	0	0	0	0	0	0
Anti-welfare state attitudes	0	0	0	0	0	−	0	0
Anti-foreign aid attitudes	0	0	0	0	0	−	−	−
Isolationist attitudes	0	0	0	−	0	−	−	−
Guttman scale errors	(1)	(0)	(0)	(0)	(0)	(0)	(0)	(0)

NOTE: Guttman's coefficient of reproducibility = .98 (.99 in all items).
Minimum reproducibility = .78.
Menzel's coefficient of scalability = .96.
Probability of arrangement occurring by chance < .001.

then be seen to constitute a simple reflection of the fact that the populations are similar in regard to this particular phenomenon. That is, the similarity of the eight scales reflects a similarity in integration of conservatism, which in turn reflects a similarity among these eight student populations.

In addition to realizing that great similarities exist among these eight student populations, we can also also recognize that the differences in ordering and scale pattern among them reveals some of the more subtle variations between these student populations in their integration of conservatism. The fact that the pattern is substantially weaker among the Mennonite students (both populations) might be taken as an indicator that they have less integration of religious and political conservatism. Given that they are a minority religious group with particularly strong religious convictions and only normatively politically conservative, this lower integration makes some sense. Also, an examination of the role of the variable fundamentalism in the southern student population's integration of conservatism reveals an ordering and pattern which is quite different from that found elsewhere. In the southern rural population, it is, in fact, the variable which is most often significantly and positively correlated with political conservatism. The southern urban population is, interestingly, the population in which we find the second greatest number of significant positive correlations between fundamentalism and political conservatism. That is, in each of the two southern populations, and

TABLE 5-9. SIGNIFICANT CORRELATIONS BETWEEN RELIGIOSITY AND POLITICAL ATTITUDES IN THE MENNONITE RURAL COLLEGE STUDENT POPULATION (N = 237)

	Ritualism	Superstition	Church Orientation	Mysticism	Fundamentalism	Altruism	Idealism	Theism
Authoritarian attitudes	+	+	+	+	+	+	0	0
Superpatriotic attitudes	+	+	+	+	+	0	0	0
Anti-foreign aid attitudes	+	0	+	+	0	0	0	0
Probusiness attitudes	+	+	+	0	0	0	0	0
Anti-civil liberty attitudes	+	+	+	0	0	0	0	0
Anti-Black attitudes	+	+	+	0	0	−	−	−
Machiavellian attitudes	+	+	+	0	−	0	−	−
States' rights attitudes	+	+	0	+	0	0	0	0
Restorationist attitudes	+	+	0	0	0	0	0	0
Isolationist attitudes	+	+	0	0	0	−	−	0
Pro-warfare state attitudes	+	+	0	0	0	−	−	−
Anti-Semitic attitudes	+	+	0	0	−	−	−	−
Laissez-faire attitudes	+	0	0	0	0	0	0	−
Anarchistic attitudes	0	0	+	0	−	0	0	−
Anti-welfare state attitudes	0	0	+	0	−	−	0	−
Guttman scale errors	(0)	(1)	(2)	(1)	(0)	(0)	(0)	(0)

NOTE: Guttman's coefficient of reproducibility = .93 (.97 in all items).
Minimum reproducibility = .84.
Menzel's coefficient of scalability = .79.
Probability of arrangement occurring in chance < .05.

TABLE 5-10. SIGNIFICANT CORRELATIONS BETWEEN RELIGIOSITY AND POLITICAL ATTITUDES IN THE MENNONITE URBAN COLLEGE STUDENT POPULATION
(N = 38)

	Ritualism	Superstition	Mysticism	Fundamentalism	Theism	Church Orientation	Altruism	Idealism
Laissez-faire attitudes	0	0	+	+	+	0	0	0
Authoritarian attitudes	+	+	+	0	0	0	0	0
Superpatriotic attitudes	+	0	+	0	0	0	0	0
Pro-warfare state attitudes	+	+	0	0	0	0	0	0
Anti-civil liberty attitudes	+	0	0	0	0	0	0	0
Restorationist attitudes	+	0	0	0	0	0	0	0
Machiavellian attitudes	+	0	0	0	0	0	0	—
Anti-foreign aid attitudes	+	0	0	0	0	0	—	0
Anti-Black attitudes	+	0	0	0	0	0	0	—
Probusiness attitudes	0	0	+	0	0	0	0	0
Isolationist attitudes	0	+	0	0	0	0	0	0
Anarchistic attitudes	0	0	0	0	0	0	0	0
Anti-Semitic attitudes	0	0	0	0	0	0	0	0
States' rights attitudes	0	0	0	0	0	0	0	0
Anti-welfare state attitudes	0	0	0	0	0	0	—	0
Guttman scale errors	(1)	(3)	(1)	(0)	(0)	(0)	(0)	(0)

NOTE: Guttman's coefficient of reproducibility = .91 (.96 in all items).
Minimum reproducibility = .87.
Menzel's coefficient of scalability = .69.
Probability of arrangement occurring by chance > .05.

only in these populations, we find the religious variable fundamentalism serving as a dominant religious variable in the pattern of integrated conservatism. This pattern certainly corresponds to the consensual social-science picture of the nature of southern conservatism. Therefore, it is fair, I believe, to say that we find the interpreting variable integration of conservatism somewhat useful in describing and interpreting that which is being scaled in the eight student populations.

It is also interesting to examine briefly the error (the deviations from a perfect scale pattern) in the various scales. For example, in the midwestern urban university student population, one-half of the errors are predicted correlations with prejudice that do not occur.

In this particular population we would expect some deviation in a liberal direction from the general conservative midwest culture among college students.

Turning our attention to the more particular pattern of findings, we might first examine religiosity in tables 5-4 through 5-12. When we take size of correlation and number of significant correlations between religious attitudes and political attitudes into account, we observe a definite order in the religious attitude variables. Of the religious attitude variables, superstition is most often positively correlated with political conservatism and is never negatively correlated with it. The dimension which is second in number of positive correlations is ritualism, following closely by church-oriented attitudes,

TABLE 5-11. SIGNIFICANT CORRELATIONS BETWEEN RELIGIOSITY AND POLITICAL ATTITUDES IN THE MIDWESTERN RURAL UNIVERSITY STUDENT POPULATION

(N = 37)

	Church Orientation	Superstition	Ritualism	Mysticism	Altruism	Idealism	Fundamentalism	Theism
Anti-civil liberty attitudes	+	+	+	+	0	0	+	0
Anarchistic attitudes	+	+	0	+	+	+	0	0
Superpatriotic attitudes	+	+	+	+	+	0	0	0
Authoritarian attitudes	+	+	+	0	0	0	0	0
Probusiness attitudes	+	+	+	0	0	0	0	0
Anti-Black attitudes	+	+	+	0	0	0	0	0
Anti-foreign aid attitudes	+	+	+	0	0	0	0	0
Restorationist attitudes	+	+	0	+	0	0	0	0
Anti-Semitic attitudes	+	+	0	0	0	0	0	0
Laissez-faire attitudes	+	+	0	0	0	0	0	0
Machiavellian attitudes	+	+	0	0	0	0	0	0
States' rights attitudes	+	0	0	0	0	0	0	0
Anti-welfare state attitudes	0	0	0	0	0	0	0	0
Pro-warfare state attitudes	0	0	0	0	0	0	0	0
Isolationist attitudes	0	0	0	0	0	0	0	0
Guttman scale errors	(0)	(0)	(1)	(1)	(1)	(1)	(0)	(0)

NOTE: Guttman's coefficient of reproducibility = .96 (.96 in all items).
　　　Minimum reproducibility = .82.
　　　Menzel's coefficient of scalability = .81.
　　　Probability of arrangement occurring by chance < .001.

TABLE 5-12. SIGNIFICANT CORRELATIONS BETWEEN RELIGIOSITY AND POLITICAL ATTITUDES IN THE MIDWESTERN URBAN UNIVERSITY STUDENT POPULATION (N = 55)

	Mysticism	Superstition	Ritualism	Church Orientation	Fundamentalism	Theism	Altruism	Idealism
Superpatriotic attitudes	+	+	+	+	+	+	+	0
States' rights attitudes	+	+	0	+	+	+	0	0
Anti-civil liberty attitudes	+	+	+	+	+	0	0	0
Restorationist attitudes	+	+	+	+	0	0	0	−
Authoritarian attitudes	+	+	+	+	0	0	0	−
Anti-Semitic attitudes	0	+	+	0	0	0	0	0
Isolationist attitudes	+	+	0	0	+	0	0	−
Anti-Black attitudes	0	+	0	0	0	0	0	−
Pro-warfare state attitudes	+	0	0	0	0	0	−	−
Laissez-faire attitudes	0	0	0	0	0	0	0	0
Probusiness attitudes	0	0	0	0	0	0	−	−
Anti-foreign aid attitudes	0	0	0	0	0	0	−	−
Anti-welfare state attitudes	0	0	−	0	0	0	−	0
Anarchistic attitudes	0	0	0	0	−	0	−	−
Machiavellian attitudes	0	0	0	0	−	−	−	−
Guttman scale errors	(2)	(0)	(1)	(0)	(1)	(0)	(0)	(0)

NOTE: Guttman's coefficient of reproducibility = .95 (.96 in all items).
Minimum reproducibility = .74.
Menzel's coefficient of scalability = .82.
Probability of arrangement occurring by chance < .001.

mysticism, and fundamentalism. The three religiosity variables with the fewest positive correlations with political conservatism and with the most negative correlations are theism, altruism, and finally, with only three positive correlations and thirty-seven negative correlations, idealism. It is interesting, in view of this, to recall Rossiter's (1962) comments bemoaning the fact that conservatism has been seen as an uncomplimentary position which is supported by the frequent and positive correlations of conservatism with superstition and the lack of positive correlations and presence of negative correlations with altruism and idealism. Perhaps the perception is a just one.

We can look at this ordering of religiosity variables in still another way. If we bisect each population into (1) those religiosity

TABLE 5-13. EXTENT AND NATURE OF CORRELATION BETWEEN POLITICAL CONSERVATISM AND THE MEASURES OF RELIGIOSITY

	Number of times in the segment of the dichotomy with the highest number of positive correlations with conservatism
Superstition	8
Church orientation	7
Ritualism	6
Mysticism	6
Fundamentalism	4
Theism	1
Altruism	0
Idealism	0

variables with the highest number of positive correlations with political conservatism and (2) those religiosity variables with the lowest number of positive correlations or the highest number of negative correlations with political conservatism, we discover the ordering found in table 5-13. Thus superstition is always in the division most highly and positively correlated with conservatism, and altruism and idealism are always in the part of the dichotomy that is not positively correlated and may be negatively correlated with conservatism.

This ordering of religiosity dimensions suggests that the dimension which is most unenlightened (superstition) is also most often positively correlated with political conservatism. Following this, we find the dimensions of church orientation and ritualism to be also frequently positively correlated with political conservatism at a significant level. This seems to suggest that the more conforming and outwardly oriented dimensions of religious attitudes are inclined to be often and positively correlated with conservatism. The dimensions of mysticism and fundamentalism fall in roughly a middle position in regard to their correlations with conservatism. If we turn our attention to the other end of the scale of correlations, we find that the dimension of idealism is hardly ever positively correlated with political conservatism and is, in fact, frequently negatively correlated. This suggests that there may be a certain affinity between orientation to principle and political liberalism. The dimension of altruism is also seldom positively correlated with political conservatism. This seems to indicate the altruistic nature obviously present in political liberalism. The position of theism in the ordering is of some interest also, for we find that it is infrequently positively correlated with political conservatism. This seems to indicate that simple

	SOUTHERN		CATHOLIC		MENNONITE		MIDWESTERN		MEAN RANK
	Rural	Urban	Urban	Rural	Urban	Rural	Rural	Urban	
Superpatriotic attitudes	3.0	1.5	2.0	2.0	2.5	2.0	3.0	1.0	2.13
Authoritarian attitudes	1.5	4.5	1.0	2.0	1.5	1.0	5.5	4.5	2.69
Anti-civil liberty attitudes	7.0	4.5	3.0	5.5	7.0	5.5	1.0	3.0	4.69
States' rights attitudes	4.0	4.5	9.5	5.5	12.5	10.0	12.0	2.0	7.50
Anti-Black attitudes	9.0	7.5	6.0	12.0	7.0	5.5	5.5	7.5	7.50
Anti-Semitic attitudes	9.0	4.5	6.0	5.5	12.5	10.0	9.5	6.0	8.00
Pro-warfare state attitudes	5.0	7.5	6.0	9.0	4.0	10.0	14.0	9.0	8.07
Probusiness attitudes	1.5	1.5	6.0	2.0	12.5	5.5	5.5	12.5	8.37
Restorationist attitudes	9.0	9.0	9.5	9.0	7.0	10.0	9.5	4.5	8.44
Machiavellian attitudes	13.0	11.0	6.0	12.0	7.0	5.5	9.5	12.5	9.56
Anti-foreign aid attitudes	13.0	11.0	13.0	14.0	7.0	3.0	5.5	12.5	9.88
Anarchistic attitudes	13.0	14.0	13.0	5.5	12.5	14.5	2.0	12.5	10.88
Laissez-faire attitudes	13.0	14.0	13.0	12.0	1.0	13.0	9.5	12.5	11.00
Isolationist attitudes	6.0	11.0	13.0	15.0	12.5	10.0	14.0	7.5	11.12
Anti-welfare state attitudes	13.0	14.0	13.0	9.0	12.5	14.5	14.0	12.5	12.81

NOTE: Coefficient of concordance = .47.
$P < .001$.

theism is more connected to liberalism than are such more specialized religious attitudes as church orientation, ritualism, mysticism, and fundamentalism.

Let us turn our attention now to a consideration of the dimensions of political conservatism. If in our analysis of the order of the political attitude variables we begin by noting the scaled orders secured from the "Guttman-like" scalings of the eight populations, we can secure an ordering or a ranking of the fifteen variables in each of the eight populations. This ranking is summarized in table 5-14. An examination of this table reveals an astonishingly constant ordering of these political variables in all eight populations. In view of the greater number of variables and the more complicated nature of the ordering, we can best demonstrate this significant constancy by employing a descriptive statistic, Kendall's coefficient of concordance.

We discover a coefficient of concordance or a W of .47, which is statistically significant at well beyond the .001 level. Therefore, the concordance is significantly high or the orderings are significantly similar.

An examination of the mean rank ordering of these variables reveals that superpatriotism and authoritarian attitudes are most often correlated positively with religiosity, followed closely by anti-civil liberty attitudes, states' rights attitudes, anti-Black and anti-

Semitic attitudes. Alternately, we find that anti-welfare and isolation-ist attitudes are typically uncorrelated or are negatively correlated with religiosity. Laissez-faire, anarchistic, anti-foreign aid, and Machiavellian attitudes are next least often positively correlated. Finally, we find pro-warfare, probusiness, and restorationist attitudes often medially correlated.

The ordering of political variables in table 5-14 shows an interesting pattern. The more "totalitarian and bigoted" dimensions are more often positively correlated with religiosity than the "staid conservative" dimensions. By "staid conservative" we mean attitudes involving notions disliking government aid and direction and favoring a return to earlier patterns of government, including isolationism. Thus totalitarian and bigoted attitudes are more often positively related to religiosity than are the staid conservative attitudes.

The totalitarian and bigoted dimensions most often related positively to religious attitudes are superpatriotism, authoritarianism, anti-civil liberties, pro-warfare, anti-Black, and anti-Semitic attitude dimensions. The dimensions included in the staid conservative set of dimensions are probusiness, restorationist, Machiavellian, anti-foreign aid, anarchistic, isolationist, and anti-welfare state attitudes.

In summary, we have noted a consistent pattern of significant positive correlation between the superstitious, externally oriented type of religious attitudes and political conservatism or between the more totalitarian types of conservatism and religiosity.

A FACTOR ANALYTIC STUDY OF RELIGIOSITY AND POLITICAL CONSERVATISM*

Another manner of analysis, which I shall now describe, does not focus upon the integration of political and religious attitudes as such but rather resolves the eight correlation matrices into their underlying clusters or factors.

The procedure is simply the factor analysis of each of the eight correlation matrices or the intercorrelations of the variables in each of the eight populations. In each population we have a 23 by 23

---

*The factor analyses reported here were performed and initially interpreted by Prof. Paul Wiebe.

correlation matrix which reports the intercorrelations of each of the scales of religiosity and political conservatism. The matrices can be found in Appendix B.

Each of these matrices was factor analyzed by the "principal components" method. The extracted factors were then orthogonally rotated to simple structure. The resulting rotated factor loadings can also be found in Appendix B. Let us, however, examine some of these resulting rotated factors.

The factor analysis of the eight populations reveals that a number of general factors appear in all or nearly all of the populations under examination. In addition to the general factors, there are also some rather specific factors. A joint interpretation of the general and the specific factors may be the most revealing approach to this analysis. We are interested in identifying the factors which underlie the intercorrelations of the variables employed in this study and in describing, through factor analysis, the populations examined in this study.

We should perhaps note initially that one of the eight populations appears somewhat at variance from the others. The population in question is the Mennonite urban sample. The sample is generally from only small cities and the number in the sample is rather small (N = 38); therefore, some of its lack of comparability might well be attributed to these facts. It was also the only population in which the scale arrangement discovered in the previous analysis was not significantly different from what could have occurred by chance.

The lowest point chosen for interpreted factor loadings is .40. Variables with loadings of less than .40 are not included in the subsequent tables of factor loadings. This point was arbitrarily selected; however, it is a rather commonly selected point. In tables 5-15 through 5-27, variables marked with two daggers will be found in all comparable factors in the various samples. Variables marked with a single dagger are found in nearly all the factors examined. The variables marked with the daggers are those used to define the factor and are considered crucial for its identification.

The first set of factors or the first general factor is one which can be labeled the "general Christianity factor." We find that the variables which occur most often and tend to identify or define the general Christianity factor are: (1) fundamentalism, a variable which we find in every population's general Christianity factor, (2) theism,

TABLE 5-15. THE GENERAL CHRISTIANITY FACTOR IN THE EIGHT POPULATIONS

	RURAL		URBAN	
	Variable	Loading	Variable	Loading
	Factor II (N = 45)		*Factor I* (N = 137)	
Southern students	†Altruism	.829	†Theism	.871
	Superstition	.785	††Fundamentalism	.844
	†Mysticism	.742	†Mysticism	.806
	†Theism	.740	†Altruism	.739
	††Fundamentalism	.715	Superstition	.695
	Idealism	.438	Church orientation	.443
	Factor II (N = 37)		*Factor II* (N = 140)	
Midwestern students	††Fundamentalism	.928	†Theism	.884
	†Theism	.857	††Fundamentalism	.859
	†Mysticism	.513	†Altruism	.755
	Idealism	.459	Church orientation	.688
	†Altruism	.407	†Mysticism	.622
	Factor II (N = 82)		*Factor II* (N = 199)	
Catholic students	†Altruism	.807	†Theism	.808
	††Fundamentalism	.696	Idealism	.746
	Anti-foreign aid	−.587	††Fundamentalism	.705
	Ritualism	.572	†Altruism	.426
	Isolationism	−.433		
	Factor II (N = 237)		*Factor II* (N = 38)	
Mennonite students	†Theism	.939	†Theism	.925
	††Fundamentalism	.925	††Fundamentalism	.921
	†Mysticism	.533	Idealism	.505
	†Altruism	.423	†Mysticism	.465

† Found in nearly all factors examined.
†† Found in all comparable factors.

found in seven of the eight populations surveyed, (3) altruism, also in seven of the eight populations, and (4) mysticism, which occurs in six of the eight samples. The clustering of these variables is not a surprising one (table 5-15).

The general Christianity factor and the loadings of some of the varying samples become somewhat more understandable when we examine some of the more specific factors. For example, we note that in the two southern student populations the variable superstition is part of the general Christianity factor and that this variable does not occur in any other population's general Christianity factor. This fact suggests that Christian religiosity in the southern sample is more inclined to be related to or to involve superstitious attitudes. The southern Christian is more a part of a tradition that includes attitudes of anti-intellectualism, religious conservatism, evangelism, and emotionally superstitious religious experience and faith (Maranell 1968). This factor pattern is further reinforced by the fact that in each of the non-southern populations we find a separate superstition factor not found in the southern sample. This tends to indicate that superstition is not involved with general Christianity elsewhere as it is found to be in the southern samples. Table 5-15 describes the general Christianity factor, and table 5-16 describes the superstition factor, as it occurs in all the non-southern samples.

In addition to discovering that superstition is found only in the general Christianity factor of the southern samples and that in all the other populations it occurs as a separate "superstition factor," we find that in the two midwestern student populations superstition and mysticism are paired in the superstition factor. This may be

TABLE 5-16. THE SUPERSTITION FACTOR IN SIX POPULATIONS

	RURAL		URBAN	
	Variable	Loading	Variable	Loading
Midwestern students	*Factor XI* (N = 37) Mysticism ††Superstition	 .682 .473	*Factor XI* (N = 140) ††Superstition Mysticism	 .780 .512
Catholic students	*Factor VII* (N = 82) ††Superstition	 .842	*Factor IX* (N = 199) ††Superstition	 .948
Mennonite students	*Factor VII* (N = 237) ††Superstition	 .906	*Factor V* (N = 38) ††Superstition Authoritarianism	 .929 .417

†† Found in all comparable factors.

taken as evidence that in these samples superstition involves a generally mystical world orientation rather than only superstition alone.

The "mysticism factor" appears to be a specifically Catholic factor which is separate from the general Christianity factor; that is, it occurs only in the Catholic samples. We note that only the Catholic samples did not have mysticism loaded on the Christianity factor (table 5-17). This suggests that in the Catholic samples mysticism is not typically a part of general Christianity, as it is elsewhere, but is a separate and perhaps even more generalized phenomenon independent of a more restricted religiosity such as that which is focused around the fundamentalism variable.

TABLE 5-17. THE MYSTICISM FACTOR IN THE CATHOLIC POPULATIONS

RURAL		URBAN	
Variable	Loading	Variable	Loading
Factor X (N = 82)		*Factor VIII* (N = 199)	
††Mysticism	−.776	††Mysticism	.841
Restorationism	.407		

†† Found in all comparable factors.

Theism was not found to be a part of the general Christianity factor in the Catholic rural population. We find that there exists a separate theism factor in this sample only (table 5-18).

The picture presented to this point suggests that (1) a rather general Christianity factor does exist, (2) that superstition is part of the southern general Christian position but exists in the other sampled areas as a factor separate from and not generally involved in the more pervasive religiosity orientation, and (3) that Catholics possess

TABLE 5-18. THE THEISM FACTOR IN THE CATHOLIC RURAL POPULATION

Variable	Loading
Factor VI (N = 82)	
Theism	.771
Probusiness	−.590

a mysticism independent of their more general Christian orientation (table 5-17). The presence of the separate Catholic rural theism factor (table 5-18) is difficult to interpret; however, in this sample theism is coupled with anti-business attitudes suggesting perhaps a general nonexpediency orientation, even a reaction of the sample to the business mentality in contrast to theism. The rural Catholic's general Christianity factor is of further interest in that it reflects an international orientation (minus loadings on anti-foreign aid and isolationism become pro-foreign aid and anti-isolationism) which is seen as a part of a more general religious stance that is centered on religious altruism. This is a familiar and even admirably enlightened factor interestingly found in a rural Catholic population.

Another interesting general factor is the "church orientation factor" (table 5-19). This general factor conceivably could be divided into two somewhat dissimilar sets of factors by applying a rough

TABLE 5-19. THE CHURCH ORIENTATION FACTOR IN THE EIGHT POPULATIONS

	RURAL		URBAN	
	Variable	Loading	Variable	Loading
	Factor VIII (N = 45)		*Factor V* (N = 137)	
Southern students	††Church orientation	–.809	†Ritualism	.740
			††Church orientation	.620
			Anti-civil liberty	.476
			Probusiness	.472
			Altruism	.412
	Factor VI (N = 37)		*Factor X* (N = 140)	
Midwestern students	†Ritualism	.893	†Ritualism	.866
	††Church orientation	.753	††Church orientation	.471
	Probusiness	.500		
	Factor IV (N = 82)		*Factor VI* (N = 199)	
Catholic students	††Church orientation	.873	†Ritualism	.797
			††Church orientation	.769
	Factor IV (N = 237)		*Factor IV* (N = 38)	
Mennonite students	††Church orientation	.911	††Church orientation	.938
	Altruism	.478		

† Found in nearly all factors examined.
†† Found in all comparable factors.

Gemeinschaft-Gesellschaft distinction to our populations. Gemeinschaft refers to a community orientation with high intimacy, whereas Gesellschaft identifies a non-intimate society of individuals who are generally unknown to each other and who place little or no value on the mutual association.

We find that the more Gemeinschaft samples do not have ritualism loaded on the factor with church orientation, reflecting a more general "church supper-bazaar" factor. The more Gemeinschaft samples would be: southern rural, Catholic rural, and the two Mennonite samples. A Mennonite student familiar with the Mennonite data pointed out that we perhaps should not call the Mennonite urban sample "urban" because of the small community orientation of the group. On the other hand, the rural midwestern sample is rural with a great participation in urban society. This is somewhat reflected in the basic urban bias in the undergraduate midwestern university student body. The difference between midwestern and southern rural areas is rather great: one is an urbanized small-town area, the other is rural in nearly every sense of the word.

When the foregoing Gemeinschaft-Gesellschaft distinction is made, we find that the factors in the Gemeinschaft samples are made up of the church-orientation variable alone except in the one case when it occurs with altruism. Whereas in the Gesellschaft samples, midwestern urban and rural, southern urban, and Catholic urban church orientation is always paired with ritualism. This may suggest that church orientation in Gesellschaft samples necessarily involves ritualism, that an individual is church oriented for formal, ritualized ceremonies and is not simply a participator in a "community" which happens to be religious. This reflects a more compartmentalized church orientation in the Gesellschaft sample and an integrated church involvement in the Gemeinschaft samples. In the Gemeinschaft samples the informal and associational is stressed, whereas in the Gesellschaft the formal and only affiliative is emphasized.

Two final sets of religious factors remain to be examined. The first of these is the "idealism factor." It is interesting to note that the variable idealism does not inevitably appear in the general Christianity factor. We find that it shows up as a separate and independent factor in nearly all the samples. This suggests an interesting isolation

TABLE 5-20. THE IDEALISM FACTOR IN THE VARIOUS POPULATIONS

	RURAL		URBAN	
	Variable	Loading	Variable	Loading
	Factor X (N = 45)		*Factor IX* (N = 137)	
Southern students	††Idealism	.815	††Idealism	.874
	Factor X (N = 37)		*Factor VIII* (N = 140)	
Midwestern students	††Idealism	−.826	††Idealism	.855
			Machiavellianism	−.489
	Factor VIII (N = 82)			
Catholic students	††Idealism	−.833		
	Pro-warfare state	.576		
	Isolationism	.484		
	Machiavellianism	.431		
	Factor VI (N = 237)		*Factor VIII* (N = 38)	
Mennonite students	††Idealism	.906	Mysticism	.733
			††Idealism	.650
			Probusiness	.421

†† Found in all comparable factors.

of lofty principle and dedication to important causes from more orthodox religious attitudes. This may reflect a certain press toward expediency in the populations studied in regard to their religious principles. Table 5-20 presents the loadings of the variables on the idealism factor.

The final of the clearly religiosity-oriented factors involves religious altruism (table 5-21). We have previously observed that altruism is a part of the general Christianity factor in all except the Mennonite samples. Altruism, it should be recalled, is a somewhat "Christian" altruism. In view of this, it should be expected to be a

TABLE 5-21. THE ALTRUISM FACTOR IN THREE POPULATIONS

	RURAL		URBAN	
	Variable	Loading	Variable	Loading
Midwestern students	Factor VII (N = 37) ††Altruism	.799		
Mennonite students	Factor XI (N = 237) ††Altruism Mysticism	–.425 –.404	Factor VII (N = 38) ††Altruism	.883

†† Found in all comparable factors.

part of the general Christianity factor. However, we find that in the case of the Mennonite populations and the midwestern rural population the variable exists as a separate specific factor. It is possible, especially in the Mennonite populations, that altruism has become a "separate" way of life and that concern for man and the brotherhood of man has become divorced and separated from the idea of the fatherhood of God. And subsequently service to others has become an end in itself.

Let us now turn our attention to the consideration of the more purely political factors. The first general political factor we shall examine is one we can perhaps best label as a "totalitarianism factor" (table 5-22). We find in each of the eight populations a clustering of variables which in each case involves authoritarian attitudes. The variables clustered with authoritarianism include anti-civil liberty attitudes, warfare state attitudes, and superpatriotic attitudes. Thus we can see that the label "totalitarian" appropriately identifies this general factor.

This particular clustering gathers together attitudes that respect

TABLE 5-22. THE TOTALITARIANISM FACTOR IN THE EIGHT POPULATIONS

	RURAL		URBAN	
	Variable	Loading	Variable	Loading
Southern students	*Factor III* (N = 45)		*Factor IV* (N = 137)	
	††Authoritarianism	−.800	†Superpatriotism	.772
	Probusiness	−.775	††Authoritarianism	.742
	†Superpatriotism	−.764	†Pro-warfare state	.407
	†Pro-warfare state	−.571	†Anti-civil liberty	.405
	†Anti-civil liberty	−.547		
	Machiavellianism	−.424		
Midwestern students	*Factor IV* (N = 37)		*Factor VI* (N = 140)	
	Anti-Semitism	.914	††Authoritarianism	.742
	Anti-Black attitudes	.860	†Anti-civil liberty	.713
	Machiavellianism	.682	†Pro-warfare state	.531
	†Anti-civil liberty	.629		
	††Authoritarianism	.553		
	†Pro-warfare state	.465		
	Superstition	.424		
Catholic students	*Factor V* (N = 82)		*Factor X* (N= 199)	
	†Superpatriotism	.905	††Authoritarianism	.803
	††Authoritarianism	.566	†Pro-warfare state	.568
	†Anti-civil liberty	.447	†Superpatriotism	.544
Mennonite students	*Factor VIII* (N = 237)		*Factor III* (N = 38)	
	††Authoritarianism	.825	†Superpatriotism	.899
	†Anti-civil liberty	.465	†Pro-warfare state	.792
	†Superpatriotism	.419	Probusiness	.745
			Machiavellianism	.663
			Anti-Black attitudes	.655
			††Authoritarianism	.597
			†Anti-civil liberty	.498
			Isolationism	.447

† Found in nearly all factors examined.
†† Found in all comparable factors.

strong leaders and obedient followers and insist upon respect for authority with attitudes that favor a restriction of civil liberties and appreciate or glorify war, even thermonuclear war, and adds to these a fanatic nationalism, a flag-waving ethnocentric, militant, super-nationalistic patriotism. This cluster of attitudes has been found in many recognized totalitarian situations. Deviation from this pattern of attitudes is held to be suspect by persons who adhere to it. Adherents feel that persons who do not hold these attitudes should be severely punished. Civil liberties and indeed the Supreme Court, they feel, shelter the suspiciously disobedient and disloyal.

Interestingly, the rural religious populations do not include warfare state attitudes in their totalitarian factors; they may have totalitarian attitudes but they are not warfare oriented, reflecting perhaps a religiously based pacifism.

We can appreciate that Machiavellian attitudes are often clustered appropriately with the other variables in the totalitarianism factor. In some instances we find anti-minority attitudes also clustered with totalitarianism, and occasionally a probusiness orientation variable is included in the cluster. We recognize that such attitudes have often been found to occur in totalitarian situations.

Only in the midwestern samples is superpatriotism missing from the totalitarianism factor. In every other population we find it clustered with the other totalitarian variables. In both of the midwestern student samples we find separate "superpatriotism factors," indicating that perhaps in these samples the linkage between totalitarianism and superpatriotism does not exist (table 5-23). The midwestern

TABLE 5-23. THE PATRIOTISM FACTOR IN THE MIDWESTERN POPULATIONS

RURAL		URBAN	
Variable	Loading	Variable	Loading
Factor VIII (N = 37)		*Factor IV* (N = 140)	
††Superpatriotism	–.816	††Superpatriotism	.749
		Probusiness	.577

†† Found in all comparable factors.

superpatriot is not as militant, as authoritarian, as warfare oriented or as anti-civil liberty oriented as the superpatriot in the other samples. For him patriotism is not so demanding, being restricted to fraternal-society opening ceremonies. He, similarly, may not suspect all others of being less patriotic than himself.

The second general factor with a purely political orientation is that which is best identified as the "bigotry factor" (table 5-24). An examination of the variables typically clustered together to form this factor demonstrates the nature and source of the labeling. The variables that define this factor are anti-Semitic, anti-Black, and anti-civil liberty attitudes. This pattern of attitudes is suspicious of minorities, considers Blacks and Jews as dangerous, overbearing groups, and further prefers to curtail the activity of all whose attitudes do not correspond to those of the "majority."

We can recognize some interesting variations in the bigotry factor in the various populations. For example, in the rural southern

TABLE 5-24. THE BIGOTRY FACTOR IN SEVEN POPULATIONS

	RURAL		URBAN	
	Variable	Loading	Variable	Loading
	Factor IV (N = 45)		*Factor VI* (N = 137)	
Southern students	††Anti-Semitism	.896	††Anti-Semitism	.821
	††Anti-Black attitudes	.831	††Anti-Black attitudes	.739
	Restorationism	.523	†Anti-civil liberty	.406
	Pro-states' rights	.496		
	Anti-civil liberty	.467		
	Factor IV* (N = 37)		*Factor I* (N = 140)	
Midwestern students	††Anti-Semitism	.914	††Anti-Semitism	.857
	††Anti-Black attitudes	.860	††Anti-Black attitudes	.758
	Machiavellianism	.682	†Anti-civil liberty	.424
	†Anti-civil liberty	.629	Restorationism	.405
	Authoritarianism	.553		
	Pro-warfare state	.465		
	Superstition	.424		
	Factor I (N = 82)		*Factor III* (N = 199)	
Catholic students	††Anti-Semitism	.880	††Anti-Black attitudes	−.819
	††Anti-Black attitudes	.773	††Anti-Semitism	−.743
	Machiavellianism	.452	Machiavellianism	−.487
	†Anti-civil liberty	.397**	Probusiness	−.415
	Factor I (N = 237)			
Mennonite students	††Anti-Black attitudes	.805		
	††Anti-Semitism	.783		
	Pro-warfare state	.585		
	Ritualism	.504		
	Superpatriotism	.499		
	†Anti-civil liberty	.474		

† Found in nearly all factors examined.
†† Found in all comparable factors.
* This cluster was also assigned previously to another general factor to aid the interpretation.
** Included because it would round to .40 and is consistent with the total pattern of loadings.

student sample bigotry is coupled with states' rights and restorationist attitudes. Apparently the rural southern student prefers to restore or return to the "good old days of bigotry"—when minority group members "knew their place" and the "tradition" of segregation was not yet challenged. There is also a coupling of bigotry with restorationistic attitudes in the midwestern urban sample. In the midwestern rural sample bigotry is clustered with attitudes of expediency, as it is in the Catholic and Mennonite samples. It should be pointed out that attitudes of expediency include Machiavellian and warfare state attitudes. Therefore, it seems that in these populations bigotry accompanies or is accompanied by militancy.

Another somewhat different political factor is that identified as the "hostility toward government factor" (table 5-25). This factor

TABLE 5-25. THE HOSTILITY TOWARD GOVERNMENT FACTOR IN THE EIGHT POPULATIONS

	RURAL		URBAN	
	Variable	Loading	Variable	Loading
Southern students	*Factor VII* (N = 45)		*Factor VII* (N = 137)	
	††Anarchy	−.878	††Anarchy	.880
	Anti-welfare state	−.519	Probusiness	.470
Midwestern students	*Factor III* (N = 37)		*Factor III* (N = 140)	
	Pro-states' rights	.844	††Anarchy	−.846
	Laissez-faire	.813		
	Restorationism	.683		
	††Anarchy	.640		
Catholic students	*Factor III* (N = 82)		*Factor VII* (N = 199)	
	Anti-welfare state	.860	††Anarchy	.841
	Anti-foreign aid	.512	Anti-welfare state	.414
	Isolationism	.460		
	††Anarchy	.409		
Mennonite students	*Factor III* (N = 237)		*Factor I* (N = 38)	
	††Anarchy	.795	††Anarchy	.858
	Anti-welfare state	.719	Anti-foreign aid	.729
	Anti-foreign aid	.580	Laissez-faire	.660
			Anti-welfare state	.618
			Isolationism	.579

†† Found in all comparable factors.

provides an interesting contrast with the previously described totalitarian factor. It is marked principally by the presence of the anarchistic attitude variable, which is featured in every sample studied. There are, however, some variations in the nature of the factor in the various samples. We find, for example, that anarchy is clustered with anti-welfare and anti-foreign aid attitudes in a number of the populations. This may be seen to indicate an antigovernment attitude deriving from an opposition to what are seen as "give-away" programs. The government is rejected because it is seen to take money from the thrifty and give it to the shiftless and lazy in this country and abroad. Those students from the midwestern rural population who are found to be anarchical are also found to favor states' rights, restoration of things associated with the past, and laissez-faire economic principles. Apparently what these persons dislike most in regard to the government is what they view as government intervention in individual affairs, economic and social. In the southern urban student sample, anarchy is coupled with probusiness attitudes. The government is here rejected for interfering with private economic activity.

Another political factor is the "isolationism factor" (table 5-26). This factor, which is also a general factor, demonstrates the coupling of anti-foreign aid and isolationist attitudes. This factor occurs in all the major samples but is missing from the rather unreliable Mennonite urban population. It ranges from a pure isolationism in the midwestern rural and urban student samples and the southern urban student population to a more complex factor involving warfare state attitudes, states' rights attitudes, laissez-faire attitudes, anti-welfare state and superpatriotic attitudes elsewhere. There are apparently economic, militant, and patriotic isolationists as well as those who simply reject international involvement of all kinds as a principle.

TABLE 5-26. THE ISOLATIONISM FACTOR IN SEVEN POPULATIONS

	RURAL		URBAN	
	Variable	Loading	Variable	Loading
Southern students	Factor I (N = 45)		Factor II (N = 137)	
	††Anti-foreign aid	.847	††Anti-foreign aid	−.815
	††Isolationism	.838	††Isolationism	−.820
	Pro-warfare state	.626		
	Pro-states' rights	.541		
	Anti-welfare state	.457		
	Laissez-faire	.456		
Midwestern students	Factor V (N = 37)		Factor V (N = 140)	
	††Isolationism	−.867	††Anti-foreign aid	.813
	††Anti-foreign aid	−.638	††Isolationism	.745
Catholic students	Factor III* (N = 82)		Factor I (N = 199)	
	Anti-welfare state	.860	††Anti-foreign aid	.848
	††Anti-foreign aid	.512	††Isolationism	.792
	††Isolationism	.459	Anti-welfare state	.672
	Anarchy	.409	Laissez-faire	.596
Mennonite students	Factor X (N = 237)			
	††Isolationism	.720		
	††Anti-foreign aid	.452		
	Superpatriotism	.438		

†† Found in all comparable factors.
* This cluster was also assigned previously to another general factor to aid the interpretation.

The last general factor we shall consider is best identified as a "states' rights–restorationism factor" (table 5-27). This factor can be

TABLE 5-27. THE STATES' RIGHTS–RESTORATIONISM FACTOR IN THE EIGHT POPULATIONS

	RURAL		URBAN	
	Variable	Loading	Variable	Loading
	Factor IV* (N = 45)		Factor VIII (N = 137)	
Southern students	Anti-Semitism	.896	†Restorationism	−.779
	Anti-Black attitudes	.831	††Pro-states' rights	−.752
	†Restorationism	.523		
	††Pro-states' rights	.496		
	Anti-civil liberty	.467		
	Factor III* (N = 37)		Factor VII (N = 140)	
Midwestern students	††Pro-states' rights	.844	††Pro-states' rights	.703
	Laissez-faire	.813	†Restorationism	.696
	†Restorationism	.683	Laissez-faire	.628
	Anarchism	.640	Pro-warfare state	.470
	Factor IX (N = 82)		Factor IV (N = 199)	
Catholic students	††Pro-states' rights	.774	†Restorationism	−.774
	Laissez-faire	.694	††Pro-states' rights	−.649
	Factor V (N = 237)		Factor X (N = 38)	
Mennonite students	†Restorationism	.789	††Pro-states' rights	.853
	Laissez-faire	.711		
	††Pro-states' rights	.685		
	Isolationism	.442		

† Found in nearly all populations examined.
†† Found in all comparable factors.
* This cluster was also assigned previously to another general factor to aid the interpretation.

found in all eight of the populations studied. It involves an emphasis upon states' rights and restorationistic attitudes. We find some interesting variations in the variables clustered with these dimensions in some of the populations. For example, in the southern rural student sample we find included both anti-Semitic and anti-Black attitudes as well as anti-civil liberties attitudes. This points up the rural South's wish to restore, under the guise of states' rights, the good old days of "institutionalized bigotry," of "holding slaves and growing cotton" as it has been put. They wish to restore a traditional past and re-establish critical racial distinctions.

In the midwestern student sample the factor is found to involve laissez-faire economics. The midwesterners wish to return to "natural laws" in a "free" economic system, before we had income taxes and acreage allotments. Crucially, the racial bigotry aspect is entirely lacking from the midwestern states' rights–restorationism factor.

In summary we have described in this chapter the interrelationships of religiosity and political conservatism. Fifteen dimensions of political conservatism were defined and measured with Likert scales. The results of a "known-group" validity study of these scales were also reported. The scales of religiosity and political conservatism were administered to eight student populations. It was discovered that the religious attitude dimensions of superstition, church orientation, ritualism, and mysticism were most highly and positively related to political conservatism. Idealism, on the other hand, was seldom positively and frequently negatively correlated with political conservatism. It was also discovered that totalitarian and bigotry variables among the political variables were most highly related to religiosity and that the more staid conservative variables are less highly and less often positively correlated with religiosity.

Following this a factor analysis of the full 23 by 23 variable correlation matrices was conducted for each of the eight student populations. The general factors identified were: (1) a general Christianity factor, (2) a church-orientation factor, (3) an idealism factor, (4) a totalitarianism factor, (5) a bigotry factor, (6) a hostility toward government factor, (7) a states' rights factor, and (8) an isolationism factor. Each of these factors was identified in each of the eight populations with only a few exceptions.

Thus this chapter attempted to clarify the religiosity-political attitude structure and outlined the general factors or clusters of variables which exist within conservatism.

6

RELIGIOSITY IN ACADEMIA*

This chapter describes the religious attitudes of college professors, focusing on religious attitude differences of differing types of college and university professors.

Evidence presented in an article published some time ago (Stark 1963) suggests the existence of a basic incompatibility between religion and science. Anderson (1968) found academics to be less oriented to religious groups in interaction and identification than people in general. Further examination of discipline and environment differences in religious attitudes seems to be called for. A study of the religious attitudes of academic persons can be a fruitful avenue for this subsequent research. Therefore, the present study attempts to identify and describe the religious attitudes of college and university professors through a mail questionnaire survey.

The attention of this survey is directed toward five areas of possible difference in the eight dimensions of religiosity: (1) region, (2) type of college, (3) size of college faculty, (4) rank of professor, and (5) discipline of professor. These variables serve to answer six general questions:

(1) Are there regional differences in the religious attitudes of college professors?

---

* Professor Robert Hickson participated in the early stages of this study. His contributions are appreciated.

(2) Do college professors in different types of colleges and universities differ in religious attitudes?

(3) Do college professors in college faculties of different size differ in religious attitudes?

(4) Do college and university professors of different rank differ in religious attitudes?

(5) Do college and university professors of different disciplines differ in religious attitudes?

(6) How do these five variables interact in "determining" differential religiosity among college and university professors?

The method of examination and analysis (factorial design analysis of variance) allows for the identification of differences between the elements analyzed, as well as for the examination of all of the possible interactions between the five areas or variables.

THE VARIABLES

Region

Region is treated as a dichotomy in this research, the two values being southern and non-southern or northern. The states classified as southern are Alabama, Arkansas, Florida, Georgia, Kentucky, Louisiana, Mississippi, North Carolina, South Carolina, Tennessee, Texas, and Virginia. The classification of these states as "southern" is in general agreement with V. O. Key, Jr. (1949) among others. The states classified as northern include Illinois, Iowa, Indiana, Michigan, Minnesota, Nebraska, New York, North Dakota, Ohio, Pennsylvania, South Dakota, and Wisconsin. The best identification of these states in this instance is that they are non-southern and serve as a group with which the southern group can be compared. It should be noted that in general these northern states lie immediately north of the southern states studied.

Type of College or University

The distinction made with this variable is one between state-supported colleges and universities and those with religious affiliation or "connection." The titles given this variable are (1) public, and (2) denominational.

Size of College or University Faculty

This variable attempts to distinguish between the larger and smaller colleges and universities. School size could also have been measured with student body size; however, since it is the faculty with which we are interested, a direct measure of faculty size was seen to be superior to a measure of student body size. The distribution of faculty size was dichotomized by cutting the total distribution into schools with faculty sizes of 130 and over and faculties of 129 and under. It should be noted that faculty sizes change, and this classification involved the data reported in the current world almanac.

Rank of Professor

This variable was also used as a dichotomy. Therefore, only full professors and assistant professors were used. It was felt that these two ranks would give us an indication of the influence of rank and would also allow us to minimize the effect of "catalogue delay," for it is realized that a great many professors listed as assistant in the catalogues are associate professors by the time the catalogue is issued. Therefore, the dichotomy is really full professors and assistant professors plus some associate professors, or full professors and non-full professors.

Discipline

Three categories of disciplines of a rather general variety were included for study. These are behavioral scientists, physical scientists, and professors of fine arts. Each of these general disciplines includes professors of two subdisciplines. The behavioral scientists are sociologists and psychologists; the physical scientists are chemists and physicists; and those in fine arts are artists and musicians.

THE POPULATIONS AND ANALYSIS

A stratified random sample of college professors was drawn from college catalogues. The sample was drawn to provide data for each of the forty-eight combinations of the five variables: region, type of college, size of college, rank of professor, and discipline (a $3 \times 2 \times 2 \times 2 \times 2$ factorial analysis of variance table). A mail questionnaire was sent to a sample of college professors from each of the forty-eight groups of professors defined by the combinations just described. In those cases where the group did not contain many professors, a questionnaire was mailed to all professors who satisfied the selection criterion. The total number of questionnaires mailed out was 1,968, slightly over 40 for each cell of analysis.

The return rate from the professors was about 50 per cent—a rather high rate considering the demanding nature of the questionnaire. However, these returned cases were unequally distributed throughout the 3 × 2 × 2 × 2 × 2 table. The distribution was such that by further sampling of the cells with extra cases and the addition of 13 mean scores (Lindquist 1953) the cell frequency could be set at 15. This step reduced the size of the analyzed sample to 720. The equality of cell frequency was demanded by the analysis form selected. It was felt the extensive analysis made possible by a 3 × 2 × 2 × 2 ×2 factorial analysis of variance more than compensated for the subjects lost, for it allows for the examination of all main effects as well as all 2, 3, 4, and 5 variable interactions. It was necessary to employ computer analysis, but an unweighted means analysis was not developed early enough at the local computer center to make its use possible. The added cases (means) were taken into account through a correction suggested by Lindquist (1953) which subtracts the number of means added from the residual degrees of freedom.

The professors who responded were on the faculties of 343 different colleges and universities. The particular number of colleges and universities of each type is:

27 small, northern, public colleges
29 small, southern, public colleges
80 small, northern, denominational colleges
66 small, southern, denominational colleges
49 large, northern, public universities
52 large, southern, public universities
27 large, northern, denominational universities
13 large, southern, denominational universities

This totals 186 denominational colleges and universities, 157 public colleges and universities, 202 small colleges, 141 large universities, 183 northern colleges and universities, and 160 southern colleges and universities.

It is, of course, realized that the questions posed by this research cannot be completely answered with a mail questionnaire; however, some valuable insight can certainly be gained with even as crude an approach as this.

In attempting to interpret the findings of this study we can employ a simple taxonomic system of the various causes of change and difference in religious attitudes of college professors. We can then recognize that all the significant differences or changes observed can be seen to involve certain combinations of these causes. There are seven basic factors which can explain the observed differences in the religious attitudes of college professors. These seven factors can be grouped into four categories.

A. Selection factors

    1. *Initial selection factor.* These differences result from the fact that individuals who hold particular attitudes choose and may be chosen by particular types of colleges and universities, or may choose particular regions, or sizes of schools, or particular disciplines. An example of this would be the situation in which a religious person might be more inclined to choose to teach in a denominational college over a state college, or that denominational schools may be more inclined to hire orthodox religious persons than unorthodox or nonreligious persons.

    2. *Accretion-mobility.* This factor is closely related to the above but involves the differential movement of individuals of particular attitude systems into more convivial environments as they carry on their professional careers. An example of this would be the movement of a religious professor into a religious environment.

    3. *Promotion selection.* This factor pertains to the bases for selection for promotion. Religiously oriented colleges may well give preferential treatment to individuals with certain types of religious attitudes. An example of this would be the use of the reward of promotion for those who are religious and who support the institutional orthodoxy rather than those with less supportive attitudes and beliefs.

B. Shift factors

    4. *Discipline shift.* Another factor is that which recognizes

that some disciplines have rather recently developed an emphasis somewhat different from that of an earlier period, say a generation ago. This difference can crucially involve generalized belief systems. Consequently such disciplines are attracting different types of individuals currently than they once did. An example of this would be the shift in emphasis in sociology from a welfare oriented to a scientifically oriented discipline.

5. *Milieu shift.* This factor recognizes that it is possible for the entire academic environment to shift from one orientation to another and somewhat different one; it is closely related to the discipline-shift factor. An example of this would be a shift in emphasis in the academic community to a more scientific and somewhat less "religious" emphasis.

C. Socialization factor

6. These differences result from the fact that individuals who take jobs in certain types of colleges, or disciplines, or regions, etc., become increasingly involved in the attitude or belief system existing in that particular environment. An example of this would be that possibly those who take jobs in denominational colleges become somewhat more religious through their interaction in the religious environment, through involvement or possibly reaction.

D. Age factor

7. Previous research suggests that older individuals are more religious than younger individuals. This suggests that the process of maturation or of being reared in another and earlier period produces differences in belief.

We can, of course, recognize that these seven factors interact with each other extensively. For example, accretion-mobility can to a great extent be the result of and also the cause of discipline shift. A particular individual because of his belief system may find himself out of tune with a department that has responded to discipline shift and may decide to move into a more convivial environment. Various other possible and common interactions can be readily imagined.

FINDINGS

As usual, we will examine the results of this study by considering each dimension in turn. It is obviously impossible to discuss all the possible explanations and differences; therefore, certain selections are necessary. The summary analysis of variance tables can be found in Appendix C; relevant probabilities will be reported in the text of this chapter.

Church Orientation

In regard to the first dimension of religiosity, we find two significant "main effect" differences and one significant interaction (table C-1, Appendix C). We find that professors in public colleges and universities are significantly less church oriented than are professors in denominational colleges. The mean church-orientation score of professors in public universities is 25.88, which is significantly lower than that of professors in denominational universities and colleges who have a mean church-orientation score of 27.39. This difference is significant at the .01 level ($F = 9.56$). We also find that full professors with a mean score of 27.98 are significantly more church oriented than assistant professors who have a mean score of 25.29. The difference between these means is significant at the .01 level ($F = 30.23$). Perhaps as important as these significant differences is the absence of significant differences in church-orientation scores between professors in the two regions studied and in the disciplines studied. The lack of significant difference in regard to size is not so surprising.

To recapitulate, older full professors and those who teach in denominational schools are more church oriented than assistant professors and those who teach in public colleges and universities. Behavioral scientists, physical scientists, and fine artists are found to be equally church oriented as are professors who teach in different-sized schools and those who teach in the two regions studied.

We can apply our taxonomy of causes to the observed "main effect" differences. The significant difference between public- and denominational-college professors can be seen to be the possible outcome of the joint, but possibly differential, operation of the initial-selection factor, socialization factor, accretion-mobility factor, promotion-selection factor, or the milieu-shift factor. That is, we can imagine church-oriented academicians choosing to teach in denominational schools as well as being more readily chosen by such schools. We can also quite easily imagine that the church-oriented environment of the denominational school would increase the church orientation of individuals teaching there. Or similarly, those academicians who are or become less church oriented could systematically remove themselves from denominational schools where promotion is slow for them, and conversely those who are or become more church oriented might be expected to migrate to church-oriented environments. Finally, we could also imagine that the church orientation of the academic world has generally shifted in a secular direction but that this is found only in public schools, which lack a vested interest in the previously more sacred church orientation.

The observed significant difference between assistant and full professors could be the result of either the milieu-shift factor or the age factor. To be more explicit, the academic world may be undergoing a systematic secular shift which can be found among the younger or "newer" academians. Another alternative or joint explanation might be that church orientation simply increases generally with age.

An examination of the significant $(F = 4.25, P < .05)$ type of college-by-rank of professor-by-discipline interaction is greatly facilitated with the diagramming of this interaction. This interaction can be diagrammed in three different ways (see figures 6-1, 6-2, and 6-3), in order to extract different information. We can observe that the seven smaller figures which make up the three different ways of diagramming this interaction describe the operation of the different hypothesized explanatory factors in the taxonomy of causes. The figures contain the following bits of information.

> Figure 6-1a diagrams the rank and type of college differences among professors of the behavioral sciences.
>
> Figure 6-1b diagrams the rank and type of college differences among professors of the physical sciences.
>
> Figure 6-1c diagrams the rank and type of college differences among professors of the fine arts.
>
> Figure 6-2a diagrams the type of college and discipline differences among full professors.
>
> Figure 6-2b diagrams the type of college and discipline differences among assistant professors.

Figure 6-3a diagrams the discipline and rank differences in denominational colleges.

Figure 6-3b diagrams the discipline and rank differences in state colleges.

The great differences observed within ranks suggest that a general age factor is in this case not a particularly effective interpreting variable. Therefore, it has been necessary to concentrate upon those factors which would account for differential increments and not general increments.

If we turn our attention to the figures, we can attempt to extract from them the pattern of findings in regard to church-orientation attitudes among college professors. Examining figure 6-1a we find that among behavioral science professors the church-orientation difference between full and assistant professors in public colleges and universities is quite small when it is compared to the rather great difference observed between the two ranks in denominational schools. Or put another way, there is relatively little difference between assistant professors in denominational and public schools and a great difference between the full professors in denominational and public schools in church-orientation attitudes.

Full professors in denominational schools are quite different from the other three groups. This difference could, of course, be due to the operation of initial-selection differences at some time past, with the more church-oriented persons having previously chosen to teach in denominational schools, or to socialization factors, which would involve recognizing that the church-oriented environment has increased the church orientation of those who have been there the longest, or to accretion-mobility factors—for example, we could easily imagine that the non-church oriented have left denominational schools by the time they reach the rank of full professor. Promotion selection can also account for some difference, for we can see that the church oriented could have been promoted more easily or rapidly.

A discipline-shift explanation is also possible in public schools at the full-professorial level; that is, the world of the behavioral scientists may have become less church oriented and the full professors in denominational schools might be either the residue that has not kept up or refugees from the previous orientation. This would, however, also involve socialization and accretion-mobility factors as well. The

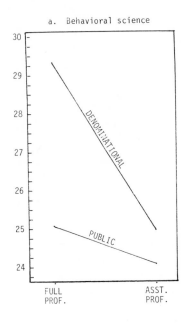

a. Behavioral science

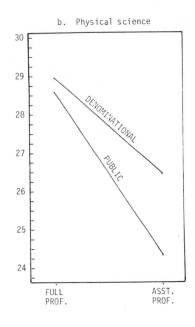

b. Physical science

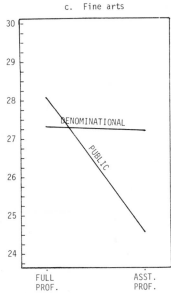

c. Fine arts

Figure 6-1. Church orientation: type of college-rank of professor-discipline interaction, form I

rather great probability of the joint operation of any and all of these possible explanations should be obvious.

Among physical science professors the rank and type of college differences are very nearly a simple reflection of the main effects alone (Figure 6-1b). For we find that full professors of physical science are more church oriented than assistant professors and that those who teach in denominational schools are more church oriented than those who teach in public schools. The differences can be initial-selection factors, in that we find a rather large difference between assistant professors in the two types of colleges. The assistant-professor–full-professor difference is probably attributable to the factor of discipline shift; that is, physical science is less church oriented now than it was in previous generations, and age or maturation factors are less likely to interact with discipline.

Among the professors of fine arts we find that the assistant professors and full professors who teach in denominational schools are very similar in church-orientation attitudes, whereas among those who teach in public colleges the assistant professors are somewhat less church oriented (figure 6-1c). The difference observed among assistant professors in denominational colleges and those in public colleges is quite likely the result of initial selection with the church oriented being chosen by denominational schools; whereas the difference between the assistant and full professors reveals that the operation of the other factors is slight in denominational schools, given the apparently more important initial-selection factor. Full professors in fine arts in public colleges are rather high in church orientation through the operation of such things as socialization, accretion-mobility, and discipline shift. The manner and operation of each of these factors can be readily reconstructed so that we realize that the factor of discipline shift is the most likely explanation. This is the case because we could hardly expect accretion-mobility to operate in this rather unlikely direction. The more church-oriented professors would not generally be expected to move into the more secular public university positions. And socialization of the sort which increases church orientation of professors in public colleges and not in denominational schools is also less than likely, leaving as the most plausible explanation the discipline-shift hypothesis. The factor in this case would suggest that those individuals now being inducted into fine arts professorial positions in public colleges and universities are somewhat different, less church oriented, than those inducted into this role at a previous period. The full-professor increment here seems to suggest a shift in what is expected of fine arts professors in state or public colleges.

In figure 6-2a we observe the results of the joint operation of the various factors. It is apparent that the greatest influence is exerted upon behavioral science professors in denominational colleges where we can well observe the full operation of such factors as socialization, accretion-mobility, and, crucially, discipline shift. It is generally recognized that the behavioral sciences have enjoyed (suffered?) the greatest discipline shift of the included disciplines in recent years, for the religious orientation of behavioral scientists has been altered significantly in the past generation. The church-orientation scores of the other full professors are indicative of apparently similar results of the operation of the explanatory factors.

In figure 6-2b we observe the operation of the initial-selection factor alone. In it we are comparing the church-orientation scores of assistant professors in denominational and public colleges for each of the three disciplines. Differences observed here cannot be accounted for by employing discipline shift, since these are all assistant professors; similarly socialization and accretion-mobility are inappropriate. This chart allows us to appraise the influence of the initial-selection factor alone. And we observe that those individuals who select and are selected by denominational colleges are slightly higher (among behavioral scientists) to moderately higher (among fine art professors) than those who select or are selected by public colleges and universities.

Figure 6-3a allows us to examine the influence of the various factors of change upon the three disciplines within denominational-college environments. We note, first of all, a complete inversion of the disciplines from the assistant- to the full-professor level. This suggests the relative operation of the identified factors that apparently exert the greatest influence upon behavioral scientists and the least influence upon fine arts professors. A great proportion of the differences observed in the behavioral science areas might be seen to be the result of discipline shift with the discipline having become less church oriented. This interpretion is not contradicted by this figure.

Finally figure 6-3b describes the influence of the various factors

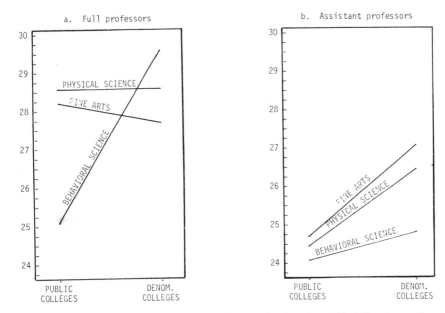

Figure 6-2. Church orientation: type of college-rank of professor-discipline interaction, form II

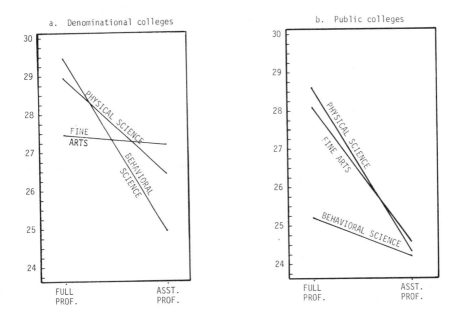

Figure 6-3. Church orientation: type of college-rank of professor-discipline interaction, form III

upon the disciplines among professors in public colleges and universities. Generally low scores are found among assistant professors in public schools and differentially high scores are found among the full professors, with the exception of the full professors of behavioral science. The low behavioral science full-professor score may reflect a receptivity of public schools to discipline shift; that is, it may reflect a receptiveness to secularization as well as to a differentially less sacred socialization and the operation of the accretion-mobility factor, which would cause the more church oriented to remove themselves from an increasingly secular world.

Ritualism

In regard to the second dimension of religiosity, we discover three significant differences among the main effects (table C-2, in Appendix C). First, we find professors in denominational colleges to be more ritualistic than those in public colleges. The mean score for professors in denominational schools is 19.621, whereas the mean ritualism score for professors in public colleges is 17.497. This difference is significant at the .01 level ($F = 9.32$). Second, we discover that full professors are more ritualistic than assistant professors. The mean ritualism score for assistant professors is 17.669 and for full professors it is 19.089. This difference is significant at the .05 level ($F = 6.03$). Third, there is a significant discipline difference in ritualism with the science professors being much less ritualistic than the art professors. The mean scores for the three disciplines are: physical scientists 16.796, behavioral scientists 16.808, and fine artists 21.533; the difference between these three means is significant at the .001 level ($F = 29.79$). In addition to these three significant main effect differences, we also observe one significant interaction in the size of college faculty-by-discipline interaction ($F = 3.66$ $P < .05$). Thus we have observed that professors in denominational schools are more ritualistic than those in public colleges, that full professors are more ritualistic than assistant professors, and that fine arts professors are more ritualistic than those in the behavioral and physical sciences.

Figure 6-4 diagrams the one significant interaction. An examination of this size of school faculty-by-discipline interaction reveals that the ritualism scores of science professors are only slightly lower in the small schools than in the large, whereas the fine arts professors in small schools are more ritualistic than those in larger schools.

This set of differences can also be interpreted in various ways. We must once again recognize the possible operation of a selection factor, an accretion factor, and a socialization factor. We find that professors in denominational colleges are significantly more ritualistic than those in public colleges; this could be the result of the operation of any of the previously mentioned factors. Either ritualistic persons tend to take jobs in denominational schools, and/or persons who take jobs in denominational schools are inducted into a ritualistic or more ritualistic position.

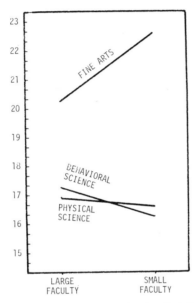

Figure 6-4. Ritualism: size of college faculty-discipline interaction

In regard to rank of professor we find that the full professors, the older men, are more ritualistic. This could be the reflection of the general operation of age in general or the socialization factor or both, or a change in the position of professors today, that is, milieu-shift in a secular direction. In regard to discipline we can observe that art professors are generally more inclined to appreciate ritual and ceremony in religion than are the science professors. This could reflect either selection or socialization; that is, scientists become less ritualistic or less ritualistic persons become scientists, or, of course, both.

The size of faculty-by-discipline interaction reveals something of a "reaction" to ritual among the small-college science professors in addition to the very high ritualism score found among the fine arts professors. One obvious interpretation, somewhat fictitious but yet appealing, is that the required religious involvement in small societies, in this case small intimate schools, causes a slight rebellion among scientists and induces, perhaps through a required high involvement in ceremony, a high ritualistic attitude among the more performance-oriented fine arts professors. Very little imagination is needed to see that at least music professors in the small schools could be called upon to participate in the institutions' ritual. The operation of differential selection among fine arts professors and not among science professors is also possible.

Altruism

An examination of academic category differences in altruism reveals that there are three significant main effect differences and one significant interaction (table C-3, Appendix C). We find that professors in denominational colleges are more religiously altruistic than those in public colleges. The mean altruism score of the professors in public schools is 29.275, whereas those in denominational schools have a mean of 30.322. This difference is significant at the .05 level (F = 5.05). We also discover that full professors are more religiously altruistic than assistant professors. The mean score of assistant professors is 28.911, whereas the mean altruism score of full professors is 30.686. The difference is significant at the .01 level (F = 14.52). The last main effect difference we observe is that the professors of the various disciplines array themselves in the following order: behavioral science professors with a mean of 28.813, physical science professors with a mean of 29.925, and fine arts professors with a mean of 30.658. The difference between these means is significant at the .05 level (F = 5.31). Thus those who teach in denominational schools, have full-professor rank, and specialize in the fine arts are more altruistic than those who teach in public schools, have assistant-professor rank, and specialize in behavioral sciences, respectively. Physical scientists fall between behavioral scientists and fine artists in regard to altruism.

These differences can, of course, also be interpreted in various ways and with various combinations of the explanatory variables. If we examine the significant difference observed between denomina- tional- and public-college professors, we find that it can be explained by initial selection, socialization, milieu shift, accretion-mobility, or any of the various combinations of these factors. For it is possible that the more religiously altruistic select denominational colleges and are selected by them, that denominational environments increase religious altruism, that a secular shift in academia has been limited to public colleges, and that the religiously altruistic have gravitated to denominational colleges from public schools.

The second significant difference involves the variable of rank of professor and indicates that full professors are more religiously altruistic than assistant professors. This difference could be inter- preted as most probably the result of milieu shift or age alone, since the other factors seem much less plausible. Socialization is not a likely explanation since the denominational–public college distinc- tion is not involved and we would not be inclined to view the entire academic world as one which socializes in a *religiously* altruistic direction. Accretion-mobility is also less than an impressive expla- nation for the same reason. Initial selection, to the extent that it is not here involved in milieu shift, is less than an impressive expla- nation. It therefore appears that the remaining factor, although it is a broad one, is the most likely explanation: that persons now at- tracted to the academic community are somewhat different from those attracted in the past. This would be a reflection of the milieu- shift factor. Another, and even more simple explanation is the more general factor of age alone, independent of academic factors. This explanation is strongly reinforced by our previous finding in regard to clergymen, that the older men are more altruistic.

The third significant difference involves discipline; and in this case we find the fine arts professors much more religiously altruistic than the scientists. This difference can be interpreted by employing the selection and the socialization factors. The other factors are not appropriate in this case, and these two appear to cover the area in- volved adequately. The sciences attract less religiously altruistic persons and do not function to increase the phenomenon through socialization.

There is one significant interaction (F = 5.52), the region-by-type of college-by-discipline interaction, which is diagrammed in figures

6-5 and 6-6. If we examine the interaction, first of all, in terms of the three disciplines, we find this relationship described in figures 6-5a, 6-5b, and 6-5c.

Among behavioral scientists we discover rather large differences between the altruism scores of professors in public and denominational colleges in the northern region and almost no difference between the two college types in the southern region. This is an interesting result, for we find something like a normative altruism among behavioral scientists in the southern region. The differences between behavioral science professors in northern denominational colleges and those in northern public colleges reflect the operation of many explanatory variables, such as (1) socialization—denominational colleges could increase religious altruism; (2) initial selection—religiously altruistic professors may choose denominational schools; (3) accretion-mobility—religiously altruistic professors may move to denominational colleges; (4) discipline shift—the behavioral sciences may have become less religiously altruistic in public schools.

Among physical scientists we find that in the South denominational colleges have professors who are more religiously altruistic than those in public colleges. This difference can be seen to reflect the possible operation of (1) socialization—these professors may have become more altruistic in these circumstances; (2) initial selection—the altruistic professors may have selected and been selected by these colleges; (3) accretion-mobility—these professors may have gravitated to this situation; (4) discipline shift—this shift may have occurred only in the more responsive public schools. Of course these factors may be combined in a great many ways.

Among the fine arts professors we observe relatively slight differences; and in view of the larger differences discussed, perhaps it would be advisable not to attempt to make a great deal out of such slight differences.

Figure 6-6a describes the denominational-public and discipline differences in northern schools. Figure 6-6b describes the same differences in southern schools. First of all we can now observe the great differences in the North between behavioral scientists in public and denominational schools. This is in marked contrast with the slight differences observed in the North in the other disciplines. Apparently the denominational schools in the North (1) select the most altruistic behavioral scientists, or (2) have a marked effect upon

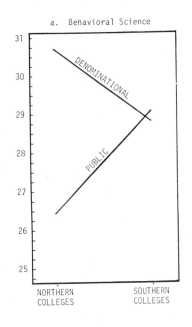

a. Behavioral Science

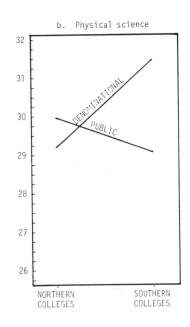

b. Physical science

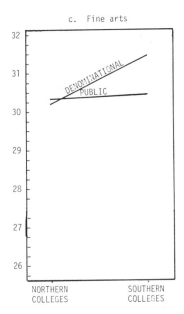

c. Fine arts

Figure 6-5. Altruism: region-type of college-discipline interaction, form I

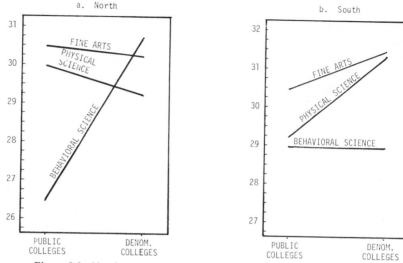

Figure 6-6. Altruism: region-type of college-discipline interaction, form II

the altruism of behavioral scientists, or (3) have not responded to a secular shift in the discipline which has occurred in public colleges. This great difference is especially interesting when we note the complex lack of a comparable phenomenon in the South. This suggests that in the South the religious influence may be equally great upon behavioral scientists in both denominational and public colleges. However, in the South we find that denominational colleges contain more religiously altruistic artists and physical scientists than do public colleges. This might indicate that in "less sensitive" areas more socialization influences are exerted and more "careful selection" takes place. I am thus suggesting that initial selection, accretion-mobility, and socialization are the probable explanations.

Fundamentalism

In regard to fundamentalism we find four significant differences in the main effect variables (table C-4, Appendix C). First of all, we observe that, surprisingly, there is no significant regional difference in fundamentalism. Second, in regard to type of college, we find that professors in denominational colleges are more fundamentalistic than professors in public colleges. The mean fundamentalism score of public-college professors is 28.68 whereas that of denominational-college professors is 33.45. This difference is significant at the .01

level $(F = 45.68)$. Third, we discover that there is a significant difference in the fundamentalistic attitudes of professors in colleges with different size faculties; professors in large schools (mean fundamentalism score of 29.84) are significantly less fundamentalistic than those in small schools (mean score of 32.29). This difference is significant at the .01 level $(F = 12.03)$. Fourth, we find that full professors are significantly more fundamentalistic than assistant professors. The mean score of assistant professors is 30.35, while the mean score of full professors is 31.78. This difference is significant at the .05 level $(F = 4.11)$. Lastly, we discover that the fundamentalism scores of professors of the various disciplines are significantly different. Behavioral science professors have the lowest fundamentalism scores with a mean of 27.99. The mean of the physical science professors is 31.92 while the art professors have a mean of 33.28. The difference between these means is significant at the .01 level $(F = 20.17)$.

The rank differences could be due to age factors or milieu-shift factors, with the older professors being more fundamentalistic because of their age or because academia is simply attracting less fundamentalistic people because of a secularistic trend. The size difference could be due to (1) selection factors—small schools are chosen by and choose more fundamentalistic individuals; (2) socialization factors—small schools in general operate to increase fundamentalism; or (3) shift factors, which involve a differential receptivity to secularism. The type of college differences could be explained in this same way. The discipline differences are conceivably the result of selection factors, with fundamentalistic people going into arts first and behavioral sciences last, and socialization factors, which would suggest that science, and behavioral science in particular, increases secularism.

There is a single significant interaction in regard to fundamentalism $(F = 4.36, P < .05)$. It is a rank-by-type of school-by-discipline interaction. This interaction is described in figures 6-7, 6-8, and 6-9, which diagram the interaction in differing ways. Figures 6-7a, 6-7b and 6-7c describe the type of college and rank differences among professors of each of the three disciplines.

Among behavioral science professors we notice a diminishing of the difference between professors in the two types of colleges at the assistant-professor level. This may indicate that (1) there has been a secular discipline shift in the behavioral sciences which is observed

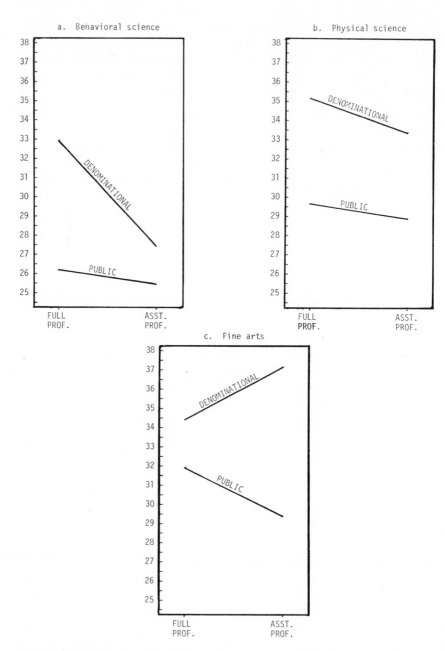

Figure 6-7. Fundamentalism: type of college-rank of professor-discipline interaction, form I

among younger men and among the more "open" public-college full professors; (2) there is a rather strong socialization effect upon behavioral scientists in denominational colleges; or (3) the more fundamentalistic selectively move into denominational schools through their careers.

Among physical science professors we find the great difference is that between professors in denominational and public colleges. And among fine arts professors we observe that there are greater differences between assistant professors in the two types of colleges than between full professors. This points to a strong initial-selection factor tempered possibly by a strange socialization factor which alienates those in denominational schools and integrates those in public schools.

Figures 6-8a and 6-8b identify rank differences in the disciplines in the two types of colleges. These figures point up the very slight fundamentalism differences in rank within public-college professors and the very great differences in denominational-college professors. It also describes a different selection and socialization influence

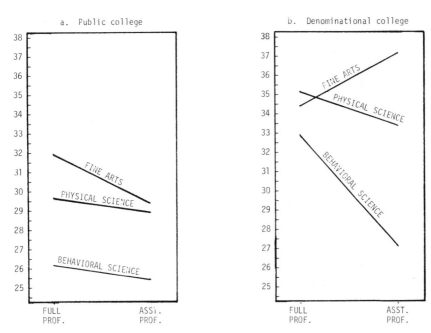

Figure 6-8. Fundamentalism: type of college-rank of professor-discipline interaction, form II

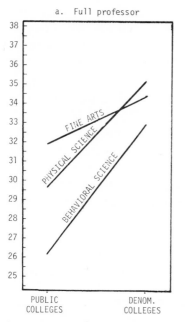
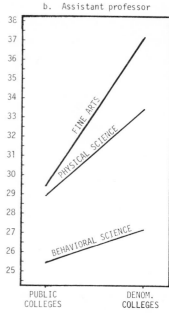

Figure 6-9. Fundalmentalism: type of college-rank of professor-discipline interaction, form III

among scientists and artists with the effect being greatest upon the behavioral scientists, whose area is more "sensitive" than the physical scientists', and being somewhat antithetical upon professors of fine arts.

Finally figures 6-9a and 6-9b clearly illustrate type-of-college influences upon the disciplines for professors of the two ranks studied. The most impressive factor is the impact of denominational colleges, which may reflect the impact of selection and socialization factors among full professors. The assistant-professor figure (6-9b) reflects the current differences in initial selection in regard to fundamentalism. Therefore, we observe that the difference between behavioral scientists being selected by the two types of schools is less great than the selection differences in either of the other two disciplines in regard to religious fundamentalism.

Theism

In theism we find three significant differences in main effect variables (table C-5, Appendix C)—in type of college, size of college faculty, and discipline. We find in regard to type of college that professors in public colleges (mean theism score of 29.06) are significantly less theistic than professors in denominational colleges (mean score of 33.62). This difference is significant at the .01 level ($F = 31.02$).

In the size-of-faculty variable, we find that professors in large colleges have a mean theism score of 29.94, whereas those in small colleges have a mean score of 32.74. This difference is significant at the .01 level ($F = 11.72$).

The third significant difference is in discipline. The mean theism score of the professors of behavioral science is 27.80; of physical science professors, 32.63; and of fine arts professors, 33.59. These means are significantly different at the .01 level ($F = 19.13$).

The explanations for these mean differences in main effects can be found in all of the sets of factors: socialization, shift, and selection. At this point it is felt to be redundant to pursue the line of conjecture followed previously in the explanation of the main effect differences, for by now the reader can easily construct each of these explanations.

Four significant interactions occur. First let us examine the

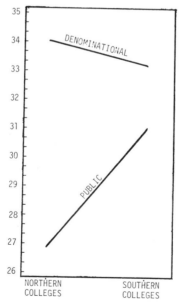

Figure 6-10. Theism: region-type of college interaction

region-by-type of college interaction (F = 6.73, P < .05). This interaction is described by figure 6-10. This figure discloses the relative constancy of theism in northern and southern denominational colleges compared with the greater difference found in public schools. The theism in southern public colleges is certainly somewhat greater than that found in northern public colleges. The figures also reveal the greater similarity of theism scores among professors in southern colleges across type of school than the northern colleges across the same variable.

An examination of figure 6-11 allows us to describe the rank-by-

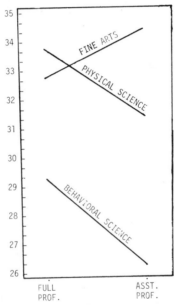

Figure 6-11. Theism: rank of professor-discipline interaction

discipline interaction (F = 3.19, P < .05). This figure reveals that assistant professors of fine arts are more theistic, or have higher theism scores, than full professors of fine arts. This reverses a previously discovered trend among science professors wherein assistant professors are less theistic than full professors.

This rank-by-discipline interaction is further elaborated by a rank-by-discipline-by-type of college interaction (F = 3.37, P < .05). This interaction is diagrammed in figure 6-12. This figure reveals that the above mentioned reversal of fine arts professors occurs only

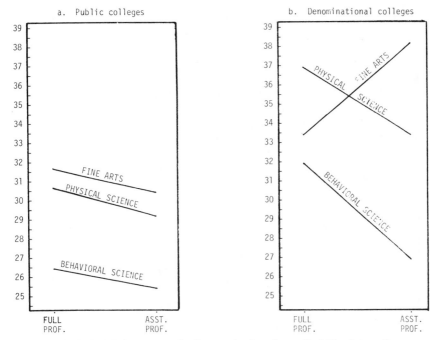

a. Public colleges

b. Denominational colleges

Figure 6-12: Theism: type of college-rank of professor-discipline interaction

in denominational colleges and not in public schools—an interesting socialization factor–selection factor effect which apparently occurs only under certain circumstances, namely, among assistant professors of fine arts in denominational colleges.

The region-by-type of college-by-rank-by-discipline interaction further clarifies the interaction described above ($F = 3.66$, $P < .05$). Figure 6-13 provides interpretive perspective. An examination of this figure discloses additional regional variations in this previously described interaction. We find that northern public college professors of science are remarkably similar, with physical scientists being slightly more theistic than behavioral scientists, and further we find that fine arts assistant professors are more theistic than full professors of fine arts (figure 6-13a). Figure 6-13b discloses a constancy through rank of theism in behavioral science professors in northern denominational colleges, which contrasts to the sharp reversal through rank of physical scientists and fine arts professors.

Figure 6-13c reveals no extremely great differences but resembles figure 6-13b. Figure 6-13d diagrams professors in southern denomi-

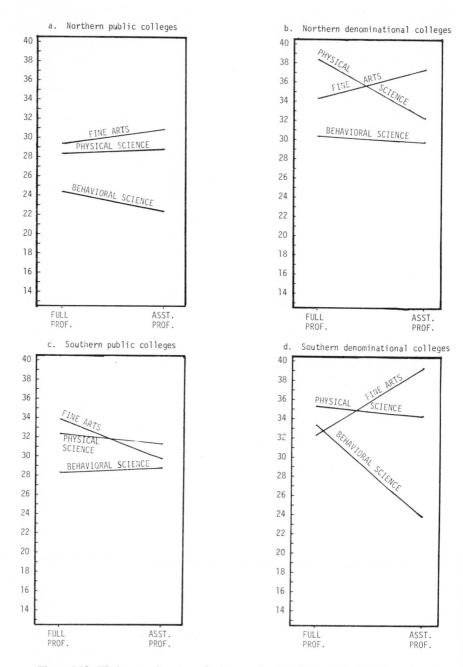

Figure 6-13. Theism: region-type of college-rank of professor-discipline interaction

national colleges and shows that startlingly great differences exist between assistant professors of the various disciplines: behavioral science assistant professors scoring very low, fine arts assistant professors scoring very high, and physical science professors in between. This reveals the reasonably strong and very different impact of the southern denominational college environment upon assistant professors of different disciplines.

Idealism

Analysis discloses that there is only one significant difference in idealism, the rank variable (table C-6, Appendix C). We find full professors to be significantly more idealistic than assistant professors. The mean idealism score of full professors is 32.01, whereas the mean score of assistant professors is 31.08. This difference is significant at the .05 level ($F = 6.20$).

There are no significant interactions in the idealism variable. Thus we have only one difference to attempt to interpret. It is somewhat surprising to find the full professors to be more idealistic than the assistant professors; however, we previously found older clergymen to be more idealistic than younger clergymen. This finding thus is best interpreted as being the result of a general age factor. The notion of youthful idealism does not seem to be supported by our evidence. However, it may be that our more youthful age groups are at a period of disenchantment which is then followed by a somewhat more realistic "idealism."

Superstition

In regard to the superstition attitude area, we find three significant differences in the main effect variables (table C-7, Appendix C). The variables in which the significant differences occur are region, type of school, and discipline.

First we discover that the mean superstition score of southern professors ($\bar{X} = 20.38$) is significantly greater than that of northern professors ($\bar{X} = 19.29$). This difference is significant at the .01 level ($F = 7.93$).

The second significant difference is in the type-of-college variable. Here we find that professors in public colleges are less superstitious than professors in denominational colleges. The mean superstition score of public-college professors is 18.92, and the mean score of denominational-college professors is 20.75. This difference is significant at the .01 level ($F = 22.59$).

The third significant difference is in discipline. In this case we find that behavioral science professors have the lowest superstition scores with a mean score of 17.87. Fine arts professors have the highest superstition scores with a mean of 21.76. The superstition scores of physical scientists fall between these other two groups (their mean score is 19.88). This difference is significant at the .01 level ($F = 34.07$).

We also observe three significant interactions. Let us examine these in order. The rank-by-discipline interaction ($F = 6.87$, $P < .01$) is diagrammed in figure 6-14. This figure reveals that there are no

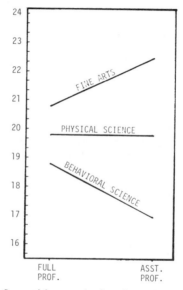

Figure 6-14. Superstition: rank of professor-discipline interaction

differences in superstition by rank of physical science professors, but that assistant professors of behavioral sciences are less superstitious than full professors while full professors of fine arts are less superstitious than assistant professors of fine arts. This seems to suggest nearly a "norming" phenomenon in superstition through time. By this I mean the development of and moving toward a normative superstition within an environment.

An examination of the next interaction, the type of college-by-rank-by-discipline interaction (F = 3.27, P < .05), discloses that the previously revealed norming pattern occurs only among professors in

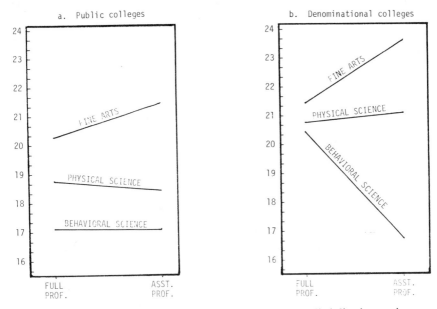

Figure 6-15. Superstition: type of college-rank of professor-discipline interaction

denominational colleges (figure 6-15). The four-variable interaction (F = 4.28, P < .05), region-by-type of college-by-rank-by-discipline, reveals further that this norming occurs mainly among southern denominational college professors, much less so in the northern region, and that the pattern is reversed in southern public schools (figure 6-16).

This suggests that the main location of the initially identified factors in regard to superstition exists in southern denominational colleges and that in this location there are radically different initial selection and antithetically operating socialization factors for behavioral scientists than for fine arts professors.

Mysticism

An examination of the mysticism variable reveals two significant differences in main effect variables (table C-8, Appendix C). We find, first of all, that full professors are significantly more mystical

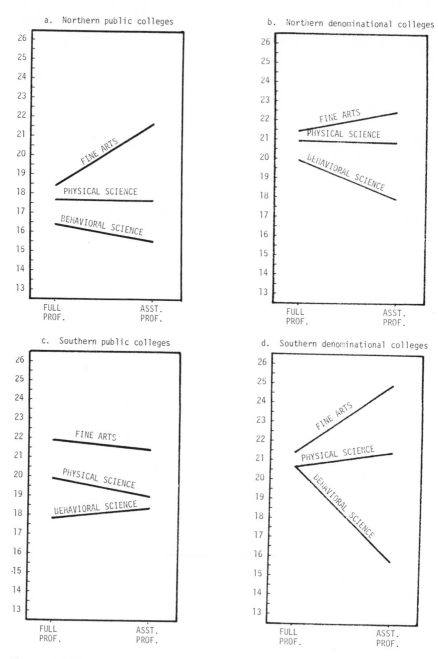

Figure 6-16. Superstition: region-type of college-rank of professor-discipline interaction

than assistant professors. The mean mysticism score of full professors is 27.64 compared to a mean score of 26.26 among assistant professors. This difference is significant at the .01 level ($F = 8.90$). The second significant difference involves discipline. We find behavioral science professors to have the lowest mean mysticism score of 24.54 compared with a mean of 26.90 for physical scientists and a mean of 29.40 for fine arts professors. This difference is significant at the .01 level ($F = 36.83$).

We also discover that there is one significant interaction ($F = 5.01$, $P < .01$), the region-by-type of college-by-rank-by-discipline interaction. This interaction can be examined in any of a great variety of diagrams. Figure 6-17 makes it possible to identify discipline and rank variations in each of the four combinations of region and type of school. Figure 6-17a discloses the differences occurring between science professors and artists in northern public colleges. The relatively high religiosity of assistant professors of fine arts in this circumstance has been isolated on other dimensions as well. Figure 6-17b reveals a real similarity of mysticism in assistant professors and full professors of physical science in northern denominational colleges in comparison to behavioral science and fine arts professors, who are both less mystical at the lower levels of rank. Figure 6-17c allows us to discover that full professors of behavioral science are conspicuously low in mysticism in comparison to artists and physical scientists. Finally figure 6-17d discloses a relatively great difference in the mysticism scores of assistant professors in southern denominational colleges in comparison to full professors.

Summary

In summary we have discovered that:
(1) Southern professors are more superstitious than northern professors. (Table C-9, Appendix C, summarizes the significant F ratios and interactions.)
(2) Professors in denominational schools are more church oriented, more ritualistic, more altruistic, more fundamentalistic, more theistic, and more superstitious than professors in public colleges.
(3) Professors in small colleges are more fundamentalistic and more theistic than professors in large colleges and universities.

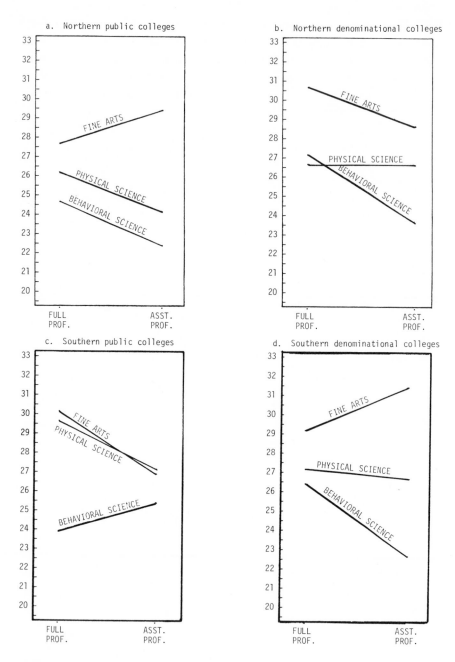

Figure 6-17. Mysticism: region-type of college-rank of professor-discipline interaction

(4) Full professors are more church oriented, more ritualistic, more altruistic, more fundamentalistic, more idealistic, and more mystical than assistant professors.

(5) Behavioral scientists are less ritualistic, less altruistic, less fundamentalistic, less theistic, less superstitious, and less mystical than other disciplines studied. Fine arts professors score highest on these same dimensions and physical science professors fall between the behavioral scientists and the artists.

In view of the complex and infrequent significant interactions, we will not attempt to summarize the few that occur. Table 6-1 summarizes the findings of this study.

TABLE 6-1. SUMMARY OF RELIGIOUS ATTITUDE DIFFERENCES AMONG COLLEGE PROFESSORS (Probabilities Listed)

	Region	Type of College	Size of College	Rank	Discipline
Church orientation	NS	.01	NS	.01	NS
Ritualism	NS	.01	NS	.05	.01
Altruism	NS	.05	NS	.01	.05
Fundamentalism	NS	.01	.01	.05	.01
Theism	NS	.01	.01	NS	.01
Idealism	NS	NS	NS	.05	NS
Superstition	.01	.01	NS	NS	.01
Mysticism	NS	NS	NS	.01	.01

It is of some interest to note that professors of the various social categories examined were found to have more and greater differences in the dimensions of fundamentalism, theism, and superstition than in idealism. They are thus more inclined to be equally idealistic than equally theistic, fundamentalistic, or superstitious.

7

RELIGIOSITY, AFFILIATION, AND SOCIAL CLASS: TWO COMMUNITY STUDIES

One area of concern to the sociologist of religion has been the relationship between religiosity and social class or stratification. Studies have rather consistently reported clear relationships between such variables as church membership or affiliation and class position (Demerath and Hammond 1969:53–59; Demerath 1965; Glock and Stark 1965: 185–200; Vernon 1962: 391–95, and Hoult 1958: 301–3). Even though persons from various class levels can be found in each denomination, studies have nevertheless discovered systematic variation. In view of this an examination of the relationship between the dimensions of religious attitude and social class seems appropriate. An examination such as this could conceivably make more understandable the nature of the more generally cited relationship between religiousness as a broad inclusive variable and social class, since it divides religiousness into some of its component variables. The general hypothesis which led to this survey is that religiosity and social class are related, though realistically we should not expect every dimension of religiosity to be significantly related to social class.

In view of this general interest and because social stratification studies are generally community oriented, available communities were selected for examination. Previous research by the author (Maranell 1968) has suggested that region is a particularly relevant variable to take into consideration in the examination of religiosity.

Recognizing this, research was conducted in two regionally different communities, one southern and one non-southern.

RELIGIOUS ATTITUDES AND SOCIAL CLASS IN A SOUTHERN COMMUNITY*

The southern community which was selected was chosen because it seemed to be an accessible, representative southern urban area. This particular community had a population of over 50,000 in 1970. The community is located in one of the states typically recognized as southern, is situated on a major river, and has a large army camp nearby. The city was found to have a rather large stratification spectrum as one might well expect. This survey was limited to the white citizens of the community. Thus we have chosen to ignore in this study, and for the time being, the investigation of the relatively important Black-White religious attitude differences.

The data used in this study were gathered through interviews with 110 persons. The interview typically involved an introduction, an attempt to secure rapport, an appraisal of socioeconomic status by the interviewer, and the making of arrangements for the completion of the religious attitude questionnaire, which was left to be filled out by the person contacted. The interviewer then either called back later for the completed religious attitude questionnaire, or if the rapport, cooperation, and understanding were sufficiently great, left an addressed, stamped envelope for returning the questionnaire.

The individual responses manifested by the subjects varied from marked suspicion (in the lower classes) to gracious cooperation with some interest expressed in the findings of the study (in the upper classes).

Variables

Religiosity was measured by means of the questionnaire described in the earlier portions of this book. An initial community survey divided the residents in the city vertically by "dwelling area" and house type. A stratified random sample was drawn from these marked areas. The questionnaire contained the final measure of vertical position or socioeconomic status.

---

* The data on which this section is based were gathered and initially analyzed by Allen McCartney.

Socioeconomic status was measured in this survey with Warner's index of status characteristics (ISC) which is made up of four status variables: (a) occupation, (b) source of income, (c) house type, (d) dwelling area (Warner et al. 1949: 121–29). Each of these is scored on a seven-point rating system. Warner provides weights which he maintains should be used when these are combined to make the index of status characteristics. The weights he suggests are: (a) occupation × 4, (b) source of income × 3, (c) house type × 3, (d) dwelling area × 2. The sum of these weighted ratings comprise the index. Warner further suggests that if all of the ratings cannot be made his alternative set of weights should be used when any single variable is missing. In this survey it was deemed impossible to secure ratings on the source of income variable, and thus the revised weights were used. These corrected weights are: (a) occupation × 5, (b) house type × 4, and (c) dwelling area × 3. These weighted totals (ISC totals) were then converted to social classes by using Warner's Jonesville conversion data (Warner 1949: 128). In this way the ISC scores were grouped into five social classes. The class breakdown of the total sample of 110 is as follows: upper class 21, upper middle 30, lower middle 32, upper lower 15, and lower lower 12.

Warner does not include the variable of education in this final ISC score. Nevertheless, we gathered data on this variable because we felt that educational differences would bear an independent examination even though they have been excluded from the stratification index.

Analysis and Findings

The general hypothesis of this study can be divided in various ways. The hypothesis is that religiosity is significantly related to socioeconomic status or social class. This hypothesis can be examined in regard to each of the dimensions of religiosity and the various indices of social class. In view of the fact that a standard approach employed in this research has involved the analytic distillation of inclusive concepts such as "religiosity," "political conservatism," etc., it is within keeping with this approach to analyze the dimensions of religiosity with each of the indicators of social status, or ISC, as well as with the total index. This approach makes possible the isolation of more specific types of relationships and the clarification of the nature of the social-class variations in religiosity. In view of this possible distillation of both religiosity and social class, we can examine the following specific relationships:

(1) The relationships between Warner's ISC and each of the eight scaled dimensions of religiosity.

(2) The relationships between each of Warner's ISC indices and the eight scaled dimensions of religiosity. These indices are (a) occupation, (b) dwelling area, and (c) house type.

(3) The relationship between education (which is not involved in ISC) and the eight scaled dimensions of religiosity.

In these series of tests for the significance of the difference between the religiosity scores of the various social classes, we will employ analysis of variance and treat each social class as a subgroup. The first social-class variable we will examine is Warner's index of social characteristics. Table D-1 in Appendix D summarizes the analysis of variance and reports the significance of the differences between the religious attitude score means across classes.

The analysis reveals that the social classes isolated by means of Warner's index of social characteristics are significantly different in three of the eight dimensions of religious attitudes. The classes differ in ritualism ($F = 4.93$, $P < .01$), superstition ($F = 3.998$, $P < .01$), and mysticism ($F = 4.59$, $P < .01$) and do not differ in church orientation, altruism, fundamentalism, theism, or idealism. Thus persons in the upper, upper-middle, lower-middle, upper-lower, and lower-lower social classes are roughly equal in these latter five dimensions of religious attitude. For example, the upper classes are not significantly more altruistic than the lower classes; the lower classes are not more fundamentalistic than the upper; and, finally, they are apparently equally theistic, and the upper classes are not more idealistic than the lower. It should be recalled that this is a southern community and consequently generally fundamentalistic, which may account for the lack of a difference in that dimension. The interpretation of the significant differences can be facilitated by an inspection of the table of means (table 7-1).

The first dimension found to differ significantly between the social classes is ritualism. An examination of the class means reveals an interesting pattern in that the ritualism scores are higher among the lower social classes than in the upper. This is contrary to expec-

TABLE 7-1. MEAN RELIGIOSITY SCORES OF THE SOCIAL CLASSES DEFINED WITH WARNER'S ISC

	Upper (N = 21)	Upper Middle (N = 30)	Lower Middle (N = 32)	Upper Lower (N = 15)	Lower Lower (N = 12)
Church orientation	30.76	30.03	28.50	33.40	31.50
Ritualism*	16.90	20.57	20.84	26.13	26.00
Altruism	33.76	32.23	33.44	35.87	32.17
Fundamentalism	38.48	39.63	40.06	43.53	42.42
Theism	39.76	40.87	41.28	42.40	39.92
Idealism	33.57	31.97	32.09	33.60	32.25
Superstition*	22.52	23.53	25.56	26.93	27.25
Mysticism*	28.52	29.17	32.88	32.93	33.25

* Significant difference ($P < .01$).

tation, for in our previously reported study of metropolitan clergymen (chapter 4) and other studies of student attitudes we have found typically that Catholics and upper-social-class Protestant groups scored higher on ritualism. However, these studies did not investigate a significant range of the class distribution. Thus, before we attempt to interpret this finding we should examine the relationship between denominational affiliation and social class as it is identified with Warner's ISC. This examination can be found in table 7-2.

Table 7-2 discloses that the community sample has a typical social-class and denomination relationship. This, in turn, suggests that when a larger social-class spectrum is investigated, at least in a southern community, the typical denominational proclivities in regard to ritualism are outweighed by an apparently stronger class influence. When a large distribution of social-class positions is involved, the lower classes are found to be more ritualistic than the upper classes, independent of the fact that in more homogeneous

TABLE 7-2. SOCIAL CLASS (WARNER'S ISC) AND DENOMINATIONAL AFFILIATION

	Upper	Upper Middle	Lower Middle	Upper Lower	Lower Lower
Episcopal	4	2	1		
Presbyterian	7	5	5		
Christian	2	2	1		
Methodist	7	6	8		1
Lutheran		2	2		
Catholic		3	3		
Baptist	1	6	5	4	5
Church of Christ		1	2	2	
Assembly of God			1	2	
Nazarene				2	
Pentecostal				1	5
Unknown or undetermined		3	4	4	1
Total	21	30	32	15	12

populations denominational ritualism differences predominate. Thus in a sample of upper-middle-class students, Catholics, Episcopalians, Presbyterians, and Lutherans are found to have higher ritualism scores than Baptists, members of the Church of Christ, etc,; and among a relatively homogeneous sample of metropolitan clergymen, these denominational differences will also appear. However, when studies are conducted in less homogeneous populations in regard to social class, these denominational differences are submerged by more powerful ritualism differences between the classes. Or when social class is ignored, denominational differences cover class variation.

The second dimension found to differ significantly between the social classes is superstition. An examination of the table of means (table 7-1) reveals that superstition increases as one progresses down the social-class structure in such a way that each successively lower class has a higher superstition score than that immediately above it. This difference is not in any way surprising in that it reflects both the increasing involvement in the culture of poverty as one passes down the class distribution and the accompanying lack of educational and other enlightening opportunities.

The third significant difference involves the mysticism dimension. An examination of the means reveals that mysticism decreases as we progress up the social-class or stratification variable and increases as we descend. This may also reflect the influence of variables like poverty and education and cultural opportunities; or it might, if we allow ourselves to cobweb a bit, involve a "flight" from the realities of a painful and underprivileged situation into a hopefully optimistic mysticism.

The differences observed in the dimension of fundamentalism approach significance ($F = 2.29$, $P < .10$) with the scores increasing in the lower end of the class distribution. Beyond this, other dimensions are not found to differ between the social classes, as they are measured with Warner's index of status characteristics, in a southern community. These similarities reflect the communalities of the religious experience and of religious belief in a southern metropolitan community.

Let us turn our attention now to a consideration of the elements involved in Warner's index of status characteristics and attempt to discover if, when they are employed individually, they lead us to the conclusions we have just drawn. Recall that these variables are (a)

TABLE 7-3. MEAN RELIGIOSITY SCORES OF THE GROUPED OCCUPATIONS

	1 (N = 17)	2 (N = 32)	3 (N = 16)	4 (N = 15)	5 (N = 13)	6 (N = 12)	7 (N = 5)
Church orientation	31.76	29.44	30.19	30.00	32.69	30.00	34.80
Ritualism*	17.88	19.66	19.44	23.67	26.54	23.75	28.00
Altruism	33.00	31.28	36.31	34.67	34.38	33.00	32.80
Fundamentalism	40.06	37.97	40.88	41.67	41.23	43.58	41.40
Theism	40.41	40.13	41.25	41.60	41.38	43.00	37.60
Idealism	32.53	31.69	33.44	32.80	33.58	33.58	31.00
Superstition*	22.65	23.22	24.06	26.53	28.38	26.00	27.40
Mysticism*	29.82	27.66	32.38	34.53	32.92	34.00	31.20

NOTE: The lower numbers indicate the higher statuses.
* Significant difference (P < .01).

occupation, (b) dwelling area, and (c) house type. The analysis of religiosity and occupation groupings involves the use of analysis of variance. The groupings are the seven ordered categories of occupation suggested by Warner and used in the ISC. The summary analysis of variance tables are presented in Appendix D (table D-2).

We find that the analysis of occupation and religiosity reaches the same results we obtained from an analysis of religiosity and ISC. This is not surprising since occupation is the highest weighted variable of the three which were used to measure ISC. Table 7-3 presents the means of the grouped occupational categories on the religiosity variables.

Significant differences between the means of the occupation groupings were found in ritualism (F = 3.61, P < .01), superstition (F = 3.74, P < .01), and mysticism (F = 5.559, P < .01). An examination of the means reveals patterns somewhat similar to the means of the social classes identified with Warner's ISC. Some of the variation from this pattern must be explained by small group size leading to greater sampling distortion. It is also obvious, however, that the other variables used in ISC had a certain influence which in this case systematized the relationship.

The second of the ISC variables which we will analyze individually is dwelling area. This variable also used seven ordered rating categories suggested by Warner, although instances were found for only six of the seven possible rating categories in the community studied. Since this variable was less heavily weighted in the ISC variable, we might expect to find greater variation in its relationship with religiosity.

The analysis of dwelling area and religious attitude reveals five significant mean differences. The analysis of variance is summarized in table D-3, Appendix D. We find significant differences in the three dimensions where differences occurred before: ritualism ($F = 3.537$, $P < .01$), superstition ($F = 2.42$, $P < .05$), and mysticism ($F = 2.78$, $P < .05$). In addition to these three differences, we now find that differences in altruism ($F = 2.44$, $P < .05$) and fundamentalism ($F = 2.92$, $P < .05$) are statistically significant. The table of means (table 7-4) will allow us to analyze these more carefully.

TABLE 7-4. MEAN RELIGIOSITY SCORES FOR DWELLING AREAS

	1 (N = 20)	2 (N = 20)	3 (N = 20)	4 (N = 20)	5 (N = 16)	6 (N = 14)
Church orientation	32.50	31.05	28.25	28.60	32.19	32.21
Ritualism**	18.45	20.80	21.70	18.95	24.63	26.93
Altruism*	33.85	32.95	32.10	32.50	37.00	32.14
Fundamentalism*	38.75	41.25	37.85	39.55	43.88	42.21
Theism	40.25	40.50	40.20	41.90	42.25	40.29
Idealism	33.80	32.55	32.40	30.50	34.50	31.79
Superstition*	23.00	23.20	24.85	25.10	26.38	27.36
Mysticism*	28.40	30.40	30.50	31.50	33.81	33.36

NOTE: The lower numbers indicate higher statuses.
* Significant difference ($P < .05$).
** Significant difference ($P < .01$).

An examination of the mean religiosity scores of the various dwelling areas again generally supports the initial social class and ritualism, superstition, and mysticism findings, with each of these variables increasing in the lower socioeconomic-status areas. The two additional significant mean differences show in regard to altruism that the next to the lowest group has an exceedingly high score and that fundamentalism increases as one progresses down the dwelling area distribution. If the variable of dwelling area had been weighted more highly on Warner's ISC, these differences might have occurred in the more general finding. The addition of these two significant differences suggests that these may be "community-like" differences stemming from associations. That is, fundamentalism is higher among those who live in certain socioeconomic areas; but when class is determined with additional variables which may well exclude persons in these areas and include persons from higher class areas who do not attend the same churches, this difference disappears. We also find that altruism is conceivably associational, that is, it derives more from dwelling area involvement and sympathies than from occupationally measured class positions.

The last of the ISC variables to be examined independently is house type. The analysis of variance which examines the differences between the religious attitude means of the ordered groups of house types is reported in table D-4, Appendix D. The scale used for the rating of house type was that suggested by Warner. Only six of his seven ratings of houses were used in this study.

This analysis of house type groupings reveals significant differences in regard to five dimensions of religious attitudes. We find in addition to significant mean differences in ritualism ($F = 3.72$, $P < .01$), superstition ($F = 2.37$, $P < .05$), and mysticism ($F = 3.79$, $P < .01$), there are now significant mean differences in the dimensions of church orientation ($F = 2.55$, $P < .05$) and altruism ($F = 2.76$, $P < .05$). The table of means (table 7-5) will allow us to analyze these differences more easily.

TABLE 7-5. MEAN RELIGIOSITY SCORES FOR THE HOUSE TYPE GROUPS

	1 (N = 14)	2 (N = 22)	3 (N = 9)	4 (N = 41)	5 (N = 19)	6 (N = 5)
Church orientation*	33.07	30.95	27.44	29.49	33.16	28.80
Ritualism**	17.93	20.14	19.44	20.95	27.11	25.20
Altruism*	34.93	32.86	30.44	33.05	35.89	29.40
Fundamentalism	39.07	40.18	39.00	39.54	43.89	40.80
Theism	40.50	40.14	39.00	41.61	42.00	38.40
Idealism	34.14	32.82	31.44	31.83	33.32	32.20
Superstition*	22.86	23.64	24.44	24.66	27.47	27.00
Mysticism**	28.07	29.45	32.56	30.95	34.84	30.80

NOTE: The lower numbers indicate higher statuses.
* Significant difference (P < .05).
** Significant difference (P < .01).

Ritualism, superstition, and mysticism follow the same general pattern we have observed before, that is, all increasing in the lower end of the class distribution. We find that church orientation is high in the highest group, according to house types, and is also high in the fifth highest group, falling off between these two peaks. The pattern discovered in regard to church orientation is interesting in that it seems to suggest that at both ends of the social class scale those with "better" houses are more church oriented, or that those who are more church oriented have better houses. Therefore, we could be led to suspect that that which separates the next to lowest house types from lowest is a matter of some community orientation which is manifested in greater church orientation or in slightly better houses. The same might well apply as an interpretation of church-orientation differences found in the upper two classes. Altruism is observed to drop in the lowest house-type group after being highest in the second group from the bottom. The relatively low altruism of the lowest group could lead us to accept an alienation hypothesis regarding those who are forced to live in the poorest housing examined. We should again note that these differences might have been observed in the ISC if this variable had been weighted more highly in that score.

Warner excluded the education variable from the index of status characteristics, but it might be of some interest to turn our attention to this variable. The analysis of the differences between the means of the ordered educational groupings will be found in table D-5, Appendix D.

We find the same statistically significant religious attitude differences among educationally different categories that we found between categories identified with Warner's ISC (see table 7-1). The means of the educational groupings are reported in table 7-6.

TABLE 7-6. MEAN RELIGIOSITY SCORES OF THE EDUCATIONAL GROUPINGS

	1 (N = 10)	2 (N = 36)	3 (N = 37)	4 (N = 11)	5 (N = 5)	6 (N = 8)	7 (N = 3)
Church orientation	30.40	30.44	29.92	31.09	33.60	30.75	37.33
Ritualism*	18.40	19.19	21.73	24.18	26.80	24.38	31.67
Altruism	32.50	33.58	32.86	35.09	35.80	32.50	31.67
Fundamentalism	39.10	38.56	40.81	42.36	42.40	42.75	44.00
Theism	41.30	40.56	40.89	41.64	39.40	40.25	44.67
Idealism	33.50	32.47	32.35	33.00	32.20	32.88	31.33
Superstition**	21.00	23.67	25.73	25.64	30.40	24.88	27.00
Mysticism*	27.40	30.06	30.92	34.09	35.60	33.13	33.67

NOTE: The lower scores indicate higher education.
* Significant difference (P < .05).
** Significant difference (P < .01).

In our examination of educational group differences in religiosity, we find the same patterns we previously discovered in our analysis of the other indices of social class. We find that ritualism (F = 2.88, P < .05), superstition (F = 3.469, P < .01), and mysticism (F = 2.78, P < .05) all generally increase when education level decreases.

In summary we have discovered three dimensions of religious attitudes which differ significantly across social classes in all of the foregoing analyses, and three dimensions of religious attitudes which have isolated instances of significant differences across social classes. These significant differences are found in the summary table (table 7-7).

TABLE 7-7. SUMMARY OF SIGNIFICANT RELIGIOSITY DIFFERENCES ACROSS SOCIAL CLASSES
(Probabilities listed)

	Warner's ISC	Occupation	Dwelling Area	House Type	Education
Church orientation	NS	NS	NS	.05	NS
Ritualism	.01	.01	.01	.01	.01
Altruism	NS	NS	.05	.05	NS
Fundamentalism	NS	NS	.05	NS	NS
Theism	NS	NS	NS	NS	NS
Idealism	NS	NS	NS	NS	NS
Superstition	.01	.01	.05	.05	.01
Mysticism	.01	.01	.05	.01	.05

It is interesting to note that altruism is related to the most "economic" of the variables of the ISC, dwelling area and house type.

A more general interpretation of the total findings of this southern community survey of religiosity and social class might take this form. First, social class differences in religiosity do not occur at all in two of the dimensions of religiosity. Theism and idealism have no social-class differences, suggesting, quite reasonably, that persons of various positions in the class structure are equally theistic or believe equally in God and are equally dedicated to principles and ideals. Thus our data do not support the notion of upper-class idealists and lower-class realists, or that the lower classes (or the upper classes for that matter) are less inclined to belief in God.

The consistency with which we have discovered certain significant differences must also be pointed out, i.e., in all tests we have found significant mean differences in ritualism, superstition, and mysticism. This points to an appreciation for ritual in the lower classes as well as to a hopeful, mystical orientation. The next most consistent finding was that involving altruism; in two separate instances we discovered significant differences in this dimension, and in both cases the social-class variable employed was noneducational. The social-class variables to which we refer are house type and dwelling area, or the house and home component of social class. In addition to this we found significant dwelling area differences in fundamentalism pointing to a locality component in this dimension. And last we found a significant house-type difference in church orientation, suggesting an interesting "structural factor" manifested in the relationship between house type and attitude to the organization and structure of the church.

We have thus accomplished some of our goals: we have demonstrated that religiosity is related to social class, but more importantly, that not all aspects are related. We can suggest from this analysis that there are within the religiosity–social class relationship a number of smaller interconnections, which may be further pursued beyond the overpowering regularities of relationship.

SOCIAL CLASS AND RELIGIOUS INVOLVEMENT IN A MIDWESTERN COMMUNITY*

An examination of social class and the dimensions of religious attitudes was subsequently conducted in a midwestern community. This survey attempts to examine more precisely the religious attitude differences between class groupings and the impact of religious involvement upon religious attitudes. The survey furthermore limits the consideration of these variables to a restricted group of religious denominations, whose differences can also be examined. By including the variables of involvement and denomination, it is possible to separate in the analysis the impact of these two variables from the social-class variable. This should allow a more refined analysis and lead to a clearer understanding of the operation of social class and religious involvement in the selected denominations.

The midwestern community selected was chosen as an accessible, representative midwestern urban area. It has a population of over 130,000, is located on a major river, and has a large air base nearby.

In view of the decision to limit the study to a small set of denominations, the first task was the selection of these groups. Those selected were Catholic, Methodist, and Baptist. These are, of course, three of the dominant denominations in the United States.

An initial questionnaire sent to all clergymen of the three denominations in the city asked the clergymen to rate all the churches of their denomination in the city according to socioeconomic status. There was substantial agreement among the responding pastors (approximately 50% responded). Churches that appeared to fit the desired status levels most closely were selected and interviews with the clergymen were arranged. Each pastor was asked for the names of thirty people who he thought belonged to a particular class level.

---

* The data reported in this section were gathered and initially interpreted by Prof. Elizabeth Almquist.

He was then asked to divide the list into the fifteen who were most highly active in the church and the fifteen who were relatively inactive. Those persons who attend church nearly every Sunday and who usually hold office in church and church-oriented groups were defined as active. Inactive members were defined as those who are members but who attend church very seldom and play little or no part in church or church-related groups.

Individuals on these lists were selected for interviewing. Each individual's occupation was first secured from the city directory. Interviews were obtained with approximately 65% of the individuals listed. A total sample of 180 was obtained; this number was sufficiently large to permit the use of a 3 × 2 × 2 factorial analysis of variance with 10 cases per cell.

Warner's index of status characteristics was used to establish the social-class level of the respondents. This study used a rating on all four characteristics: occupation, source of income, house type, and dwelling area. The weightings suggested by Warner were used, as were his suggested cutting points between classes. These weights are presented in the study of the southern community reported earlier in this chapter. Three socioeconomic-status groupings were employed in this analysis: upper middle, lower middle, and lower.

The religious attitudes were measured with the eight scales previously described in this volume.

Findings

This study employed a factorial analysis of variance design. This technique allows for the examination of differences between socioeconomic classes, involvement categories, and denominations as well as interactions. In view of the use of the two additional factors, the results of this study will be reported separately for each scale or dimension of religious attitude.

Church Orientation. The analysis of variance, which is summarized in table D-6, Appendix D, reveals two significant main effects differences. There is a statistically significant difference ($F = 11.21$, $P < .01$) in church orientation between active members (mean score of 31.5) and inactive members (mean score of 28.6). There is also a significant difference in church orientation across the three class levels with the upper-middle group having a mean score of 28.9, the lower-middle category a mean of 28.8, and the lower socioeconomic class a mean score of 32.5. (F = 7.74, P < .01). In addition, there is a significant denomination-by-involvement interaction (F = 5.20, P < .01).

We find, therefore, that church orientation is higher in the lower social class, which is consistent with what we discovered in the previously reported study of a southern city. The lower socio-economic-class individual may see the church as one of the few available avenues through which to interact with others who share an aspiration for mobility and conventionality. An examination of the items in the scale reveals that this dimension involves a belief that church members are particularly good people to associate with in order to be accepted.

It is not surprising that the active members are more church oriented than the inactive. A church orientation clearly involves high activeness, and in turn activeness involves a substantial church orientation.

The involvement-by-denomination interaction is diagrammed in figure 7-1. This diagram reveals the interesting fact that active and inactive Baptists are nearly equally church oriented, suggesting perhaps that for Baptists church membership or church orientation is more of an identity than an association—like being a Democrat in the South. Catholics and Methodists, conversely, are church oriented only if they are active members of congregations.

Ritualism. This analysis is summarized in table D-7 in Appendix D. The analysis of ritualism reveals three significant differences. Members of the three socioeconomic classes differ significantly, as do members of the three denominations and the two categories of involvement. In regard to social class, we find that the upper-middle-class category has a mean of 22.9, the lower middle class has a mean of 19.7, and the lower socioeconomic class has a mean of 24.1 (F = 4.84, P < .01).

Further we find, not too surprisingly, that active church members are more ritualistic (mean score of 24.2) than inactive members (mean score of 20.2) (F = 11.02, P < .01).

Finally, the three denominations are predictably different in this variable. The Catholics score highest with a mean of 27.6, the Methodists are next high with a mean score of 20.8, and the non-

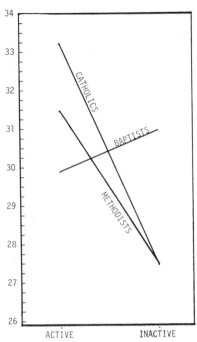

Figure 7-1. Church orientation: denomination by religious involvement interaction

ritualistic Baptists score lowest with a mean of 18.3 (F = 21.78, P < .01). These denominational differences conform to previous patterns of findings, such as the clergyman survey reported in chapter four.

Altruism. The analysis of altruism, which is summarized in table D-8, Appendix D, reveals two statistically significant differences. The first is between active church members, who have a mean of 33.3, and inactive members, who have a mean score of 31.6. This difference is significant at the .01 level (F = 21.46). Thus we find that concern for others is higher or greater among active church members than inactive members. This suggests that the association with the church and its rhetoric has some influence, or that altruism increases participation in a church.

The second significant difference is between classes (F = 3.24, P < .05). We find high altruism scores among the members of the lower class, who have a mean score of 33.9. We also find that the other two class groupings have lower and similar scores of 32.0 for the upper-middle class and 31.5 for the lower-middle class. The lack of any denominational difference should be noted, for it indicates that denominations are similarly altruistic.

Fundamentalism. The analysis of fundamentalism, summarized in table D-9, Appendix D, indicates that there are statistically significant differences between denominations, levels of involvement, and social classes.

In regard to socioeconomic-class differences we find that fundamentalism increases as one proceeds down the status hierarchy. This pattern is consistent with that discovered in the study of a southern city reported in the first section of this chapter. The lower-class group has the highest fundamentalism score with a mean of 38.4, followed by the lower-middle group with a mean score of 35.6, and the upper-middle group with a mean score of 32.4. These differences are significant at the .01 level $(F = 13.21)$.

An examination of fundamentalism differences across the two levels of religious involvement indicates that those who are actively involved are higher in fundamentalism (a mean of 38.1) than those who are less active (a mean score of 32.8). This difference is significant at the .01 level $(F = 32.32)$.

The third area of difference is that between denominations. Here we find that the Baptists are highest (a mean of 37.6), that Catholics (a mean of 35.0) are second, and that both are more fundamentalistic than the Methodists (a mean score of 33.6). These differences are significant at the .01 level $(F = 6.85)$. These findings are in general agreement with those presented in chapter four, which describes a national survey of clergymen.

Theism. The pattern of difference in regard to theism is very similar to that found in the previous examination of fundamentalism. The analysis of this variable is summarized in table D-10, Appendix D. Theism, we find, differs across social-class categories, across degrees of involvement, and across the three denominations.

First, in regard to social class, we find that theism increases as one moves down the status hierarchy. The upper-middle class has the lowest mean (34.2), followed by the lower-middle class (a mean of 37.6), followed lastly by the lower-class category (a mean of 39.8). These differences are significant at the .01 level $(F = 9.59)$.

The second area of significant difference is between degrees of involvement. The active members (a mean score of 39.9) are significantly more theistic than the inactive members (a mean score of 34.4). This difference is significant at the .01 level (F = 28.36).

The third area of difference is in regard to denomination. We find that Catholics are the most theistic (a mean of 39.2), followed closely by Baptists (a mean of 38.5), and that Methodists score lowest (a mean of 33.8). These differences are significant at the .01 level (F = 10.54). These findings conform to the pattern established in the clergyman survey and in the study of religious attitude differences across social-class groupings in a southern city, reported earlier in this chapter.

Idealism. There is only one significant difference in idealism. It is found to be significantly higher among active church members (a mean score of 33.3) than among inactive members (a mean score of 29.6). This difference is significant at the .01 level (F = 16.43). The analysis of variance is summarized in table D-11, Appendix D. Again we can see some attitude influence in active participation in a church. We find that active members become or remain idealistic or that idealists are more inclined to maintain an active involvement in a church.

Superstition. The analysis of superstition, which is summarized in table D-12, Appendix D, indicates that active and inactive church members differ in superstition, as do members of the three class categories. The analysis also indicates that there are two significant interactions, denomination-by-involvement, and social class-by-involvement.

First, we find that active church members are less superstitious (a mean of 23.7) than the inactive (a mean of 24.3). This difference is significant at the .05 level (F = 5.69). This is a somewhat surprising finding and suggests interestingly that controls on superstitious thinking might be provided by church attendance and involvement, or that less superstitious people are more active in their churches.

Second, we find the members of the lower-class category are more superstitious (a mean of 27.3) than the lower-middle-class category (a mean score of 23.7) or the upper-middle-class category (a mean score of 22.8). These differences are significant at the .01 level (F = 4.92). This pattern strongly conforms to that found in the southern sample reported earlier in this chapter.

The first of the significant interactions is that which examines denomination-by-religious involvement differences. This interaction is significant at the .01 level (F = 6.94). An inspection of the diagram of this interaction (figure 7-2) indicates that active members of all three denominations have similar superstition scores but that, in addition to the fact that inactives are more superstitious, the inactive Baptists are much more superstitious than inactive Catholics or Methodists.

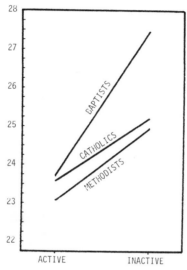

Figure 7-2. Superstition: denomination by religious involvement interaction

The second significant interaction is concerned with social class and religious involvement. This interaction is significant at the .05 level (F = 3.84). A diagram of this interaction can be found in figure 7-3. This diagram of mean scores indicates that inactive members of the lower class are the most highly superstitious but that inactivity seems to make members of the upper-middle class less superstitious. Alternatively, superstition might create an inactivity in church, particularly among the members of the lower socioeconomic classes. We can provide some insight into understanding this pattern by revealing that it follows very closely the years-of-schooling pattern. Lower-class inactives have the lowest mean years of school (11.1 years), followed in turn by lower-class actives (a mean of 11.7), lower-middle-class inactives (a mean of 12.9), lower-middle-class actives (mean of 13.1), upper-middle-class inactives (mean of 16), and upper-middle-class actives (a mean of 15.1). Superstition, it seems, varies rather directly with years of schooling.

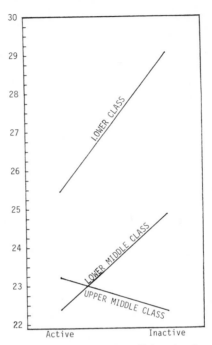

Figure 7-3. Superstition: social class by religious involvement interaction

Mysticism. The analysis of variance of mysticism is summarized in table D-13, Appendix D. The analysis reveals a significant mysticism difference across social classes as well as a significant denomination-by-class interaction. In examining the social-class differences in mysticism, we find that it increases as status decreases. The most mystical group is the lower class with a mean of 34.9; the next lower group is the lower-middle group with a mean of 29.9; and the upper-middle group has the lowest mean score of 29.8. The difference between the lower and the two middle-class groups is significant at beyond the .01 level (F = 16.76). This finding is consistent with the findings of the previously reported study of social class and mysticism in a southern city.

An examination of the significant (F = 2.57, P < .05) denomination-by-class interaction reveals the high lower-class mysticism and explicitly points up the exceptionally high lower-class-Catholic mys-

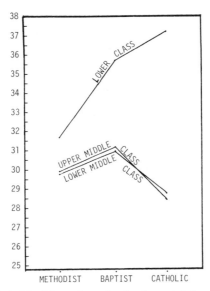

Figure 7-4. Mysticism: denomination by social class interaction

ticism. Figure 7-4 diagrams this interaction. This pattern among the Catholics in the community studied indicates that the lower-class members are the most ardent participants in the mysticism of that church.

In summary we have found significant social-class differences in seven of the eight dimensions of religious attitudes. The only exception is idealism. Secondly, we found that active church members differed from inactive members on seven of the eight dimensions—all but mysticism. Finally, the denominations studied differ on only

TABLE 7-8. SUMMARY OF SIGNIFICANT DIFFERENCES IN RELIGIOSITY BETWEEN SOCIAL CLASSES, LEVELS OF INVOLVEMENT, AND DENOMINATIONS
(Probabilities listed)

	Social Class Difference	Religious Involvement Difference	Denomination Difference
Church orientation	.01	.01	NS
Ritualism	.01	.01	.01
Altruism	.05	.01	NS
Fundamentalism	.01	.01	.01
Theism	.01	.01	.01
Idealism	NS	.01	NS
Superstition	.01	.05	NS
Mysticism	.01	NS	NS

three of the eight scales. These, crucially, are ritualism, on which Catholics score high, fundamentalism, on which Baptists score high, and theism, on which Methodists score lower than the other two denominations. The significant differences are summarized in table 7-8. These findings generally replicate findings of related studies and serve still further to underscore the value of an analytic approach to variables like religious attitude.

8

RELIGIOUS ATTITUDES
AND THREE SITUATIONALLY
CONSTRUCTED VARIABLES

This chapter describes three studies which employ the measurement of situationally constructed variables. The three studies investigate the relation between social arrogation or derogation, suggestibility, perceptual rigidity and religious attitudes. The three studies are described in a common chapter because they all involve either the manipulation of subjects or a measurement that can be obtained only in a physically or socially controlled situation. We will find that the results of the three studies are also somewhat related.

RELIGIOUS ATTITUDES AND EXPERIMENTALLY INDUCED SOCIAL DEROGATION AND ARROGATION

The first study involves the creation of an experimental situation within which individuals are made to feel rejected or accepted by others. The study employs a falsified feedback of others' opinion to create the feeling of rejection or undue acceptance.

A few years ago the late Manford H. Kuhn conducted an experiment (unfortunately never published) which identified and demonstrated some of the effects of social rejection or derogation and arrogation upon self-conceptions. He discovered that the effects were contingent upon the presence of "religious" self-identifications. More precisely, he discovered that social anchorage scores increased markedly among those subjects who made religious self-identifications on the "before measure" and were "subjected to the experimental variable."

Noting this contingency upon religious self-identifications, an additional experiment concerned with the effect of derogation and arrogation upon religious attitudes seems to be called for. We might ask, in other words, what are the effects of experimentally induced rejection or "derogation" and acceptance or "arrogation" upon religious attitudes.

The dependent variable is, of course, religiosity. And this experiment employed the previously described instrument to measure eight dimensions of religiosity. The eight dimensions are church orientation, ritualism, altruism, fundamentalism, theism, idealism, superstition, and mysticism.

The profound impact of the presence or absence of social or sensory support upon human behavior has been a recurring finding in social psychology. The relevant research ranges from such early studies as those of Asch (1952) and Sherif (1952), among others, through the sensory deprivation research (Solomon et al. 1961). We are aware of the profound impact of such variables, for on a more personal level we can occasionally note the extreme discomfort caused by an unfavorable personal evaluation by others. The effect of positive and negative social reaction on self, as well as the presence or lack of "sensory support," is an area of useful but difficult experimentation. Recently, many of the potential concerns have been impressed upon the public as well as the researchers. Appropriately, research of this variety should be entered into hesitantly and most carefully.

Procedure

The problem of this experiment is to determine the effects of derogation and arrogation upon the responses made on the eight scaled dimensions of religiosity. Kuhn's experiment used small discussion groups made up of individuals drawn from several classes who volunteered to meet separately, but the present experiment was conducted in one medium-sized college class in a southern university. The subjects had been classmates for nearly a semester in an introductory sociology class.

In preparation for the experiment a questionnaire containing the previously mentioned scales of religious attitudes was administered to the class two months before the experiment proper was conducted. This constituted the "before measure."

The experiment involved a certain amount of necessary manipulation. On a Monday the students in the particular class were asked to select six or so of their classmates in the course and rate or appraise them on a series of questionnaires. The prepared questionnaires contained the names of all the students in the class, and from this list the six were to be selected. After selecting six of their peers, they rated or appraised each of them with a set of questions which involved appraisals of competence, intellectual or academic interest, social attractiveness, contribution to the class, and general personality. The exact questionnaire filled out by the students can be found in Appendix E. They were asked not to discuss the ratings.

At the next class meeting, on Wednesday, some of the students in the class were given what appeared to be and was described to them as "summaries of the ratings they received from their classmates." These "summaries" were given to two-thirds (2/3) of the class with the explanation that the instructor had not had time to complete all the summaries but would return those thus far completed and the others could pick theirs up later in the day at his office or get them Friday in class. They were told that the remaining summaries would be completed by a definite time that afternoon in order to make the story seem more plausible. The returned and unreturned "summaries" created the following experimental and control groups:

A. The one-third (1/3) of the class that did *not* receive a summary was a randomly selected group of students who by virtue of receiving no experimentally false ratings served as the control group in the experiment. This group received: "Before Measure"—No Experimental Variable—"After Measure."

B. The remaining two-thirds (2/3) of the class served as the two experimental groups. They were randomly divided into two groups: experimentally derogated and experimentally arrogated.

   B₁ The first of these groups was experimentally derogated. This one-third of the class (one-half of the experimental two-thirds) received summaries which indicated that about ten of their classmates had rated them and that all or nearly all of them had rejected and disliked them. This group received: "Before

Measure"—Experimental Variable (Derogation)—"After Measure."

B₂ The second half of the experimental two-thirds of the class (one-third of the total class) received summaries which indicated that about ten of their classmates had rated them, and that all or nearly all of these classmates had rated them very highly. These persons were highly complimented, they were told that about ten of their peers considered them to be "splendid people." This group received: "Before Measure" —Experimental Variable (Arrogation)—"After Measure."

It was not possible to anticipate who would be absent from class on the day of the experiment. Because of absences the groups were not all the same size: the control group numbered 14; the arrogated group size was 15; and there were 16 in the final derogated group.

The two sets of false "summaries" were designed to summarize how their classmates had rated the subject on each question. Thus in both the derogation and arrogation summaries, the subject found question after question on which they were either "clobbered" time after time, or "flattered" time after time. In order to gather the possible impact of each form of summary, an example false summary of each type is included in Appendix E.

Throughout the experiment (on both Monday and Wednesday) the subjects were seated in such a way that they could not see any other than their own ratings and summary of ratings. Thus they encountered the derogating or arrogating summary appraisal "alone," and no one could reduce the impact by sharing it or denying it. In order to intensify the impact the instructor told them just before they received their summaries that most of the ratings were "average —as you would expect" and that hardly any were either highly favorable or highly unfavorable. This was done in order to make their rejection or arrogation even more theirs alone, that is, that they alone were highly liked or disliked.

Right after the summaries were distributed the subjects were asked to fill out the religiosity questionnaire. There was no explanation for the repeating of this measure which they had taken some months before. And frankly most (the experimental two-thirds) of the members of the class were so self-oriented at this time that they asked for no explanation. There is considerable evidence that the constructed situation and the false summaries were accepted as real and "honest" by all or most of the subjects. For example, the derogated subjects were all very sober and quiet, and a couple of girls cried softly. The arrogated subjects appeared to be elated, smiling broadly. The researcher was so intensely sympathetic with the derogated subjects that the experiment was terminated as quickly as possible. After it was terminated and the questionnaires were collected, the researcher explained the experiment and attempted to reassure the subjects and reduce their anxiety. At this point the experimentally arrogated subjects became "upset" for they suddenly discovered that their "glowing summaries" were not real and that they did not have evidence of great acceptance and affection by their peers.

After the nature and purpose of the experiment was explained, the subjects were asked to comment on their feelings during the experience and upon the experiment itself. Their responses seem to assure us that they accepted the summaries as real, for they admitted to being taken in when they would no doubt have liked to say that they had known what was going on all along. Some representative comments from subjects in both experimental groups follow:

Derogated Subjects

"It was a horribly nasty, inhuman kind of a trick (sociological study if you prefer) and I've never felt so miserably rejected by my 'friends.' " [This was from an A student.]

"I just wanted to shrivel up and die."

"I was sort of sort of stunned and couldn't think too clearly."

"I was upset."

"I was thoroughly convinced that these [the ratings] were real."

"It was a fantastic blow to 'pride.' "

"The only thing that worried me or made me doubt a little about the authenticity of this were the 'waste time' ratings. Then I decided 'they hate me because I make better grades' and it's really amazing the amount of irrational rationalizing you do in such a situation." [This was from an honor student.]

"On the religious survey I must have reread the same questions fifty times."

"It was awful."

"I rationalized by thinking—'Oh well, perhaps they just don't know me.' "

"I thought it was very real and it affected me—I felt quite rejected and outcast."

"When I saw the first page, I could hardly believe it, and I was afraid to go on to the next page. I was ready to change my personality."

"Yes, I did think it was real. I kept thinking how I was going to revamp my personality to make myself socially acceptable."

"My self-confidence was considerably shaken."

"My main feeling was that somehow I had wronged all these people."

"I didn't know how to feel. There was a sad sort of feeling inside."

"I felt somewhat depressed and rejected however I tend to say 'to hell with what he thinks of me anyway.' "

Arrogated Subjects

"I thought it was a very good survey. When I received this summary I was well pleased and surprised."

"I did think it was real, I had no reason to think otherwise."

"I did think the ratings were true, but thought it strange that everyone felt about the same way."

"I believed it."

"It's very frustrating to have your ego built up then torn down all in a matter of minutes! I would like to see the real results, if possible."

"I hoped it was real."

Thus, I believe, there is evidence to suggest that these false ratings and summaries were accepted as real. In fact, the reactions observed in the students (crying, etc.) were sufficiently intense and emotional to lead the investigator to give up plans he had to repeat the experiment the next week in another class. The extent of reaction was also so great that it was feared the experiment would be widely discussed so that a replication would be impossible.

Results

In the analysis of this experiment we will attend to the presence and direction of religious attitude change in each dimension of religiosity rather than the extent of shift and mean score differences. The analysis will involve the comparison of the two experimental groups and the control group. We will examine the groups in pairs, thus allowing us to employ a fourfold table without collapsing two categories into one, and we can thus place the total analysis in a simple format. Throughout the total analysis we will group "non-changes" with those whose score has decreased in regard to the particular dimension. This will create a dichotomy allowing us to use the fourfold table. The dichotomy is: (1) those who increase in the particular score and (2) those who do not change or decrease in the particular score.

Church Orientation. In regard to church orientation, the first dimension to be examined, we find that 50% of the control group increased in score or became more church oriented and that the remaining 50% either didn't change or became less church oriented. We find the same breakdown in the derogated group. The experimentally arrogated group contained five persons who became more church oriented and ten persons that did not. These score changes, which are revealed in table 8-1, suggest that the experimental variable did not affect church orientation attitudes.

TABLE 8-1. THE IMPACT OF ARROGATION AND DEROGATION UPON CHURCH-ORIENTED ATTITUDES

	Increased Score	Unchanged-Decreased Score	Total
Derogation†			
Derogated group	8 (50%)	8 (50%)	16 (100%)
Control group	7 (50%)	7 (50%)	14 (100%)
Total	15	15	30
Arrogation††			
Arrogated group	5 (33%)	10 (67%)	15 (100%)
Control group	7 (50%)	7 (50%)	14 (100%)
Total	12	17	29

† Q = .00   X² = .00   P > .05
†† Q = .33   X² = .83   P > .05

Ritualism. In regard to ritualism, we observed that 25% of the experimentally derogated group became more ritualistic, that 36% of the control group increased in ritualism, and that 73% of the arrogated group increased in ritualism, (see table 8-2).

The following table discloses that the arrogated subjects became significantly more ritualistic than the control subjects and much more ritualistic than the derogated subjects. This suggests that arrogation works to create greater ritualism; and when it is com-

	Increased Score	Unchanged-Decreased Score	Total
Derogation†			
Derogated group	4 (25%)	12 (75%)	16 (100%)
Control group	5 (36%)	9 (64%)	14 (100%)
Total	9	21	30
Arrogation††			
Arrogated group	11 (73%)	4 (27%)	15 (100%)
Control group	5 (36%)	9 (64%)	14 (100%)
Total	16	13	29
Arrogation-Derogation‡			
Arrogated group	11 (73%)	4 (27%)	15 (100%)
Derogated group	4 (25%)	12 (75%)	16 (100%)
Total	15	16	31

† $Q = .25$ $X^2 = .407$ $P > .05$
†† $Q = .66$ $X^2 = 4.14$ $P < .05$ (also significant by Fisher Exact Probability Test)
‡ $Q = .78$ $X^2 = 7.24$ $P < .05$ (also significant by Fisher Exact Probability Test)

pared with derogation, the influence is even more apparent, for derogated subjects have a slightly increased tendency to become less ritualistic or remain unchanged.

We might ask ourselves why interpersonal flattery or arrogation should increase an individual's appreciation for aesthetic liturgy and standardized ritual. Any answer to this puzzle must be recognized as purely conjectural. Perhaps having been strongly reinforced for being as they are, the arrogated subjects are more inclined to endorse items that connote appreciation for stability in religion as a reflection for an appreciation of stability in general. In fact, the third study described in this chapter will show ritualism to be related to perceptual rigidity. Perhaps having been relieved of interpersonal anxiety by the objective evidence indicating acceptance of themselves by others, they (the arrogated) can manifest increased liturgical sensitivity. The reaction of the derogated subjects might reflect a rejection of stability in a world they have suddenly found to be unstable and an increase of concern in interpersonal relations leading in turn to diminution of interest in things of beauty.

Altruism. We find that 50% of the control group, 37.5% of the derogated, and 60% of the arrogated group increased in altruistic attitudes. Table 8-3 shows the effects of arrogation upon altruism.

Thus we find a slight and nonsignificant difference in the influ-

TABLE 8-3. THE IMPACT OF ARROGATION AND DEROGATION UPON ALTRUISTIC ATTITUDES

	Increased Score	Unchanged-Decreased Score	Total
Derogation†			
Derogated group	6 (37.5%)	10 (62.5%)	16 (100%)
Control group	7 (50%)	7 (50%)	14 (100%)
Total	13	17	30
Arrogation††			
Arrogated group	9 (60%)	6 (40%)	15 (100%)
Control group	7 (50%)	7 (50%)	14 (100%)
Total	16	13	29

† Q = .25   X² = .47   P > .05
†† Q = .20   X² = .29   P > .05

ence of derogation and arrogation upon altruism. The direction indicates that arrogation increases altruism and derogation decreases it. However, since the relationship is not significant, we should only note the consistency of direction of the impact of arrogation in the case of altruism as well as ritualism.

Fundamentalism. In examining fundamentalism we find that 50% of the control group, 50% of the derogated group, and 30% of the arrogated group experienced an increase in fundamentalistic religious attitudes. Table 8-4 summarizes the effect of the experimental variables upon fundamentalism.

TABLE 8-4. THE IMPACT OF ARROGATION AND DEROGATION UPON FUNDAMENTALISTIC ATTITUDES

	Increased Score	Unchanged-Decreased Score	Total
Derogation†			
Derogated group	8 (50%)	8 (50%)	16 (100%)
Control group	7 (50%)	7 (50%)	14 (100%)
Total	15	15	30
Arrogation††			
Arrogated group	6 (40%)	9 (60%)	15 (100%)
Control group	7 (50%)	7 (50%)	14 (100%)
Total	13	16	29

† Q = .00   X² = .00   P > .05
†† Q = .20   X² = .29   P > .05

We observe that the experimental variable does not result in significant alterations of the fundamentalism scores of the subjects;

neither arrogation nor derogation alters fundamentalism scores significantly.

Theism. In regard to the theism dimension, we observe that 43% of the control group, 31% of the derogated group, and 27% of the arrogated group increased in theism. Table 8-5 discloses an apparent lack of relationship between arrogation-derogation and change in theistic attitude.

TABLE 8-5. THE IMPACT OF ARROGATION AND DEROGATION UPON THEISTIC ATTITUDES

	Increased Score		Unchanged-Decreased Score		Total	
Derogation†						
Derogated group	5	(31%)	11	(69%)	16	(100%)
Control group	6	(43%)	8	(57%)	14	(100%)
Total	11		19		30	
Arrogation††						
Arrogated group	4	(27%)	11	(73%)	15	(100%)
Control group	6	(43%)	8	(57%)	14	(100%)
Total	10		19		29	

† $Q = .245$ $X^2 = .436$ $P > .05$
†† $Q = .35$ $X^2 = .837$ $P > .05$

The experimental variables do not create differential effects in theism scores.

Idealism. In regard to this dimension we observe that 27% of the control group, 37.5% of the derogated group, and 67% of the arrogated group increased in idealism. We can observe the differential effects in table 8-6.

We observe that the control group and derogated group are not

TABLE 8-6. THE IMPACT OF ARROGATION AND DEROGATION UPON IDEALISTIC ATTITUDES

	Increased Score		Unchanged-Decreased Score		Total	
Derogation†						
Derogated group	6	(37.5%)	10	(62.5%)	16	(100%)
Control group	4	(27%)	10	(73%)	14	(100%)
Total	10		20		30	
Arrogation††						
Arrogated group	10	(67%)	5	(33%)	15	(100%)
Control group	4	(27%)	10	(73%)	14	(100%)
Total	14		15		29	

† $Q = .20$ $X^2 = .27$ $P > .05$
†† $Q = .67$ $X^2 = 4.213$ $P < .05$ (also significant by Fisher Exact Probability Test)

significantly different. Apparently derogation does not influence idealism. However, the arrogated group is significantly more idealistic than the control group. Apparently, one effect of interpersonal confidence of the variety created by arrogation is to turn one's attention toward lofty principles in the same way that arrogation increases one's sensitivity to religious liturgy and ritual.

Superstition. The next dimension to be examined is superstition (see table 8-7). In regard to this variable we discover that

TABLE 8-7. THE IMPACT OF ARROGATION AND DEROGATION UPON SUPERSTITIOUS ATTITUDES

	Increased Score	Unchanged-Decreased Score	Total
Derogation†			
Derogated group	6 (37.5%)	10 (62.5%)	16 (100%)
Control group	8 (57%)	6 (43%)	14 (100%)
Total	14	16	30
Arrogation††			
Arrogated group	6 (40%)	9 (60%)	15 (100%)
Control group	8 (57%)	6 (43%)	14 (100%)
Total	14	15	29

† $Q = .38$ $X^2 = 1.163$ $P > .05$
†† $Q = .33$ $X^2 = .85$ $P > .05$

57% of the control group, 37% of the derogated group, and 40% of the arrogated group increased in superstition scores. Thus we find that there are not significant differential effects of arrogation or derogation upon superstition. Apparently superstition is unaffected by this particular variable.

Mysticism. The last dimension to be examined is mysticism. By examining table 8-8 we find that 36% of the control group, 37.5% of the derogated group, and 53% of the arrogated group increased in mysticism scores. Thus we find that mysticism is not affected by either arrogation or derogation.

In general we have discovered that:

(1.) Derogation does not have a substantial impact upon any of the various dimensions of religiosity.

(2.) Arrogation has a small, but in some instances significant, impact upon religiosity.

(3.) Idealism and ritualism show significant increases as the result of arrogation.

	Increased Score	Unchanged-Decreased Score	Total
Derogation†			
Derogated group	6 (37.5%)	10 (62.5%)	16 (100%)
Control group	5 (36%)	9 (64%)	14 (100%)
Total	11	19	30
Arrogation††			
Arrogated group	8 (53%)	7 (47%)	15 (100%)
Control group	5 (36%)	9 (64%)	14 (100%)
Total	13	16	29

† Q = .04   X² = .01   P > .05
†† Q = .35   X² = .91   P > .05

The comparative impact of arrogation and derogation is somewhat surprising. It appears that flattery leads to a profound increase in certain dimensions of religiosity, whereas derogation leads to no significant change. It is possible that individuals are more insulated against rejection than flattery, or perhaps the subjects were so upset by rejection that they merely responded automatically which in turn yielded no change. It is possible that those who were arrogated experienced an expansiveness which increased their responsiveness to the aesthetic aspects of ritualism, liturgy, and idealistic principles. Therefore, the observed differences may be the result of an increase in self-satisfaction, which is the result of arrogation and which, in turn, results in changes in a more aesthetic and idealistic direction. On the other hand those individuals who were rejected simply might not have experienced the self feelings which would allow them to direct their attentions to principle and aesthetics. They may have been so self-concerned as a result of their rejection that they responded automatically or unthinkingly, simply giving the same answers they had before.

Summary

In summary we have observed significant changes in the religious attitudes of individuals subjected to experimental arrogation in only two dimensions of religiosity, idealism and ritualism. Experimentally induced rejection did not lead to any significant changes in any of the dimensions of religiosity studied.

RELIGIOUS ATTITUDES AND SUGGESTIBILITY*

The major objective of this particular study is to ascertain if there are religious attitude differences between suggestible and non-suggestible subjects. In this study suggestibility is measured by the extent to which individuals are induced to alter their reports of a perception by the reports of their peers. The religious attitudes of the subjects were measured with the religiosity questionnaire described earlier in this book. The religious attitude measurements were made some weeks prior to the measurement of suggestibility.

Suggestibility can be seen to take many forms. Eysenck (1947) conceived that there are at least three types of suggestibility: (1) primary—the process through which individuals carry out motor movement upon suggestion without conscious participation; (2) secondary —the process through which persons perceive and recall the thing suggested; and (3) prestige—the process through which persons change opinion toward that which they are told is held by a prestigious person. Symington (1935), Hoffman (1953), and Dreger (1952) found religious conservatives to be high on prestige suggestibility. Howells (1928) and Sinclair (1928) found religious conservatives to be high on primary suggestibility. Thus, there is evidence that religious persons are inclined to be high in primary and prestige suggestibility. Eysenck (1947) found neurotics to be suggestible; and others, Brown and Lowe (1951) and Maranell (see chapter 10 of this book) have found religious persons to be more neurotic, especially high in hysteria. Thus, this also supports the notion of a relationship between religious conservatism and suggestibility.

Procedure

The particular method used in this study to measure suggestibility was suggested by various classical studies of phenomena resembling suggestibility (Asch 1952, Sherif 1952, Hovland et al. 1953). By this I mean we gathered from Asch the notion of confederates influencing reported perceptions and from Sherif the notion of using a vague, ambiguous stimulus object. The economics of the situation

---

* The data presented in this section were gathered by the author and Mrs. Analee Beisecker (née Burns).

were such that it was necessary to gather data from more than one critical subject at a time. It was not possible to employ a device as demanding of special circumstances as the autokinetic effect.

I have in past situations used a crumpled piece of string in classroom demonstrations of norm formation. In these demonstrations a crumpled length of string was held up in a "wad" and the students were asked to estimate its length. Group discussion of the length was solicited, and through subsequent judgments the development of norms can be demonstrated by re-examination of the series of individual judgments.

The measurement situation was a university classroom; the class, an undergraduate sociology class. Following Asch and others, confederates were employed in this study. A previous arrangement was made with a number of the relatively high prestige students in the class regarding their responses, and they were coached to make a particular type of response when called upon in this constructed situation. In the experimental situation judgments were solicited only from confederates, and when called upon, they presented their prepared opinions.

The situation involved presenting a university class with an ambiguous stimulus object, which in this case was a crumpled length of string. The string was hastily presented in a crumpled ball. The subjects were then asked to write their individual estimates of the length of the string in inches. After each individual had made an estimate and recorded it, individuals in the class were "randomly selected" and asked to report their estimates to the class. These "randomly selected" students were all confederates and they reported their prepared estimates aloud.

There were ten confederates, and the confederates were instructed to make a guess of over 100 inches. In the classroom demonstration of norm formation previously referred to, it has been noted that in such comparable situations the mean estimates are about 60 inches with a usual range of from 30 to 80 inches. In view of this the coached estimates solicited of over 100 inches were felt to be well beyond the usual expected range. The estimates made in the study situation by the confederates were 110, 115, 118, 103, 130, 116, 72, 110, 112, 150, 115 with a mean of 113.7 or 114. The one instance where an estimate of under 100 inches was made is explained by confusion in the soliciting of the confederates' opinions so that one nonconfederate responded aloud. The influence of this, according to the Asch study, would be one of diminishing the influence of the confederates.

During the study the naive subjects were apparently very "upset" by these strangely long and homogeneous estimates. An early nervous laughter developed into a rather horrified silence as confederate after confederate threw doubt upon the subjects' perception.

From the class only seventeen subjects could be used in this study. Seven subjects were not affected by the suggestion in any way and ten subjects were definitely influenced, which they demonstrated by increasing their estimates, thus moving in the direction of the confederates' suggestions.

Results

The significance of the difference between the means on the religiosity dimensions of the two groups, suggestible and nonsuggestible, was tested with the t test. The results can be found in table 8-9.

TABLE 8-9. MEAN RELIGIOUS ATTITUDE SCORES OF SUGGESTIBLE AND NON-SUGGESTIBLE STUDENTS

	Suggestible (N = 10)	Non-suggestible (N = 7)	t Value
Church orientation	25.10	23.00	.516
Ritualism	15.40	9.00	1.850*
Altruism	24.60	27.14	1.26
Fundamentalism	25.10	23.00	.504
Theism	28.60	22.86	1.15
Idealism	25.80	32.57	2.89**
Superstition	19.10	19.71	.33
Mysticism	26.50	24.86	.468

* P < .05
** P < .01

We find that suggestible individuals are significantly more ritualistic than the nonsuggestible, and suggestible persons are significantly less idealistic than the nonsuggestible. We can note also that the suggestible individuals are inclined to be less altruistic and more theistic, but not significantly so. Thus, we find that only certain dimensions of religiosity and not religiosity in general are related to suggestibility.

A possible interpretation of these findings can, in the case of ritualism and idealism, be accomplished by pointing to the fact that ritualism has been found to be related significantly to various aspects of neuroticism—anxiety, general maladjustment, dependency, and social alienation (see chapter 10 in this book)—and idealism has been found to be inversely related to anxiety. Thus, the suggestibility finding could conceivably be accounted for by means of an anxiety, which corresponds to previously cited findings by Eysenck (1947) and Brown and Lowe (1951).

Other interpretations could be suggested as well. For example, if we recognize that ritualism involves an excessive attention to the external world and implies a responsiveness to this external world, we can recognize that it is essentially a conformity oriented position. The ritualistic individual is impressed by external behavior and ceremony and is especially impressed by the shared nature of this external behavior. It is thus possible that ritualistic individuals are thereby inclined to be conforming and unduly influenced by the behavior of others. Such inclinations would certainly lead to high suggestibility and would permit us to observe that suggestible persons are ritualistic.

The idealistic individuals, in contrast with the ritualistic, feel that one should not be seduced by the pressures of conformity. In fact the idealist might well be suspicious of highly structured, conformity oriented situations. He maintains that principles and ideals should be followed regardless of what other people are doing. Therefore, it is not surprising to find that idealistic individuals are low in suggestibility and that nonsuggestible individuals are idealistic.

In summary we have found only ritualism and idealism to be related to suggestibility, with the suggestible individuals being found to be ritualistic and nonidealistic, and the nonsuggestible individuals being nonritualistic and idealistic.

RELIGIOUS ATTITUDES AND PERCEPTUAL RIGIDITY*

This section describes an examination of the relationship between religious attitudes and perceptual rigidity. Some investigators (Swindell and L'abate 1970, Warner and Kawamura 1967) have

---

*The data presented in this section were gathered by Professor George Nielson and the author.

found religiosity correlated with dogmatism, so that there is some reason to explore the subtleties of the relationship.

Frenkel-Brunswik (1949) maintained that variables such as rigidity and intolerance of ambiguity can be measured by measuring the response an individual makes to ambiguous visual stimuli. She further maintains that this, in turn, provides clues to the degree of an individual's prejudice and authoritarianism since these attitudes have been found to be related to rigid outlook. Frenkel-Brunswik sought an objective and relatively precise instrument for measuring rigidity. The present study uses a measurement which is a modified version of her approach.

The concept of rigidity refers to the perseveration of, and resistance to change in, the visual perception of a gradually changing and ambiguous visual stimulus. The longer a person clings to the original or the familiar image in the face of changing and ambiguous stimuli, the more perceptually rigid he is held to be.

The approach employed by Frenkel-Brunswik was first to show the subjects a picture of a dog. Following this a number of pictures were shown representing transitional stages leading finally to the picture of a cat. At each stage in the transformation the subject was asked to identify the object in the picture. Prejudiced subjects tended to hold on longer to the first perception and to respond more slowly to the changing stimulus. Frenkel-Brunswik reports that there was a greater reluctance on the part of the prejudiced subjects to give up the original perception about which they had felt relatively certain.

The instrument developed for the present study is a modification of that described above. Frenkel-Brunswik has suggested that objects less similar than a cat and dog should be selected as stimulus objects. The original picture in the present study was a tree which was changed through twenty serially modified pictures into a picture of a house. The pictures were reproduced on 35 mm slides and shown to the subjects with a tachistoscopic device. This device permitted the limiting of the exposure time for each picture. By using a tachistoscopic device the ambiguity was increased. Ambiguity in the stimuli or its presentation permits the material to be perceived in more than one way. In this case it allows for the operation of personality factors. Completely unambiguous stimuli would not allow for the operation of perceptual rigidity as a variable.

It was discovered in several pilot tests that it was necessary to use an exposure speed of .01 of a second. The measurement situation thus involved presenting twenty serially changing slides to the subjects for .01 of a second each. The first slide was shown for a longer period to make certain that it was correctly perceived. The subjects recorded on twenty numbered blanks what they perceived on each of the serially presented slides. This recording took place during a pause which followed the exposure of each slide.

It was assumed that the longer a subject held on to the original image—the tree—in the face of a changing ambiguous stimulus, the greater was the subject's perceptual rigidity. This was seen to be true since rigidity involves the tendency to cling to the familiar and the known when ambiguous stimuli are presented. The perceptual rigidity score for a person was the number of the picture, or exposure, to which he last responded with "tree"; that is, it was the last picture in which he perceived the tree he had seen originally. A score of twenty means that he never perceived anything but a tree; and a score of four means that the fourth picture was the last in which he perceived a tree. Reporting that one did not know what one had perceived was, of course, scored as perceiving something other than a tree.

Following the measurement task the subjects completed the eight religious attitude scales. They also took an authoritarianism scale and a superpatriotism scale which were added as independent measures of attitude variables which should be related to perceptual rigidity. The scales and the perceptual rigidity test were administered to five undergraduate classes. Questionnaires completed by students with visual handicaps were excluded from the analysis. The final number of subjects is 268.

Findings

The method of analysis selected in this study of the relationship between perceptual rigidity and the religious attitude variables is simply a nonparametric measure of association, Gamma, and a measuse of statistical significance, Chi square. This mode of analysis was selected since it permits a visual inspection of the associations. The mode of analysis used works best when the variables are reduced to smaller sets of categories. It was decided to reduce the religious attitude variables to dichotomies and to employ a three-category division of the perceptual rigidity variable. The division of the total sample on the variables was made in such a way that the subgroups created were as nearly equal in size as possible.

Church Orientation. Table 8-10 summarizes the relationship between church orientation and perceptual rigidity. An examination of this table shows that the percentage of perceptually rigid individuals in the high and low church-orientation categories is very similar. Therefore, no relationship of substantive or statistical significance appears to exist between perceptual rigidity and church orientation.

TABLE 8-10. THE ASSOCIATION BETWEEN PERCEPTUAL RIGIDITY AND CHURCH ORIENTATION

	CHURCH ORIENTATION		
	High	Low	Total
Perceptual rigidity†			
High	50%	50%	100% (84)
Medium	49%	51%	100% (87)
Low	45%	55%	100% (97)
Total	48% (129)	52% (139)	100% (268)

† $X^2 = .4743$ $P > .05$
Gamma = .06

Ritualism. It is apparent in table 8-11 that a significant relationship exists between perceptual rigidity and ritualism. Those who score high or medium on the perceptual rigidity scale tend to be

TABLE 8-11. THE ASSOCIATION BETWEEN PERCEPTUAL RIGIDITY AND RITUALISM

	RITUALISM		
	High	Low	Total
Perceptual rigidity†			
High	58%	42%	100% (84)
Medium	61%	39%	100% (87)
Low	42%	58%	100% (97)
Total	48% (129)	52% (139)	100% (268)

† $X^2 = 7.6269$ $P < .05$
Gamma = .22

Religious Attitudes and Three Situational Variables [197]

ritualistic, while those with low perceptual rigidity scores—those who are more flexible—tend to receive low scores on the ritualism scale. The relationship between ritualism and perceptual rigidity is significant at the .05 level.

Altruism. We find that no significant relationship exists between perceptual rigidity and altruism (see table 8-12).

TABLE 8-12. THE ASSOCIATION BETWEEN PERCEPTUAL RIGIDITY AND ALTRUISM

| | ALTRUISM | | |
	High	Low	Total
Perceptual rigidity†			
High	55%	45%	100% (84)
Medium	53%	47%	100% (87)
Low	54%	46%	100% (97)
Total	54% (144)	46% (124)	100% (268)

† $X^2 = .06$ $P > .05$
Gamma $= .01$

Fundamentalism. In table 8-13 we find that there is no significant relationship between fundamentalism and perceptual rigidity.

TABLE 8-13. THE ASSOCIATION BETWEEN PERCEPTUAL RIGIDITY AND FUNDAMENTALISM

| | FUNDAMENTALISM | | |
	High	Low	Total
Perceptual rigidity†			
High	49%	51%	100% (84)
Medium	51%	49%	100% (87)
Low	49%	51%	100% (97)
Total	49.6% (133)	50.4% (135)	100% (268)

† $X^2 = .05$ $P > .05$
Gamma $= .01$

Theism. The data indicate that there is a very slight tendency for flexible people to be nontheistic (see table 8-14); however, the relationship between perceptual rigidity and theism is not statistically significant.

TABLE 8-14. THE ASSOCIATION BETWEEN PERCEPTUAL RIGIDITY AND THEISM

	THEISM		
	High	Low	Total
Perceptual rigidity†			
High	51%	49%	100% (84)
Medium	52%	48%	100% (87)
Low	45%	55%	100% (97)
Total	51% (136)	49% (132)	100% (268)

† X² = 1.26 P > .05
Gamma = .10

Idealism. We find that the distribution of perceptual rigidity categories between high and low idealism scores is similar (see table 8-15), with a slight trend for those who are low on perceptual rigidity to be high on idealism. The relationship is not significant, however.

TABLE 8-15. THE ASSOCIATION BETWEEN PERCEPTUAL RIGIDITY AND IDEALISM

	IDEALISM		
	High	Low	Total
Perceptual rigidity†			
High	50%	50%	100% (84)
Medium	48%	52%	100% (87)
Low	54%	46%	100% (97)
Total	51% (136)	49% (132)	100% (268)

† X² = .55 P > .05
Gamma = −.05

Superstition. Table 8-16 indicates that no significant relationship occurs between perceptual rigidity and superstition. This is somewhat surprising; however, it is consistent with the finding in regard to suggestibility which was presented in the second section of this chapter.

Mysticism. The eighth and final religiosity variable to be examined is mysticism (see table 8-17). Although the relationship between perceptual rigidity and mysticism is not statistically significant, there is a noticeable tendency for perceptually rigid people to be high on mysticism, or for mystical people to be perceptually rigid.

Religious Attitudes and Three Situational Variables [199]

TABLE 8-16. THE ASSOCIATION BETWEEN PERCEPTUAL RIGIDITY AND SUPERSTITION

| | SUPERSTITION | | |
	High	Low	Total
Perceptual rigidity†			
High	46%	54%	100% (84)
Medium	49%	51%	100% (87)
Low	47%	53%	100% (97)
Total	48% (128)	52% (140)	100% (268)

† $X^2 = .16$ $P > .05$
Gamma $= -.01$

Two variables, superpatriotism and authoritarianism, were included as potential validity checks for the perceptual rigidity variable. That is, if perceptual rigidity is operating as expected, it should be related to both of these variables. Furthermore, the perceptually rigid should be superpatriotic and authoritarian.

TABLE 8-17. THE ASSOCIATION BETWEEN PERCEPTUAL RIGIDITY AND MYSTICISM

| | MYSTICISM | | |
	High	Low	Total
Perceptual rigidity†			
High	62%	38%	100% (84)
Medium	47%	53%	100% (87)
Low	46%	54%	100% (97)
Totals	51% (137)	49% (131)	100% (268)

† $X^2 = 5.75$ $P > .05$
Gamma $= .21$

The relationships between superpatriotism, authoritarianism, and perceptual rigidity are significant, as is shown in tables 8-18 and 8-19. The relationships are also in a positive direction. Thus we find that superpatriotism is positively related to perceptual rigidity. That is, superpatriots are inclined to be perceptually rigid (see table 8-18). A similar pattern exists in regard to authoritarianism and perceptual rigidity (see table 8-19). There is a significant relationship between perceptual rigidity and authoritarianism. Authoritarian persons are disproportionately perceptually rigid.

TABLE 8-18. THE ASSOCIATION BETWEEN PERCEPTUAL RIGIDITY AND SUPERPATRIOTISM

| | SUPERPATRIOTISM | | |
	High	Low	Total
Perceptual rigidity†			
High	62%	38%	100% (84)
Medium	52%	48%	100% (87)
Low	40%	60%	100% (97)
Total	51% (136)	49% (132)	100% (268)

† $X^2 = 8.53$ $P < .05$
Gamma = .29

In this study we found in summary that:

(1) Ritualism alone among the religious attitude variables is significantly associated to perceptual rigidity.

(2) The measure of perceptual rigidity is predictably associated to authoritarianism and superpatriotism.

TABLE 8-19. THE ASSOCIATION BETWEEN PERCEPTUAL RIGIDITY AND AUTHORITARIANISM

| | AUTHORITARIANISM | | |
	High	Low	Total
Perceptual rigidity†			
High	60%	40%	100% (84)
Medium	53%	47%	100% (87)
Low	41%	59%	100% (97)
Total	51% (136)	49% (132)	100% (268)

† $X^2 = 6.26$ $P < .05$
Gamma = .24

GENERAL SUMMARY

The three studies summarized in this chapter reveal that:

(1) Social arrogation increases ritualism.

(2) Social arrogation increases idealism.

(3) Ritualistic persons are suggestible (or) suggestible persons are ritualistic.

(4) Idealistic persons are nonsuggestible (or) nonsuggestible persons are idealistic.

(5) Ritualistic persons are perceptually rigid (or) perceptually rigid persons are ritualistic.

We now have evidence that ritualistic individuals are unduly suggestible, or conforming, and are also perceptually rigid which indicates perhaps that they are suggestible only to the extent that they can or will perceive the nature of model forming behavior. Furthermore we found that ritualism is increased through social arrogation. Reinforced self-regard or social acceptance thus increases ritualism, which is, in turn, associated with rigidity and suggestibility. This suggests the existence of an interesting pattern of selective perception, or tunnel vision, and conformity which is reinforced by strong social acceptance. The social acceptance is, of course, what one sees in the selectively perceived world or in one's restricted circles of interaction.

Idealism on the other hand is also increased by social acceptance; but it is not related to perceptual rigidity, and it is associated with being nonsuggestible. This suggests the importance of social support even for persons with principled independence of perception, as was indicated by the suggestibility study.

9

RELIGIOUS ATTITUDES
AND SCHOLASTIC APTITUDE

The basic question in regard to this area of concern is, "do religious persons have more or less scholastic ability than nonreligious persons?" or "are the scholastically able more or less religious than the less able?" Studies in general have found negative correlations between indices of religious commitment, or religious conservatism, and measures of academic or scholastic ability. Argyle (1958) has summarized the research findings in this area and has pointed out that there are consistently discovered differences in IQ and achievement between denominations, and that success in particular fields of endeavor varies with denomination; for example, scientists are largely Protestants. Argyle further stated that "intelligent children grasp religious concepts earlier" but that "they are also the first to doubt the truth of religion" and that "intelligent students are much less likely to accept orthodox beliefs and rather less likely to have pro-religious attitudes or mystical experiences" (Argyle 1958: 96). Individuals who are more intelligent are felt to be less influenced by social pressure and, because of this, can be expected to be less orthodox in religious belief.

A study by Kosa and Schommer (1961), however, found religiosity to be positively correlated with scholastic aptitude. This finding, it should be realized, is in contradiction to the usual findings in this area which have been summarized by Argyle.

In view of this contradictory set of results we will examine this study in a bit more detail. These researchers, Kosa and Schommer, used a population of Catholic college students. Religiosity was measured with the "Le Moyne Religion Test," which measures *religious knowledge*. Scholastic aptitude was measured with reading speed, comprehension, spelling, math, grade point, etc. Verbal skills were found to be more highly correlated than such things as math or spelling.

The obvious distinction between "religious knowledge" and "religious belief" might help us to account for these contradictory findings, as could the nature of the population. We could well imagine that in a Catholic environment the students with the highest scholastic aptitude would secure the highest scores on a test of religious knowledge. We might also recognize that the possibly restricted range of religious belief within a conservative Catholic college student population could itself obscure a high negative correlation which exists over a larger segment of the religious belief spectrum.

In view of these findings it is felt to be of some interest to discover the pattern of relationship between various dimensions of religiosity and some selected indices of scholastic ability. Is there a consistent pattern of negative correlation, with religiosity uniformly associated with lower scholastic aptitude? Or does this only occur in certain dimensions of religiosity, and perhaps in only certain regional subcultures? These and other questions can best be answered through an examination of the relationships between the dimensions of religiosity and some measures of scholastic ability in at least two different regional subcultures.*

POPULATIONS STUDIED

This research was conducted in two university undergraduate populations. The first is a group of 133 undergraduate students at a southern university. The second sample is a group of 131 undergraduate students at a midwestern university.

---

* The midwestern data reported in this chapter were gathered by Miss Jean Leonard.

VARIABLES

Religious Attitudes

Measurements of religious attitudes were secured for this study with the religiosity scales previously described in this book. These scales were designed to provide measurements of church orientation, ritualism, altruism, fundamentalism, theism, idealism, superstition, and mysticism.

Scholastic Aptitude

Slightly different measures of scholastic aptitude were secured in the two populations studied. In each population the scores used were those secured on the tests administered to the freshmen during their orientation and testing periods. In view of these differences in measurements between the two populations, we will discuss the tests used in each population separately.

Measures used in the Southern student population:

(1) The American Council of Education Psychological Examination for College Freshmen (ACE) 1952) ed.

This test measures six different skills: (a) sentence completion, (b) figure analogies, (c) arithmetic, (d) same-opposite relationships, (e) number series, and (f) verbal analogies. A single summed score was all that was available for this test in this population. The reliability and validity of this test are discussed in the usual sources; see Cronbach (1960), for example. Strong positive correlations have been found to exist between ACE and college grades; and both split-half and test-retest reliabilities (correlations) have been found to be greater than .90.

(2) The Cooperative English Test (published by the Cooperative Testing Service of the American Council on Education).

This test was used by the southern university to measure reading speed, level of comprehension, and vocabulary. All three scores were employed.

Measures used in the Midwestern student population:

(1) The School and College Ability Test (SCAT), form 1C (pub-

lished by the Cooperative Testing Division of the Educational Service, Princeton, N.J.).

This test measures quantitative and verbal ability. The test is divided into four parts but only one quantitative and one verbal are administered and used at the midwestern university; thus only two scores were available.

(2) The Cooperative English Test (this is the same test as is used at the southern university).

The midwestern university uses more sections of this test than the southern university. Both schools use form 2C for vocabulary and reading speed and the midwestern university also uses form OM sections on usage and spelling. This involves appraisals of grammar, diction, punctuation, sentence structure, and capitalization. This test yielded four scores which were employed in this research.

The relationship between each of the dimensions of religiosity and the various measures of scholastic aptitude was examined in each of the two populations with coefficients of correlation. The results of this analysis can be found below.

RESULTS

The Southern University Student Population

The results of the analysis of the southern student population can be found summarized in table 9-1 and figure 9-1. An examination of this table and figure reveals the following general conclusions.

(1) All the coefficients of correlation except two (both of these in regard to idealism and neither significant) are negative. This reflects a strong pattern in the southern population of scholastic aptitude being associated with less strong religiosity; or, inversely, high religiosity is associated with low scholastic ability.

(2) The lack of strong and even consistent correlations between idealism and scholastic aptitude reflects a lack of relationship between these variables in the southern population.

(3) All indices of scholastic aptitude are correlated significantly and negatively with at least six of the eight dimensions of religiosity.

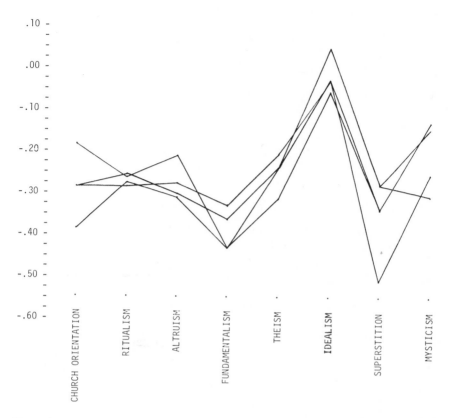

Figure 9-1. The general pattern of correlations between religious attitudes and academic aptitude in the southern student population

(4) An examination of the mean correlations of all scholastic ability indices with each dimension of religiosity reveals that in the southern sample fundamentalism is most highly related to scholastic aptitude $(\bar{X}_r = -.38)$ followed closely by superstition with a mean correlation of $-.36$. Following superstition, in order, we have theism $(\bar{X}_r = -.282)$, church orientation $(\bar{X}_r = -.28)$, altruism $(\bar{X}_r = -.27)$, ritualism $(\bar{X}_r = -.265)$, mysticism $(\bar{X}_r = -.20)$, and finally idealism $(\bar{X}_r = +.02)$.

(5) The general pattern of the relationship is revealed in figure 9-1, which reflects the uniqueness of the idealism dimension coupled with a relatively consensual pattern in all variables. (For specific correlations, see table 9-1.)

Table 9-1. The Correlations between Religiosity and Academic Aptitude in the Southern Student Population

	ACE	Reading Speed	Reading Comprehension	Vocabulary	$\bar{X}_r$ of row
Church orientation ..	—.28**	—.38**	—.18*	—.28**	—.28
Ritualism	—.28**	—.27**	—.26**	—.25**	—.265
Altruism	—.27**	—.31**	—.21**	—.29**	—.27
Fundamentalism	—.32**	—.42**	—.42**	—.36**	—.38
Theism	—.20*	—.31**	—.23**	—.23**	—.2825
Idealism	+.06	—.05	—.02	+.08	+.02
Superstition	—.27**	—.33**	—.51**	—.27**	—.36
Mysticism	—.31**	.—12	—.24**	—.13	—.20

* Correlation is significant at the .05 level.
** Correlation is significant at the .01 level.

The Midwestern University Student Population

The results of the analysis of the relationships in the midwestern population are revealed in table 9-2 and figure 9-2.

Table 9-2. The Correlations between Religiosity and Academic Aptitude in the Midwestern Student Population

	SCAT Verbal	SCAT Quantitative	Vocabulary	Reading Speed	English Usage	Spelling
Church orientation	—.18*	—.01	—.10	—.15	—.08	—.13
Ritualism	—.32**	—.20*	—.22**	—.22**	—.03	—.05
Altruism	—.06	+.07	.00	—.13	+.14	+.05
Fundamentalism	—.23**	—.12	—.12	—.14	+.02	—.09
Theism	—.17*	—.18*	—.08	—.12	.00	—.16
Idealism	+.15	+.14	+.24**	+.19*	+.22**	+.12
Superstition	—.25**	—.13	—.13	—.17*	—.10	—.15
Mysticism	—.12	—.17*	—.02	—.07	+.03	—.17*

* Correlation is significant at the .05 level.
** Correlation is significant at the .01 level.

(1) The correlations between scholastic aptitude and religiosity in the midwestern population are in general less highly negative and more highly positive than are the correlations in the southern population. This general pattern is found in the higher placement of the correlation lines in the midwestern sample (figure 9-2).

(2) We can also note that idealism is always positively correlated with scholastic aptitude in the midwestern population.

(3) Superstition is always negatively correlated with scholastic aptitude in the midwestern population.

(4) Altruism is the only dimension of religiosity having no significant correlation with scholastic aptitude.

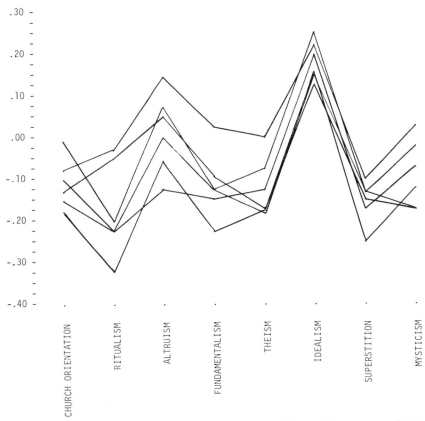

Figure 9-2. The general pattern of correlations between religious attitudes and academic aptitude in the midwestern student population

(5) All significant correlations are negative with the exception of the idealism–scholastic aptitude correlation mentioned above.

(6) The measures of religiosity most often significantly correlated with scholastic aptitude are ritualism and idealism (three of seven and four of seven significant). Idealism is positively correlated with scholastic aptitude, whereas the ritualism correlations are all negative.

(7) The measure of scholastic aptitude most often significantly correlated with religiosity is SCAT verbal (four of eight significant at .01 level).

A comparison of the correlations within the two populations reveals:

(1) Religiosity and scholastic aptitude are more highly and negatively correlated in the southern student population than in the midwestern student population.

(2) In the midwestern population idealism is positively correlated with scholastic aptitude, whereas in the southern population the two are not correlated.

(3) In the southern population fundamentalism and scholastic aptitude have the highest (negative) correlations, whereas in the midwestern population none of these correlations is even significant.

(4) Altruism and scholastic aptitude are significantly and negatively correlated in the southern student population, whereas in the midwestern populations none of the these correlations is significant.

(5) Church orientation, superstition, and theism are all significantly and negatively correlated in the southern student population whereas in the midwestern student population only a very few of these correlations are significant.

(6) The correlations between ritualism and scholastic aptitude are always significant and negative in the southern populations whereas only four out of six corresponding correlations are significant in the midwestern population.

The picture which emerges from the study of the comparative correlations of religiosity and scholastic aptitude among students in a southern and a midwestern university suggests a much greater salience of religiosity in the southern student population. In the southern population we find frequent and moderate negative correlations between the variables of these two clusters of attitudes and scores (religiosity and scholastic aptitude) which do not, in general, occur in the midwestern student population, suggesting that in regard to scholastic aptitude religiosity of certain types may be an active detriment for southern students. The pervasive and generally restrictive nature of southern religiosity appears to be reinforced once again. The southern student's religiosity may be seen to have a greater and distressingly restrictive impact upon scholastic aptitude which midwestern religiosity does not share.

10

RELIGIOSITY AND PERSONALITY ADJUSTMENT

An area of interest to those concerned with religion and religious attitudes is the interrelationship between religiosity and personality adjustment.

Individuals both favorably and unfavorably disposed to orthodox religion have very definite notions (scarcely hypotheses) regarding the relationship between these two sets of variables. Those who are favorably disposed toward religious orthodoxy are inclined to maintain that religiosity is positively related to adjustment, whereas those hostile to orthodox religion maintain that religiosity is inversely related to adjustment.

An examination of previous research discloses some interesting, if unclear, results. Broen (1955) discovered that the more religious male university students score significantly higher on the MMPI Pa (Paranoia) scale. Funk (1956) found manifest anxiety correlated with religious doubts, guilt about not living up to religion, and need for religious consolation. Rokeach (1960) found that believers scored significantly higher on manifest anxiety than nonbelievers. Wilson and Miller (1968) found anxiety moderately correlated with religiosity. Bohrnstedt and Borgatta (1968) found MMPI scales correlated negatively but at a low level with religiosity. Lindenthal et al. (1970) report finding negative correlations between psychopathology and a number of reported religious activities. It should be noted that religiosity in these earlier studies sometimes involves beliefs and sometimes reported affiliation and behavior. Stark (1971) suggests that a great deal of the research which has discovered positive corretions between psychopathology and religious commitment has employed inappropriate samples, has overlooked the need for comparison groups, and has used incompetent methods. He also suggests that membership in a stable social group such as a church should be expected to be inversely correlated with psychopathology. Stark may be correct—the correlations between religious commitment and insanity and/or severe psychopathology would be expected to be inverse—however, this does not preclude the possibility that less severe personality maladjustment such as dependency or anxiety might still be positively correlated with religious commitment. A subsequent and reasonable suggestion would be that there are several forms of religious commitment some of which may be quite differentially related to personality adjustment of different types. Religious commitments which involve passive acceptance of certain forms of authority could be expected to be correlated with such variables as dependency, and other types of commitment which stress the threatening aspects of religion might be correlated with anxiety. In the face of this somewhat confusing picture, it is my purpose to attempt to shed some further light upon the nature of this relationship. Therefore, I intend to attempt to identify the relationship between the dimensions of religious attitudes and personality adjustment.

Personality adjustment is a construct which can be measured in any of a great variety of manners. From the rather great array of instruments, it was decided to select certain scales from the Minnesota Multiphasic Personality Inventory (MMPI), because it is one of the most frequently used personality inventories and because a relatively great amount of reliability and validity research has been conducted on it.

A problem obviously inherent in this research revolves around the fact that the results may, instead of indicating the relationship between adjustment and religiosity, simply indicate the existence of a "religious" or "antireligious" bias in the instruments. However, an examination of the items involved in each scale leads us, I believe, to the conclusion that the extent of "built-in" bias is very small.

PROCEDURE

The dimensions of religiosity were measured with the scales which have been previously described in this book. These scales measure eight dimensions of religiosity: church orientation, ritualism, altruism, fundamentalism, theism, idealism, superstition, and mysticism.

The selection of the MMPI scales used in this study might appear somewhat arbitrary, but this is only slightly true. The major scales, or basic scales—hypochondriasis (Hs), depression (D), hysteria (Hy), psychopathic deviates (Pd), sexual inversion (Mf), paranoia (Pa), psychasthenia (Pt), schizophrenia (Sc), hypomania (Ma), and Introversion (Si)—were not used in this research because of a greater interest in the less serious maladjustments and also in more general and/or subtle relationships. An examination of the available MMPI scales revealed the following scales which appeared to be of interest: dependency, ego strength, manifest anxiety, general maladjustment, and social desirability. These MMPI scales are not, of course, completely independent of one another; for example the first two mentioned above (dependency and ego strength) share some items which are scored antithetically on the two scales.

In view of the fact that the MMPI scales used in this study are not the basic scales, a word or two describing each might be of some value. The MMPI scales have generally been employed in only medical situations; therefore, most of the validity studies are concerned with psychiatric and other medical populations.

Dependency

The dependency scale, which was developed by Navran (1954), was originated by securing, first of all, ratings of items by a panel of judges in regard to this characteristic and, secondly, by performing an internal consistency analysis of the items secured. The scale has been used successfully in studies of dependency among ulcer groups (Ruesch 1948), epileptics and tuberculous groups (Warn 1958). The items involve indecision, low self-confidence, unaggressiveness, high sensitivity to criticism, shyness, being easily embarrassed, quickly yielding, seeking advice, as well as many having more explicitly dependent characteristics.

Ego Strength

The ego strength scale was devised by Barron (1953). The criterion employed for scale development was response to treatment.

The items selected point out pretreatment attributes which are related to degree of improvement shown by subjects after psychotherapy. The scale's predictive power has been found to be superior to the judgment of a panel of clinicians. The *MMPI Handbook* suggests that "the best single index of control within the MMPI seems to be the ego strength scale" (Dahlstrom and Welsh 1960:303).

Manifest Anxiety

The manifest anxiety scale was developed by Taylor (1953). Judges were asked to select items indicative of manifest anxiety. The resulting scale was further distilled by internal consistency analysis. The scale is made up, in part, of items related to physical symptoms from which anxiety is inferred. Other items indicate existence of tension, nightmares, poor sleep, worry, restlessness, excessive sweating, general anxiety, excitability, and nervousness. The scale has been very widely used and evidence indicates it is generally reliable (Dahlstrom and Welsh 1960).

General Maladjustment

The general maladjustment scale was devised by Welsh (1952). The scale is made up of the items which appear on three or more of the basic clinical scales. The scale has been found to be highly correlated with over-all profile elevation. This scale, therefore, in part provides us with insight regarding the relation between the religiosity variables and the over-all elevation on the basic scales.

Social Desirability

This scale was devised by Fordyce (1956) and revised by Edwards (1957). Various writers have demonstrated that the probability of endorsement is related to the rated desirability of the item content. Therefore, sensitivity to undesirable aspects of the items is a variable included in most scales. The particular scaled dimension involved measures the tendency of individuals to select the socially desirable response to self-description items.

Thus the problem becomes one of ascertaining the correlation between these aspects of personality adjustment and the various dimensions of religiosity. The use of correlations and populations including persons of many degrees of religiosity provides the comparisons Stark (1971) correctly indicates are necessary.

POPULATIONS

In view of the fact that there are regional differences in religiosity (see chapters 4–7 and 9; and Maranell 1968), the correlations between religiosity and personal adjustment were examined in two somewhat different regions. Included is a population of midwestern students and a southern student population. The students were enrolled in introductory sociology classes at their respective schools.

RESULTS

The Southern Population

An examination of table 10-1 reveals the following general patterns of relationship.

TABLE 10-1. THE CORRELATIONS BETWEEN RELIGIOSITY AND PERSONALITY ADJUSTMENT (MMPI) IN THE SOUTHERN STUDENT POPULATION (N = 109)

	Taylor Manifest Anxiety	General Mal-adjustment	Dependency	Ego Strength	Social Desirability
Church orientation	.14	.05	.25**	—.23*	—.15
Ritualism	.30**	.06	.33**	—.23*	—.21*
Altruism	.35**	.37**	.43**	—.36**	—.25**
Fundamentalism	.10	—.01	.23*	—.26**	—.13
Theism	.20*	.01	.27**	—.29**	—.14
Idealism	.04	—.78**	.08	—.04	—.01
Superstition	.35**	.23*	.38**	—.30**	—.25**
Mysticism	.25**	.07	.35**	—.34**	—.22*

* Correlation is significant at the .05 level.
** Correlation is significant at the .01 level.

(1) Dependency and ego strength are the adjustment variables most often correlated with religious attitude. The correlations between dependency and religiosity are positive, indicating that dependency increases with religiosity, or religiosity increases with dependency. Ego strength is inversely correlated with religiosity. This indicates that low ego strength accompanies high religiosity and high ego strength accompanies low religiosity or religious emancipation. Thus, it appears that religious belief accompanies low ego strength and dependency, and that reli-

gious faith may be a manifestation of dependency or that dependency is manifest in such faith.

(2) There is no correlation between idealism and either ego strength or dependency. This is the only dimension of religiosity which is not related to these two adjustment variables. Therefore, we find that subscribing to visionary principles is not related to dependency or ego strength.

(3) Only one of the remaining adjustment variables is generally positively correlated with the religiosity dimensions; that variable is anxiety. Only idealism, church orientation, and fundamentalism are not significantly correlated with anxiety in the southern student population.

(4) General maladjustment is positively correlated with altruism and superstition. This seems to indicate that altruistic individuals in the southern student population manifest general maladjustment. In addition, superstitious individuals are inclined to score high on general maladjustment. More important, however, is the high (−.78) negative correlation we find between idealism and general maladjustment. This correlation indicates that idealistic individuals are inclined to personality adjustment and that nonidealistic individuals are inclined to score high on maladjustment. This is particularly interesting when we note the fact that altruism is positively correlated with maladjustment and that there are some similarities between altruism and idealism. The differences between these two scales are more important, however. We can easily notice that the altruism items are much more "religious," even more "Christian," than the more humanistic idealism items.

(5) Social desirability is inversely correlated with four religiosity variables: altruism, superstition, mysticism, and ritualism. This suggests that altruistic, superstitious, mystical, and ritualistic responses are inversely related to the tendency of students to select socially desirable responses. The choosing of superstitious responses, for example, involves inattention to the social desirability aspect in the items and in superstition generally.

The Midwestern Population

From an examination of table 10-2, the following observations can be made.

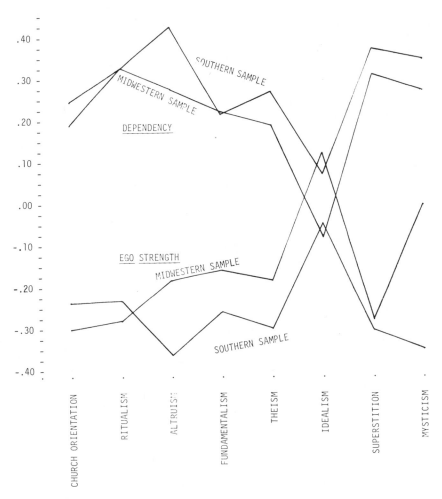

Figure 10-1. The correlations between religious attitudes and dependency and ego strength (MMPI)

(1) Dependency and ego strength are again the "adjustment" variables most often correlated with religiosity. Dependency is positively correlated with every religiosity variable but idealism. Ego strength is negatively correlated with all religiosity variables except fundamentalism, idealism, and mysticism. Again we have observed that, in general, as religiosity increases in the

population studied, dependency increases and ego strength decreases.

(2) General maladjustment is related only to superstition (+.30) and ritualism (+.28) in this population.

(3) Anxiety is also less related to religiosity in the midwestern population. Only ritualism and superstition are significantly correlated with anxiety in a positive direction, and idealism is significantly and inversely correlated with anxiety. These are, though statistically significant, not very important correlations.

(4) Social desirability is significantly and inversely correlated only with ritualism. This indicates a slight tendency for those select-

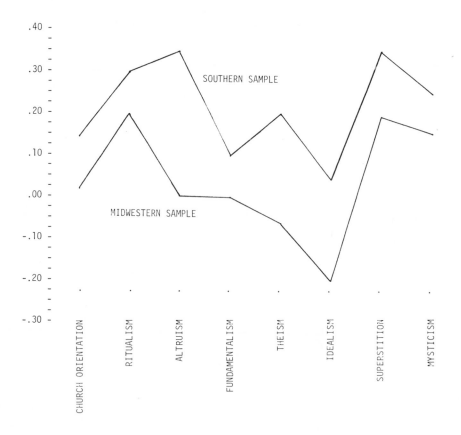

Figure 10-2. The correlations between religious attitudes and anxiety (MMPI)

TABLE 10-2. THE CORRELATIONS BETWEEN RELIGIOSITY AND PERSONALITY ADJUSTMENT (MMPI) IN THE MIDWESTERN STUDENT POPULATION

(N = 96)

	Taylor Manifest Anxiety	General Maladjustment	Dependency	Ego Strength	Social Desirability
Church orientation	.02	—.03	.19*	—.29**	—.01
Ritualism	.20*	.28**	.33**	—.27**	—.30**
Altruism	.01	—.11	.28**	—.18	—.08
Fundamentalism	.00	.01	.24*	—.16	—.03
Theism	—.06	—.04	.19*	—.18	.06
Idealism	—.20*	—.13	—.07	.12	.10
Superstition	.19*	.36**	.31**	—.27**	—.12
Mysticism	.16	.11	.27**	.00	—.14

* Correlation is significant at the .05 level.
** Correlation is significant at the .01 level.

ing ritualistic responses to select socially undesirable responses as well.

These two sets of findings are summarized in the following figures, which also allow for interregional comparisons and serve to reveal the more general patterns of relationship.

Figure 10-1 reveals the complementary nature of the dependency scale results and the ego strength scale results in both populations.

Figure 10-2 reveals the pattern of higher correlations discovered within the southern population between anxiety and religiosity, especially ritualism, altruism, superstition, and mysticism.

Figure 10-3 describes the correlations between general maladjustment and religiosity. The nature of the regional differences in ritualism and idealism are apparent in this figure.

Figure 10-4 summarizes the relatively small and ambiguous correlations which occur between social desirability and the various dimensions of religiosity in the regional populations examined.

We are thus led to the following general conclusion: Religiosity of an orthodox variety is correlated with certain varieties of personality maladjustments. We find, for example, that a strong attachment to religious faith involves a certain dependency and that conversely ego strength can well lead to, or possibly result from, a decrease of religious faith. We also find that religious dogma in certain forms is related to higher anxiety, or that high anxiety is related to an acceptance of religious dogma.

In general this study does reveal that religious persons are in-

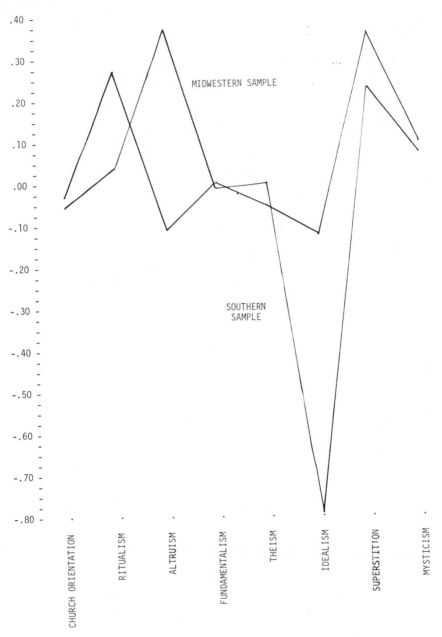

Figure 10-3. The correlations between religious attitudes and general maladjustment (MMPI)

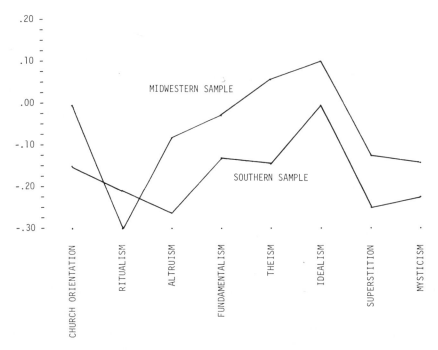

Figure 10-4. The correlations between religious attitudes and social desirability (MMPI)

clined to be less well adjusted than the irreligious or less religious. In addition we find that within this "world of commitment" a commitment to principle alone is associated with greater personality adjustment.

11

A COMPARISON WITH OTHER RELIGIOUS ATTITUDE SCALES

The relationship between the eight scaled dimensions of religiosity described in this book and other different measures of religious attitudes is another topic of interest. Any of a very large number of scales and questions regarding religious attitudes could have been selected for this study. Among those available are Putney and Middleton's (1961a), Ferguson's (1944), Thurstone and Chave's (1929). Of this very rich assortment, an arbitrary selection was made; however, it is seen as a selection which would allow both for the investigation of the relationship between the scales and for some additional information about the dimensions of religiosity employed in this book. Not only can we compare the analyses of religious attitudes, but we can gather some data regarding the nature of two sets of scales.

The scales selected for this comparative study are those developed by Putney and Middleton. These were selected because they were seen to relate rather orthogonally to the set of scales employed in this book. Putney and Middleton report research results using three scales and a single question to ascertain: (1) religious orthodoxy, (2) religious fanaticism, (3) importance of religion, and (4) religious ambivalence. Ambivalence was measured with a single question. In view of this, only the first three of Putney and Middleton's scales were used in this study.

The general purpose of this chapter is to ascertain the relationship between the scales of religious orthodoxy, religious fanaticism, and the importance of religion, on one hand, and those of church orientation, ritualism altruism, fundamentalism, theism, idealism, superstition, and mysticism, on the other. These two sets of scales are seen to be two somewhat different ways of dividing the area of religious attitude. The logical relation of any two of the many possible conceptualizations of religious attitude can be seen to range from orthogonality or complete independence to congruence. Therefore, the nature and degree of relationship between these two conceptualizations will be ascertained in this particular study.

It is, of course, expected that certain areas will be more highly correlated than others. This does not detract from the logical orthogonality of the two sets of scales. Thus we would expect, and be most surprised if we did not discover, that orthodoxy and theism are very highly correlated and that fanaticism is less highly correlated with theism than theism is with orthodoxy.

THE SCALES

Putney and Middleton's three aspects of religious attitudes are measured with Likert scales. The orthodoxy scale ascertains the extent to which individuals hold such orthodox beliefs as: (1) there is a physical hell where people are punished after death for their sins, (2) there is a supernatural being, the Devil, who attempts to lead people into sin, (3) saving souls is the most important thing a church can do, (4) there is life after death, (5) prayers are more than psychologically beneficial, and (6) there is a Divine plan for every person and thing.

The fanaticism scale ascertains the extent to which individuals feel that (1) it is their duty to help those who are confused about religion, (2) they must argue with people in order to enlighten them about religion, (3) things would be much better if everyone shared their own religious beliefs, (4) other people's beliefs must be changed when they are wrong, and (5) the world's problems are aggravated by the many people who are misguided about religion.

The importance scale ascertains the extent to which individuals (1) feel that their religious beliefs are the most important part of their philosophy of life, (2) feel particularly interested in religion, (3) think about matters related to religion very often, (4) feel that their religious beliefs influence all their other beliefs, and (5) feel that if their religious beliefs were different they would be different.

POPULATIONS

The dimensions of religiosity to be compared with these are described in the foregoing parts of this book. It was decided that since this was to be a survey of student (university) attitudes it would be wise to attempt to secure at least two different student populations. College students are not always the best subjects—but then again they are not, as is apparently sometimes assumed, the worst either. Putney and Middleton used university students in their research on religious attitudes. Many other researchers have been inclined to conduct correlational studies of religious attitudes in university undergraduate populations (Gilliland 1940; Brown and Lowe 1951; Mull, 1947, to cite but a few). The inclusion of a second and regionally different student population was designed to permit some comparative examination and extend the possibility of generalizing.

The students used in the two surveys reported here were undergraduate students in general sociology classes at two state universities. One population of 284 was gathered at a southern university and the other of 120 at a midwestern university.

RESULTS

The results of this examination of the relationship between the previously described dimensions of religiosity and the three alternative scales can be found in table 11-1 and figures 11-1 and 11-2.

TABLE 11-1. CORRELATIONS BETWEEN THE DIMENSIONS OF RELIGIOSITY AND THE THREE PUTNEY-MIDDLETON SCALES IN TWO SELECTED POPULATIONS

	SOUTHERN POPULATION			MIDWESTERN POPULATION		
	Orthodoxy	Importance	Fanaticism	Orthodoxy	Importance	Fanaticism
Church orientation	.50**	.39**	.40**	.57**	.45**	.26**
Ritualism	.17**	.06	.14*	.35**	.30**	.20**
Altruism	.45**	.49**	.17**	.59**	.57**	.45**
Fundamentalism	.75**	.53**	.48**	.84**	.57**	.56**
Theism	.74**	.55**	.41**	.88**	.66**	.47**
Idealism	.34**	.43**	.27**	.44**	.43**	.49**
Superstition	.52**	.38**	.31**	.79**	.48**	.36**
Mysticism	.47**	.43**	.22**	.65**	.51**	.39**

* Correlation is significant at the .05 level.
** Correlation is significant at the .01 level.

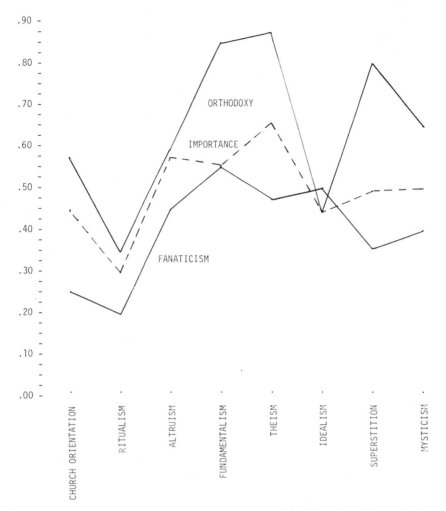

Figure 11-1. The pattern of correlation between the dimensions of religious attitudes and orthodoxy, fanaticism, and the importance of religion in the midwestern sample

An examination of this table and these figures reveals some interesting patterns.

(1) We find that the highest correlations, in general, in both populations are between the various dimensions of religiosity and orthodoxy and that the lowest correlations, in general, are between fanaticism and the dimensions studied. The only excep-

tions are: (a) In the southern population altruism is more highly correlated with importance than with orthodoxy; (b) In the southern population idealism is more highly correlated with importance than with orthodoxy; (c) In the midwestern population idealism is more highly correlated with fanaticism than with orthodoxy.

(2) The dimensions most highly correlated with orthodoxy are fundamentalism and theism in both the midwestern and southern student populations.

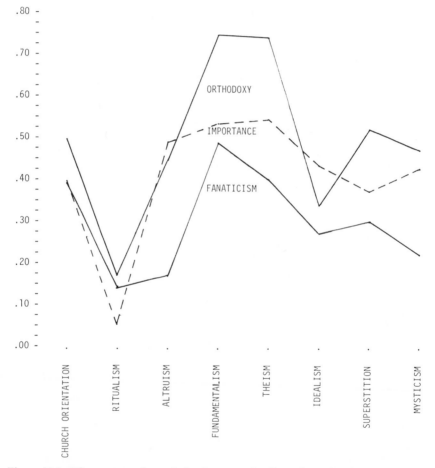

Figure 11-2. The pattern of correlation between the dimensions of religious attitudes and orthodoxy, fanaticism, and the importance of religion in the southern sample

(3) The dimensions most highly correlated with importance are theism, fundamentalism, and altruism in both populations.

(4) The dimensions most highly correlated with fanaticism are fundamentalism and theism in the southern population, and fundamentalism, idealism, theism, and altruism in the midwestern population.

(5) The only correlations of less than substantive significance are between ritualism and the three other variables (orthodoxy, importance, and fanaticism) in the southern population. This may reflect the basic Protestantism of the southern student population.

(6) The general similarity of the correlations in the two populations indicates a generally comparable pattern of association between the variables examined.

In each population the three highest correlations are between orthodoxy and the three aspects of religiosity (theism, fundamentalism, and superstition) that make up the first factor in the clergyman study (reported in chapter fourteen of this book). This suggests that "the old time religion" factor identifies Christian orthodoxy variables as orthodoxy is identified and defined by Putney and Middleton. Similarly, the variable with the lowest correlations (ritualism) was the single variable not loaded on either factor previously identified in the clergyman study.

In view of the generally lower coefficients of correlation we would have to recognize that apparently idealism and ritualism are not crucial aspects of orthodoxy. However, the variables of altruism and idealism are interestingly more highly correlated with fanaticism in the midwestern student population than in the southern student population. This may suggest that these sympathetic, principled attitudes are more associated with the assertive-fanatic in this region than in the southern student population.

12

RELIGIOSITY AND ALIENATION

A concept which is currently attracting a considerable amount of attention is "alienation." The concept is not new but we are currently witnessing a renewed concern with the phenomenon. Behavioral scientists have devised various scales to measure alienation and have employed these scales in a variety of research (Srole 1956; Roberts and Rokeach 1956; Nettler 1957; Dean 1961, 1968; Dean and Reeves 1962).

Melvin Seeman has conceptually analyzed alienation in an attempt to clarify the phenomenon and has provided us with a classification of the uses of the concept. His classification includes five varieties of alienation: (1) powerlessness—which he defines as "the expectancy or probability held by the individual that his own behavior cannot determine the occurrence of the outcomes, or reinforcements, he seeks"; (2) meaninglessness—which Seeman defines as "when the individual is unclear as to what he ought to believe—when the individual's minimal standards for clarity in decising-making are not met," and also when an individual has a "low expectancy that satisfactory predictions about future outcomes of behavior can be made"; (3) normlessness—this involves "a high expectancy that socially unapproved behaviors are required to achieve given goals"; (4) isolation—which involves assigning "low reward value to goals or beliefs that are typically highly valued in the given society" and also involves an "apartness from society"; (5) self-estrangement—which

Seeman defines as the "degree of independence of the given behavior upon anticipated future rewards—rewards that lie outside the activity itself" (Seeman 1959: 784, 786, 788, 789, 790).

Dean (1961) translated powerlessness, normlessness, and social isolation into attitude scales and discovered correlations ranging from +.40 to +.70 between the three components of alienation he investigated. He found generally low (−.06 to −.26) negative correlations between occupation, education, income, community, and alienation. He also discovered low correlations (−.03 to +.14) between age and the components of alienation studied.

The interrelations of religiosity and alienation have not been the subject of extensive investigation though research in this area would provide us with useful insight into the nature of both. Therefore, we are concerned with ascertaining the extent and direction of the relationship between the various dimensions of religiosity and the various aspects of alienation. Although the specific goal of this research is somewhat unique, others have examined the relationship between alienation and religious affiliation and orthodoxy. Dean and Reeves (1962) examined the relationship of occupational prestige and religious differences to normlessness or anomie and found that Protestants exhibit a greater degree of anomie than Catholics. Keedy (1958) using Srole's scale found anomie to be related to religious orthodoxy among Protestants; and Bell (1957) found no correlation between anomie and general affiliation using the same scale. Dean (1968) found powerlessness to be related to church attendance.

The particular object of this study is to describe the correlation between the various dimensions of religious attitude and the various elements of alienation. In view of the "normative" nature of religious attitudes in the various populations studied, the particular correlations of interest will be examined in a student population. The students studied were 107 undergraduates enrolled in introductory sociology classes at a midwestern university.

VARIABLES

The variables employed in this research are:

(1) The Dean scale of alienation which yields four different scores: (a) powerlessness, (b) normlessness, (c) social isolation, and (d)

total alienation. This scale was used in preference to others which are available for various reasons. First, it derives directly and clearly from Seeman's conceptual analysis, which serves to distill the phenomenon analytically. Second, Dean (1961) points out that the Srole scale (which could have been used) did not meet judging and item analysis criteria. Third, reliability estimates are available for the Dean scale; and they are moderately high, ranging over .73 on all scales. In view of these reasons, the Dean scale was selected for this research.

(2) The scales of religiosity previously described in this book, which yield scores on eight dimensions of religiosity: church orientation, ritualism, altruism, fundamentalism, theism, idealism, superstition, mysticism.

The analysis involves the examination of coefficients of correlation between the religiosity variables and the alienation variables.

RESULTS

The results of this study are presented in table 12-1 and figure 12-1.

TABLE 12-1. THE CORRELATIONS BETWEEN THE DIMENSIONS OF RELIGIOSITY AND ALIENATION

	Powerlessness	Normlessness	Social Isolation	Total Alienation
Church orientation	+.14	—.10	+.11	—.02
Ritualism	+.16	+.03	+.14	+.13
Altruism	+.21*	—.08	—.05	+.13
Fundamentalism	+.15	—.19*	+.02	+.04
Theism	+.11	—.27**	+.03	—.02
Idealism	—.46**	—.25**	—.35**	—.64**
Superstition	+.24**	+.05	+.15	+.18*
Mysticism	+.16	—.06	+.02	+.11

* Correlation is significant at the .05 level.
** Correlation is significant at the .01 level.

We can abstract the following general findings from the preceding table and figure.

(1) We observe that only one dimension of religiosity is consistently and significantly correlated with all the measures of alienation as well as total alienation. Idealism is inversely and significantly related in every instance. These correlations (between idealism and alienation) also include the highest correlations discovered.

Responses to Religion

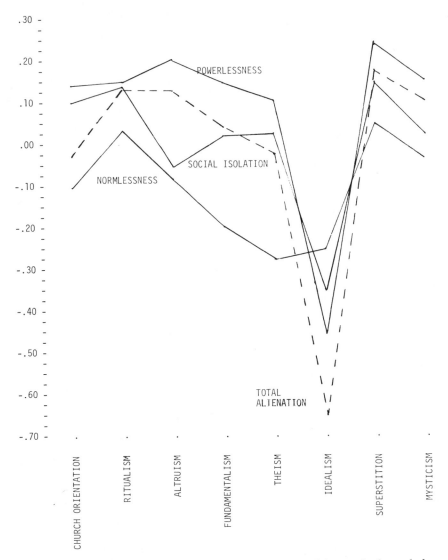

Figure 12-1. The correlations between the dimensions of religious attitudes and the dimensions of alienation

In the figure we see that idealism is differently related to alienation than any of the other religiosity dimensions. Note the great "dip" in the relationships (to negative) at this point only. Thus we find that idealistic students are not inclined to feel normless, powerless, isolated, or "alienated," whereas the non-idealistic are somewhat inclined to alienation, powerlessness, isolation, and normlessness. Idealism clearly does not accompany alienation.

(2) Among the other significant correlations we find one between theism and normlessness. Theistic students tend to score low on normlessness, or theistic students are not inclined to be norm-less. This should not surprise us, since theism implies a particular set of norms in our society.

(3) Superstition is found to be significantly correlated with power-lessness and total alienation. That superstition increases with both powerlessness and alienation or that those who feel power-less or alienated are superstitious is similarly not surprising.

(4) Altruism is also correlated significantly with powerlessness. Those feeling powerless are inclined to be altruistic. This I believe is interestingly contrasted with the relationship between idealism and powerlessness. The altruistic feel powerless—or those who feel powerless are altruistic; however, the idealistic do not feel powerless.

(5) Also we find that fundamentalism is inversely related to norm-lessness. That is, the fundamentalist is not inclined to feel normless—which is also not surprising, since for the fundamentalist the Bible serves as the ever-ready source of norms.

(6) There are some apparent differences between the dimensions of alienation as well, for we find that in general powerlessness is positively related to religiosity (with the exception of idealism), whereas normlessness is generally negatively related to religiosity. Religiosity serves, to extrapolate from this difference, as a norm source but does not apparently convey in general any particular feeling of power. This finding may well reflect a particular aspect of Christianity and may not appear in populations with other than a Christian tradition.

13

SEX AND RELIGIOSITY

A common impression in American society is that women are more religious than men. One of the most consistent findings in regard to the various indices of religiosity is the generally higher scores secured by females in comparison to males.

Women have been found to show greater interest in the church and to manifest attitudes more favorable to the church than men (Terman and Miles 1936; Newcomb and Svehla 1937; Kirkpatrick 1949; Spoerl 1952). An examination of particular beliefs, e.g. "after-life," etc., shows the same result (Katz and Allport 1931; Allport et al. 1948; Ross 1950; Gorer 1955). Females are also more inclined to read the Bible at home and say private prayers daily (Allport et al. 1948; Ross 1950; Gorer 1955). Also the same differences are found in regard to church membership and attendance statistics. Argyle (1958) reports, in his survey of the literature, that women are found to be more religious than men on all criteria.

In view of this astonishingly consistent pattern of findings, an investigation of sex differences among college students in the various dimensions of religiosity may provide further and more specialized evidence. Are these sex differences in religiosity present on any or all of the dimensions of religiosity? The previous research suggests that we should expect females to score higher on all or at least most of the religiosity scales. Therefore, the question becomes whether females are more church oriented, altruistic, ritualistic, fundamentalistic, theistic, idealistic, superstitious, and mystical than males. Questions such as this are obviously answered with large and representative samples. However, an initial examination in two university student populations may provide us with some preliminary evidence.

The measurements for this research were secured with a questionnaire. The questionnaire was made up of the previously mentioned religious attitude scales and a question ascertaining the sex of the respondent.

The populations examined were undergraduate students at two universities, one southern and one midwestern. The population sizes were:

Southern Population: Females N = 91, Males N = 91.
Midwestern Population: Females N = 103, Males N = 74.

RESULTS

All comparisons were made within each of the two populations. The results of this investigation are summarized in table 13-1. The

TABLE 13-1. SEX DIFFERENCES IN THE DIMENSIONS OF RELIGIOSITY IN TWO REGIONAL POPULATIONS

	Midwestern Students t score	Southern Students t score
Church orientation	.485	−.6807
Ritualism	.386	.797
Altruism	1.842	2.555*
Fundamentalism	1.81	2.222*
Theism	2.728**	3.079**
Idealism	2.719**	1.800
Superstition	1.000	1.71
Mysticism	2.208*	2.934**

* P < .05
** P < .01

scores of the female students exceed those of the male students in all the comparisons but one—in the southern population in regard to church orientation. The significant differences are identified in table 13-1.

Beyond this first general finding we discover that the sex differences in religiosity are not statistically significant in all of these comparisons. Of the sixteen comparisons, only seven of the differences are statistically significant. Importantly, however, we find that males are significantly less theistic and mystical than females in both of the populations studied. Therefore, female students in each of the two populations are more inclined to believe in God and trust more in mystical approaches to knowledge. This general finding may be an indication of the underlying nature of the more general differences in the religious attitudes and behaviors of females that have led to the commonly discovered sex differences. That is, the evidence presented here suggests that the only general sex differences are those in the areas of theism and mysticism.

In addition to these general differences we find some sex differences that are unique in each of the two populations. First, we find that southern female students are significantly more fundamentalistic and altruistic than southern male students. It is interesting to note that the sexes differ in the southern population on fundamentalism, which is generally found to be higher in the South than elsewhere. Second, in the midwestern population we find that female students are significantly more idealistic than male students.

In summary, we have found southern female students to be significantly more fundamentalistic, theistic, mystical, and altruistic than southern male students; and midwestern female students are significantly more theistic, mystical, and idealistic than the midwestern male students.

14

FACTOR ANALYSIS
OF THE SCALES
IN THREE POPULATIONS

Analyses to this point have been concerned with the examination of differences in the religious attitudes of various samples and subgroups of populations and with the inspection of selected correlates of the various dimensions. Following these descriptions of the significant differences and correlations in each of the areas, an examination of the clustering of the scales in various populations seems to be of some interest. There are many forms of cluster analysis which could be undertaken, each of which would provide us with various and yet interesting data. One of the possible analyses involves examination of the intercorrelations of these eight dimensions of religious attitudes. Such examination can be edifying in view of some of the populations available for study. The metropolitan clergymen of the several denominations, the college and university professors, and others can provide us with insight into the patterning of these religious attitudes in populations that are differentially religiously sophisticated. In view of this, the clergymen's scores on the eight dimensions were correlated, as were those of the professors and a group of adults from two Methodist churches in a midwestern community. These three of the many populations were selected for comparison since they are all adult populations. Further, they are as nearly equivalent in status as three divergent populations can easily be.

The clergymen were analyzed and described in chapter four of this volume; the professors were analyzed and described in chapter six. The additional population is made up of the members of two generally middle-class Methodist churches in a midwestern city. The city is a state capital with a population of over 130,000. The Methodist church was selected as a "typical" major Protestant denomination. It is one of the liberal orthodox cluster described in chapter four. The members of the two Methodist churches were asked to complete the eight scales as part of a program of self-analysis encouraged by a committee of the local church as well as by the general conference of the church.

Appendix F contains tables which report the correlations within these three populations. These correlation matrices were then factor analyzed by the principal components method (Thurstone 1947; Harmon 1967; Horst 1965; Rummel 1970). The resulting factors in each of the three populations were rotated orthogonally in order to obtain meaningful factors. The number of factors to be rotated was determined by the unit eigenvalue criteria. The rotation used attends to both simple structure and positive manifold. Tables 14-1,

TABLE 14-1. THE ROTATED FACTOR LOADINGS OF THE EIGHT RELIGIOUS ATTITUDE VARIABLES IN THE CLERGYMAN SAMPLE

	Factor One	Factor Two
Church orientation	.38	.68†
Ritualism	.18	.37
Altruism	.16	.83†
Fundamentalism	.91†	.16
Theism	.91†	.17
Idealism	−.09	.82†
Superstition	.73†	.18
Mysticism	.46	.61†
Variance accounted for	32.35%	30.09%

† Variables employed in the interpretation of factors (highest loadings).

TABLE 14-2. THE ROTATED FACTOR LOADINGS OF THE EIGHT RELIGIOUS ATTITUDE VARIABLES IN THE PROFESSOR SAMPLE

	Factor One	Factor Two
Church orientation	.64†	.44
Ritualism	.73†	−.14
Altruism	.46	.72†
Fundamentalism	.72†	.49
Theism	.72†	.48
Idealism	−.03	.88†
Superstition	.74†	.16
Mysticism	.66†	.48
Variance accounted for	39.76%	27.98%

† Variables employed in the interpretation of factors (highest loadings).

	Factor One	Factor Two
Church orientation	.40	.72†
Ritualism	−.14	.85†
Altruism	.79†	.35
Fundamentalism	.82†	.15
Theism	.87†	.12
Idealism	.64†	−.09
Superstition	.17	.58†
Mysticism	.68†	.45
Variance accounted for	39.11%	24.22%

† Variables employed in the interpretation of factors (highest loadings).

14-2, and 14-3 report the rotated factor loadings in the three populations.

Let us consider the resulting factors in each sample studied.

FACTOR NUMBER ONE AMONG THE CLERGYMEN

The following variables or dimensions are heavily weighted on the clergyman's first factor:

(1) Fundamentalism—This variable has a loading of .91 on the first factor. Recall that this involves the literal interpretation of the Bible.

(2) Theism—This variable has a loading of .91 on the first factor also. Recall that this variable involves only the belief in God.

(3) Superstition—This variable has a loading of .73 on the first factor. It involves irrational and antiscientific beliefs.

This factor describes an interesting set of intercorrelations. The variables in the cluster make it rather easy to label. This factor involves, I believe, the elements of Protestant tent meetings, a heavy reliance upon the Bible, a devout belief in God, and a participation in the magic irrationality of superstition. Clergymen cluster these three variables together and separate them clearly from altruism, idealism and ritualism. For this sample of clergymen, fundamentalism and theism are part of an "old time religion" factor which includes an antiscientific world view and excludes such things as altruism. The variables in the factor reflect a somewhat sacred, fundamentalistic, and clearly Protestant Christianity.

FACTOR NUMBER ONE AMONG UNIVERSITY PROFESSORS

The following variables are heavily loaded on the professors' first factor:

(1) Superstition—This variable has a loading of .74 on the first factor. It involves irrational, magical, and antiscientific beliefs.

(2) Ritualism—This variable has a loading of .73 on the professors' first factor. It involves an appreciation for the ritual of worship.

(3) Fundamentalism—This variable has a loading of .72 on the professors' first factor. It involves seeing the Bible as being literally true.

(4) Theism—This variable also has a loading of .72 on the professors' first factor. A belief in God is the central facet of the variable or dimension.

(5) Mysticism—This variable has a loading of .66 on the first factor. This variable involves an appreciation for, and a belief in, the availability of knowledge through silent meditation.

(6) Church Orientation—This variable has a loading of .64 on the first factor among professors. The dimension is concerned with an appreciation for the church and its members as a traditional and a valued association.

This factor differs clearly from the first factor we found among the clergymen. It does contain heavy loadings on the theism and fundamentalism variables, as well as on superstition; however university professors cluster these three variables with ritualism, mysticism, and church orientation. It seems that professors have clustered together attitudes that pertain clearly to religion and have isolated them from altruism and idealism. The "other worldliness" of religion is apparently separate from the "this worldliness" of concern for others and visionary principles. For the professors the first factor is a more general "Christianity" or even a "religiosity" factor.

FACTOR NUMBER ONE AMONG THE METHODIST CHURCH MEMBERS

The following dimensions are heavily weighted on the Methodist's first factor:

(1) Theism—This dimension, which involves basically a belief in God, has a weighting of .87.

(2) Fundamentalism—This variable, with a loading on the first factor of .82, involves a belief that the Bible is everlastingly true.

(3) Altruism—The third variable, weighted heavily on the first factor (.79), involves a concern for others.

(4) Mysticism—This variable has a first factor loading of .68 and involves an emphasis upon silent worship and transcendent states.

(5) Idealism—This variable has a loading of .64 on the first factor. The dimension is concerned with the holding of visionary principles.

Among the Methodist church members we find a first factor which clusters altruism, mysticism, and idealism with theism and fundamentalism, indicating that these church members do not separate the more clearly theological or religious aspects from the more visionary or principled or from the performance of good works. Both the clergymen and the professors seem to separate these two aspects. The first factor for the Methodist church members is a Christian altruism factor.

FACTOR NUMBER TWO AMONG THE CLERGYMEN

The following variables or dimensions are heavily weighted on the second factor among the clergymen:

(1) Altruism—This variable has a loading of .83 on the second factor. It, one will recall, involves an unselfish concern for others.

(2) Idealism—This variable has a loading of .82 on the second factor. It involves a dedication to lofty principles.

(3) Church Orientation—This variable has a loading of .68 on the second factor. It involves attitudes which value church membership and association.

(4) Mysticism—This variable has a loading of .61 on the second factor. It involves contemplation, transiency, passivity, and inexpressibility.

This factor also describes how clergymen cluster religious attitudes. This is a somewhat more secular factor—notice, for example, the absence of theism and fundamentalism. It is a more welfare oriented and organizationally oriented cluster. Although this is a familiar cluster of attitudes, it is however, somewhat difficult to name.

FACTOR NUMBER TWO AMONG THE UNIVERSITY PROFESSORS

The variables loaded on the second factor are:

(1) Idealism—This variable has a loading of .88 on the second factor. This dimension involves subscribing to visionary principles.
(2) Altruism—This variable has a loading of .72 on the second factor. It involves a concern for the welfare of others.

This second factor suggests further that professors tend to isolate subscription to principles and attitudes favoring aid and concern for others from the more general religious attitudes. That is, the isolated, "this worldly" good works are separated from the "otherworldly" concerns of religion in general.

FACTOR NUMBER TWO AMONG THE METHODIST CHURCH MEMBERS

Among the members of the Methodist churches studied, we find the following variables heavily loaded on the second factor:

(1) Ritualism—This variable has a loading of .85 on the second factor. This variable involves an appreciation for the ritual of worship.
(2) Church Orientation—This variable has a loading of .72 on the second factor. It involves an appreciation for the church as an historic body with which to be affiliated.
(3) Superstition—This variable has a loading of .58 on the second factor. The variable involves irrational and antiscientific beliefs.

The Methodists' second factor clusters the more liturgical ritualism, appreciation for the church as an institution, and antirational superstition. These three attitudes are separated from the more clearly Christian first factor and perhaps include the aspects of religion they feel do not belong with theism and the other dimensions.

CONCLUSIONS

This chapter reports the factor analysis of the eight scales of religious attitudes in three different adult populations. The three populations were a sample of clergymen of eleven denominations, a sample of college and university professors, and members of two Methodist congregations. Two factors were discovered in each analysis by unit eigenvalue criteria. The two factors were rotated for interpretation; and a comparison revealed that interestingly different and meaningful clusters of religious attitudes exist in the groups studied.

In view of the fact that this is a factor analytic study, I should point out that in the preceding pages of this book we have found extensive evidence that demonstrated the independence of each of these eight scales of religious attitudes in other situations. Although some of these variables have been found to be members of a common factor, in other situations they operate independently and even antithetically to each other; and indeed they cluster quite differently in the three populations examined. For example, altruism and idealism are, in each analysis, members of a common factor; but altruism has been found to have a positive correlation with personality maladjustment and idealism has been found to have a high *negative* correlation with the same variable in one sample studied.

15
SUMMARY

In this attempt to summarize the research described and reported in this book we will examine each of the eight dimensions of religiosity in turn and describe in a generalized manner the composite picture of findings which emerge. This summary will take the form of a rather detailed list of results obtained in all of the foregoing studies as these results pertain to each of the eight dimensions.

We will summarize the findings by overlooking population and study design differences. This focus will orient us, at this point, to each of the particular dimensions and will obscure the smaller differences between them. We will by this device acquire a broader perspective and more general understanding of the nature of each dimension. The resulting pictures will, of course, be seriously overgeneralized and overly expansive.

Such an approach will provide us with ample evidence to indicate that religiosity is indeed not a unitary phenomenon. It will also allow us to appraise the importance and utility of each of the dimensions examined and permit us to focus subsequent research upon those areas which are of particular importance or which have a particular relevance to the behavior or orientation systems with which we are concerned.

CHURCH ORIENTATION

1. Methodist, Catholic, and Disciples of Christ clergymen are high-

est in church orientation; Unitarian-Universalist and Presbyterian clergymen are lowest.

2. Southern clergymen are highest in church orientation, followed by Pacific Coast clergymen and New England clergymen. Midwestern clergymen are lowest in church orientation.
3. Older clergymen are higher in church orientation than younger.
4. Professors in church-affiliated colleges and universities are higher in church orientation than those in public schools.
5. Full professors are higher in church orientation than assistant professors.
6. Church orientation is often related to political conservatism in college student populations.
7. Church orientation is not generally related to socioeconomic status in the southern community studied.
8. Church orientation is inversely associated with socioeconomic status in the midwestern community studied; i.e., members of the lower socioeconomic status are highest in church orientation.
9. Active church members are higher in church orientation than are inactive members.
10. Church orientation is not affected by arrogation or derogation.
11. Church orientation is not related to suggestibility.
12. Church orientation is not related to perceptual rigidity.
13. Church orientation is inversely (low) correlated with scholastic aptitude in a southern student population.
14. Church orientation is positively related to an MMPI based measure of dependency and inversely related to ego strength as measured by an MMPI based scale.
15. Church orientation is moderately correlated with orthodoxy, less so with importance of religion, and least with fanaticism.
16. Church orientation is not related to alienation.
17. There are no significant sex differences in church orientation.
18. Church orientation is clustered in clergymen's attitude system with altruism, idealism, and mysticism, and not with ritualism, fundamentalism, theism, or superstition.
19. Church orientation is clustered in professors' attitude system with superstition, ritualism, fundamentalism, theism, and mysticism, and not with altruism or idealism.
20. Church orientation is clustered in the Methodist congregation members' attitude system with ritualism and superstition.

RITUALISM

1. Catholic and Episcopalian clergymen are highest in ritualism; Church of Christ, Unitarian-Universalist, Seventh-Day Adventist and Baptist clergymen are lowest.
2. There are no significant regional differences in the ritualism scores of clergymen.
3. There are no significant age differences in the ritualism scores of clergymen.
4. Professors in denominational colleges are more ritualistic than professors in public colleges.
5. Full professors are more ritualistic than assistant professors.
6. Science professors are less ritualistic than professors of fine arts.
7. Ritualism is often correlated with political conservatism.
8. Ritualism scores are higher in the lower socioeconomic classes than in the upper in the southern community studied.
9. Ritualism is directly related to socioeconomic status in the midwestern community studied; that is, persons in the lower and lower-middle classes have the highest ritualism scores.
10. Active church members score higher in ritualism than inactive members.
11. Ritualism scores are increased by experimentally induced arrogation.
12. Suggestible individuals score higher in ritualism.
13. Ritualism is positively related to perceptual rigidity.
14. Ritualism is inversely (moderate) correlated with scholastic aptitude.
15. Ritualism is significantly correlated (low) with the MMPI anxiety scale.
16. Ritualism is significantly correlated (low) with the MMPI dependency scale and inversely with the ego strength scale on the MMPI.
17. Ritualism is significantly correlated (low) with the MMPI general maladjustment scale.
18. Ritualism is significantly (low) correlated with orthodoxy, fanaticism, and the importance of religion in the midwestern population, and much less so in the southern population.
19. Ritualism is not correlated with alienation.
20. There are no significant sex differences in ritualism.
21. Ritualism is clustered in neither the fundamentalism, theism, or

superstition factor, nor the idealism, altruism, church orientation, and mysticism factor of clergymen.

22. Ritualism is clustered in the professors' attitude system with all the dimensions except altruism and idealism.
23. Ritualism is clustered in the Methodist church members' attitude system with church orientation and superstition and *not* with altruism, fundamentalism, theism, mysticism or idealism.

ALTRUISM

1. Catholic, Seventh-Day Adventist, Church of Christ, and United Church of Christ clergymen are highest in altruism, whereas Lutheran, Episcopal, Presbyterian, and Unitarian-Universalist clergymen are lowest.
2. There are no significant regional differences in the altruism scores of clergymen.
3. Older clergymen are significantly more altruistic than younger clergymen.
4. Professors in denominational colleges and universities are significantly more altruistic than professors in public colleges.
5. Full professors are significantly more altruistic than assistant professors.
6. Professors of fine arts are more altruistic than physical science professors, who are, in turn, more altruistic than behavioral science professors.
7. Altruism is seldom positively correlated, and often is negatively correlated, with political conservatism.
8. Altruism scores of the various socioeconomic classes are not significantly different in the southern community studied.
9. Altruism is found to be highest among the members of the lower socioeconomic classes in the midwestern community studied.
10. Active church members are more altruistic than inactive members.
11. Altruism scores are not altered by either experimental arrogation or derogation.
12. Altruism is not related to suggestibility.
13. Altruism is not related to perceptual rigidity.
14. Altruism is inversely correlated with scholastic aptitude in the southern student population studied.

15. Altruism is significantly correlated with MMPI anxiety scores in the southern student population.
16. Altruism is significantly and positively correlated with dependency and inversely correlated with ego strength as both are measured by the MMPI.
17. Altruism is significantly correlated with scores of general maladjustment on the MMPI in the southern student population.
18. Altruism is correlated (moderately) with orthodoxy and the importance of religion in general.
19. Altruism is correlated (moderately) with fanaticism in the southern student population.
20. Altruism is generally not related to alienation.
21. Altruism is significantly higher among southern females than among southern males.
22. Altruism is clustered with idealism, church oriented attitudes, and mysticism among clergymen.
23. Altruism is clustered with idealism alone in the attitude system of university professors.
24. Altruism is clustered with theism, fundamentalism, mysticism, and idealism among Methodist church members.

FUNDAMENTALISM

1. Seventh-Day Adventist, Lutheran, Catholic, Church of Christ, and Baptist clergymen are highest in fundamentalism, whereas Unitarian-Universalist clergymen are lowest.
2. Southern clergymen are most fundamentalistic, followed in order by those of the Pacific Coast, New England, and lastly by those in the Midwest.
3. Older clergymen are significantly more fundamentalistic than the younger clergymen.
4. Professors in denominational colleges and universities are significantly more fundamentalistic than those in public universities.
5. Professors in larger colleges and universities are less fundamentalistic than those in small colleges.
6. Full professors are significantly more fundamentalistic than assistant professors.
7. Behavioral science professors are significantly less fundamental-

istic than professors of physical science and fine arts professors, who are the most fundamentalistic.

8. Fundamentalism is not often positively correlated with political conservatism.

9. Fundamentalism scores of the various socioeconomic classes of a southern city are not significantly different.

10. Fundamentalism is inversely related to socioeconomic status in the midwestern community studied; that is, fundamentalism is highest in the lowest class and lowest in the highest class.

11. Active church members score higher on fundamentalism than inactive members.

12. Fundamentalism is not affected by either arrogation or derogation.

13. Fundamentalism is not related to suggestibility.

14. Fundamentalism is not related to perceptual rigidity.

15. Fundamentalism is generally inversely correlated with scholastic aptitude in the southern student sample only.

16. Fundamentalism is significantly and positively correlated with dependency and inversely correlated with ego strength as both are measured by the MMPI.

17. Fundamentalism is highly related to orthodoxy; less, but significantly correlated with fanaticism and the importance of religion.

18. Fundamentalism is not generally correlated with alienation.

19. Fundamentalism is significantly higher among southern female students than among southern male students.

20. Fundamentalism is clustered with theism and superstition in a common factor among clergymen.

21. Fundamentalism is clustered with superstition, ritualism, theism, mysticism and church orientation and not with altruism or idealism in the attitude system of professors.

22. Fundamentalism is clustered with theism, altruism, mysticism, and idealism and not with church orientation, ritualism, or superstition in the attitude system of Methodist church members.

THEISM

1. Catholic, Lutheran, Seventh-Day Adventist, and Church of Christ clergymen are highest in theism; Unitarian-Universalist clergymen are lowest.

2. Southern clergymen are the most theistic, followed in order by clergymen from the New England region, the Pacific Coast states, and the midwestern states.

3. Older clergymen are significantly more theistic than younger clergymen.

4. Professors in denominational colleges and universities are significantly more theistic than professors in public colleges and universities.

5. Professors in large universities are significantly less theistic than professors in small colleges.

6. Professors of behavioral science are less theistic than professors of physical science who are in turn less theistic than professors of fine arts.

7. Theistic attitudes are seldom positively correlated, and are often negatively correlated, with political conservatism.

8. Theistic attitude scores of the various socioeconomic classes of a southern city are not significantly different.

9. Theistic attitude scores increase as one proceeds down the status hierarchy in the midwestern community studied.

10. Active church members are more theistic than inactive members.

11. Theism scores are not altered by either experimental arrogation or derogation.

12. Theism is not related to suggestibility.

13. Theism is not related to perceptual rigidity.

14. Theism is inversely correlated with scholastic aptitude in the southern student population.

15. Theism is significantly and positively correlated with dependency and inversely correlated with ego strength as both are measured by the MMPI.

16. Theism is significantly correlated with MMPI anxiety scores in the southern student population.

17. Theism is highly correlated with orthodoxy; moderately correlated with the importance of religion and fanaticism.

18. Theism is not related to alienation.

19. Theistic attitude scores are significantly higher among female students than among male students.

20. Theistic attitudes are clustered with fundamentalistic attitudes and superstitious attitudes among clergymen.

21. Theistic attitudes are clustered with all the dimensions but idealism and altruism by professors.
22. Theistic attitudes are clustered with all the dimensions except church orientation, ritualism, and superstition by the members of the Methodist congregation.

IDEALISM
1. Catholic and Methodist clergymen score highest in idealism, whereas Lutheran, Presbyterian, Episcopal, and Seventh-Day Adventist clergymen are lowest.
2. There are no significant regional differences in the idealism scores of clergymen.
3. Older clergymen are significantly more idealistic than younger clergymen.
4. Full professors are significantly more idealistic than assistant professors.
5. Idealism is never positively correlated and is often negatively correlated with political conservatism.
6. Idealism scores of the various socioeconomic classes are not significantly different in the southern city studied.
7. Idealism scores of the various socioeconomic classes are not significantly different in the midwestern city studied.
8. Active church members are more idealistic than inactive members.
9. Idealism scores are increased significantly by arrogation and flattery.
10. Non-suggestible students are significantly more idealistic than suggestible students.
11. Idealism is not related to perceptual rigidity.
12. Idealism is positively correlated with scholastic aptitude in the midwestern population.
13. Idealism is inversely correlated with general maladjustment (as measured by the MMPI) in the southern population. That is, idealists are not maladjusted.
14. Idealism is inversely correlated with anxiety (as measured by the MMPI) in the midwestern population. That is, midwestern idealists are less anxious than nonidealists.
15. Idealism is moderately correlated with orthodoxy and belief in the importance of religion.

16. Idealism is moderately correlated with fanaticism in the midwestern student population and has only a low correlation with fanaticism in the southern student population.
17. Idealism is inversely correlated with alienation. That is, idealists are not alienated.
18. Idealism is significantly higher among midwestern females than among midwestern males.
19. Idealism is clustered with altruism, mysticism, and church orientation among clergymen.
20. Idealism is clustered with altruism alone by the college and university professors.
21. Idealism is clustered with theism, fundamentalism, altruism, and mysticism and not with church orientation, ritualism, or superstition among the Methodist church members.

SUPERSTITION

1. Catholic, Baptist, and Seventh-Day Adventist clergymen are highest in superstition, whereas Unitarian-Universalist clergymen are lowest.
2. There are no significant region differences in the superstition scores of clergymen.
3. Older clergymen are significantly more superstitious than the younger clergymen.
4. Professors in southern colleges and universities are significantly more superstitious than professors in northern colleges and universities.
5. Professors in public colleges and universities are significantly less superstitious than professors in denominational colleges and universities.
6. Professors of fine arts are more superstitious than professors of physical science, who are in turn more superstitious than behavioral science professors.
7. Superstition is the religiosity variable which is most often significantly and positively correlated with politically conservative attitudes.
8. Superstition scores are higher in the lower socioeconomic classes than in the upper classes in the southern community studied.
9. Superstition is inversely related to socioeconomic status in the

midwestern community studied; that is, the lower classes are the most superstitious.

10. Active church members are less superstitious than inactive members.

11. Superstition scores are not altered by either experimental arrogation or derogation.

12. Superstition is not related to suggestibility.

13. Superstition is not related to perceptual rigidity.

14. Superstition is inversely and significantly correlated with scholastic aptitude in the southern student population studied.

15. Superstition is significantly correlated with the MMPI anxiety scale.

16. Superstition is significantly correlated with general maladjustment as measured by the MMPI.

17. Superstition is significantly correlated with dependency and inversely with ego strength as both are measured by the MMPI.

18. Superstition is highly correlated with orthodoxy in the midwestern student population, and only moderately in the southern student population.

19. Superstition is moderately correlated with the importance of religion and fanaticism.

20. Superstition is generally not related to alienation.

21. The sexes are not significantly different in superstition.

22. Superstition is clustered with fundamentalism and theism in a common factor among clergymen.

23. Superstition is clustered with all the religious attitude dimensions except idealism and altruism among professors.

24. Superstition is clustered with only church orientation and ritualism among Methodist church members.

MYSTICISM

1. Mysticism is highest among Methodist, United Church of Christ, Catholic, and Seventh-Day Adventist clergymen and lowest among Unitarian-Universalist, Lutheran, and Presbyterian clergymen.

2. There are no significant regional differences in the mysticism scores of the clergymen studied.

3. Older clergymen are significantly more mystical than younger clergymen.
4. Full professors are significantly more mystical than assistant professors.
5. Behavioral science professors are less mystical than physical science professors, who in turn are less mystical than fine arts professors.
6. Mysticism is rather often positively correlated with politically conservative attitudes.
7. The lower socioeconomic classes in the southern city studied are significantly more mystical than the upper socioeconomic classes.
8. Mysticism is inversely related to socioeconomic status in the midwestern community studied; that is, the lower-class categories are most mystical and the highest status categories are the lowest in mysticism.
9. Mysticism scores are not altered by either arrogation or derogation.
10. Mysticism is not related to suggestibility.
11. Mysticism is not related to perceptual rigidity.
12. Mysticism is inversely (low) correlated with scholastic aptitude. That is, the more mystical are less scholastically capable.
13. Mysticism is, in general, correlated positively with dependency as measured by the MMPI and inversely with MMPI-based ego strength scores.
14. Mysticism is correlated with MMPI anxiety scores in the southern student population studied.
15. Mysticism is moderately correlated with orthodoxy, fanaticism, and the importance of religion.
16. Mysticism is not, in general, related to alienation.
17. Females are significantly more mystical than males.
18. Mysticism is clustered in a common factor with the attitude dimensions of idealism, altruism, and church orientation among clergymen.
19. Mysticism is clustered in a factor with all the dimensions of religious attitudes except idealism, and altruism by college and university professors.
20. Mysticism is clustered in a factor with theism, fundamentalism, altruism, and idealism by the Methodist church members studied.

APPENDIXES
BIBLIOGRAPHY
AND
INDEX

APPENDIX A

Analysis of Variance Summary Tables for the Clergyman Survey

TABLE A-1. TOTAL RELIGIOSITY OF CLERGYMEN

Source of Variation	Sum of Squares		df	Mean Square	F Ratio
	Unadjusted	Adjusted			
By denomination and region					
Region	45.660	68.208	3	22.736	2.023
Denomination	4878.180	4900.728	10	490.073	43.605**
Region x denomination	487.633	465.085	30	15.503	1.379
Within	5608.187		499	11.239	
Total	11019.660		542		
By denomination and age					
Age	509.840	462.773	2	231.386	21.609**
Denomination	4517.280	4470.213	10	447.021	41.748**
Age x denomination	185.878	232.945	20	11.647	1.088
Within	5054.032		472	10.708	
Total	10267.030		504		

** P < .01

TABLE A-2. CHURCH ORIENTATION OF CLERGYMEN

Source of Variation	Sum of Squares		df	Mean Square	F Ratio
	Unadjusted	Adjusted			
By denomination and region					
Region	315.480	344.057	3	114.686	3.675*
Denomination	2233.750	2262.327	10	226.233	7.249**
Region x denomination	658.633	630.056	30	21.002	.673
Within	15573.808		499	31.210	
Total	18781.671		542		
By denomination and age					
Age	1370.090	1261.215	2	630.608	21.979**
Denomination	2036.530	1927.655	10	192.766	6.719**
Age x denomination	425.629	534.504	20	26.725	.931
Within	13542.392		472	28.692	
Total	17374.641		504		

* P < .05
** P < .01

TABLE A-3. RITUALISM OF CLERGYMEN

Source of Variation	Sum of Squares		df	Mean Square	F Ratio
	Unadjusted	Adjusted			
By denomination and region					
Region	150.970	66.296	3	22.099	.610
Denomination	10999.291	10914.617	10	1091.462	30.148**
Region x denomination	607.077	691.751	30	23.058	.637
Within	18065.714		499	36.204	
Total	29823.052		542		
By denomination and age					
Age	450.960	137.114	2	68.557	1.912
Denomination	10147.441	9833.594	10	983.359	27.419**
Age x denomination	477.761	791.607	20	39.580	1.104
Within	16927.850		472	35.864	
Total	28004.012		504		

** P < .01

TABLE A-4. ALTRUISM OF CLERGYMEN

Source of Variation	Sum of Squares		df	Mean Square	F Ratio
	Unadjusted	Adjusted			
By denomination and region					
Region	31.710	27.925	3	9.308	.324
Denomination	2536.310	2532.526	10	253.253	8.823**
Region x denomination	692.289	696.074	30	23.202	.808
Within	14322.612		499	28.703	
Total	17582.921		542		
By denomination and age					
Age	1291.750	1272.955	2	636.477	25.348**
Denomination	2455.450	2436.655	10	243.665	9.704**
Age x denomination	1002.006	1020.802	20	51.040	2.033**
Within	11851.645		472	25.109	
Total	16600.851		504		

** P < .01

TABLE A-5. FUNDAMENTALISM OF CLERGYMEN

Source of Variation	Sum of Squares		df	Mean Square	F Ratio
	Unadjusted	Adjusted			
By denomination and region					
Region	170.920	201.221	3	67.074	2.737*
Denomination	32185.561	32215.862	10	3221.586	131.475**
Region x denomination	1210.611	1180.311	30	39.344	1.606*
Within	12227.240		499	24.503	
Total	45794.332		542		
By denomination and age					
Age	212.860	365.968	2	182.984	7.174**
Denomination	29933.081	30086.189	10	3008.619	117.947**
Age x denomination	353.556	200.448	20	10.022	.393
Within	12039.925		472	25.508	
Total	42539.422		504		

* P < .05   ** P < .01

Source of Variation	Sum of Squares		df	Mean Square	F Ratio
	Unadjusted	Adjusted			
By denomination and region					
Region	356.300	413.059	3	137.686	5.110**
Denomination	36922.411	36979.170	10	3697.917	137.233**
Region x denomination	1589.860	1533.102	30	51.103	1.896**
Within	13446.171		499	26.946	
Total	52314.742		542		
By denomination and age					
Age	310.930	427.911	2	213.956	7.453**
Denomination	34235.481	34352.462	10	3435.246	119.662**
Age x denomination	527.788	410.807	20	20.540	.715
Within	13550.103		472	28.708	
Total	48624.302		504		

** P < .01

Source of Variation	Sum of Squares		df	Mean Square	F Ratio
	Unadjusted	Adjusted			
By denomination and region					
Region	100.430	104.928	3	34.976	1.842
Denomination	1457.110	1461.608	10	146.161	7.697**
Region x denomination	363.868	359.370	30	11.979	.631
Within	9475.542		499	18.989	
Total	11396.950		542		
By denomination and age					
Age	431.380	400.708	2	200.354	11.037**
Denomination	1345.510	1314.838	10	131.484	7.243**
Age x denomination	395.751	426.423	20	21.321	1.175
Within	8568.339		472	18.153	
Total	10740.980		504		

** P < .01

Source of Variation	Sum of Squares		df	Mean Square	F Ratio
	Unadjusted	Adjusted			
By denomination and region					
Region	132.570	131.575	3	43.858	2.580
Denomination	2763.370	2762.375	10	276.237	16.251**
Region x denomination	707.929	708.925	30	23.631	1.390
Within	8481.931		499	16.998	
Total	12085.800		542		
By denomination and age					
Age	154.000	140.940	2	70.470	4.052*
Denomination	2592.350	2579.290	10	257.929	14.829**
Age x denomination	270.289	283.349	20	14.167	.815
Within	8209.521		472	17.393	
Total	11226.160		504		

* P < .05   ** P < .01

TABLE A-9. MYSTICISM OF CLERGYMEN

Source of Variation	Sum of Squares		df	Mean Square	F Ratio
	Unadjusted	Adjusted			
By denomination and region					
Region	14.630	11.298	3	3.766	.127
Denomination	2976.240	2972.908	10	297.291	10.041**
Region x denomination	1558.763	1562.095	30	52.070	1.759**
Within	14774.457		499	29.608	
Total	19324.090		542		
By denomination and age					
Age	405.960	353.187	2	176.594	6.008**
Denomination	2726.000	2673.228	10	267.323	9.094**
Age x denomination	405.061	457.834	20	22.892	.779
Within	13873.939		472	29.394	
Total	17410.960		504		

** P < .01

APPENDIX B

Correlation Matrices, Factor Matrices, Means, and Standard Deviations for the Study of Religious and Political Attitudes

Key to attitude dimensions in the tables of Appendix B.

1. Church-oriented attitudes
2. Ritualistic attitudes
3. Altruistic attitudes
4. Fundamentalistic attitudes
5. Theistic attitudes
6. Idealistic attitudes
7. Superstitious attitudes
8. Mystical attitudes
9. Authoritarian attitudes
10. Probusiness attitudes
11. Anti-civil liberty attitudes
12. Anarchistic attitudes
13. Anti-Black attitudes
14. Anti-Semitic attitudes
15. Anti-foreign aid attitudes
16. Pro-warfare state attitudes
17. Isolationist attitudes
18. Classical laissez-faire economic attitudes
19. Machiavellian attitudes
20. States' rights attitudes
21. Superpatriotic attitudes
22. Anti-welfare state attitudes
23. Restorationist attitudes

TABLE B-1. MEANS AND STANDARD DEVIATIONS FOR THE SOUTHERN AND MIDWESTERN POPULATIONS

	Southern Rural		Southern Urban		Midwestern Rural		Midwestern Urban	
	means	s.d.	means	s.d.	means	s.d.	means	s.d.
1	26.62	5.84	26.58	6.31	28.92	6.07	26.75	6.32
2	18.04	6.57	17.93	7.95	20.57	7.91	17.63	7.78
3	27.71	5.78	28.28	5.97	30.84	4.41	28.74	5.58
4	33.18	9.40	30.66	8.74	34.57	8.00	31.56	7.63
5	34.04	9.38	33.38	9.73	35.73	8.10	32.59	9.26
6	27.49	4.87	27.74	4.62	30.51	5.28	28.93	4.80
7	21.09	5.28	21.27	6.24	22.57	5.60	21.87	4.74
8	27.33	5.77	26.42	5.63	28.43	5.02	26.29	4.80
9	18.31	6.33	17.12	5.57	18.41	5.05	18.17	5.18
10	15.64	4.57	15.26	4.18	15.97	4.68	16.39	4.47
11	14.71	5.03	13.64	4.48	14.68	4.46	13.83	4.26
12	15.40	4.39	15.07	3.77	16.78	4.79	15.97	4.02
13	13.78	7.72	12.21	7.25	10.54	7.22	11.27	7.91
14	10.96	5.43	10.48	5.02	10.46	5.95	9.54	5.73
15	13.60	7.47	12.17	5.99	15.32	6.85	14.42	5.73
16	17.67	5.70	17.00	4.44	18.08	4.59	16.94	4.28
17	14.84	5.82	13.88	4.60	15.05	4.87	13.96	4.28
18	14.07	4.74	13.96	5.25	13.30	5.07	13.16	5.42
19	14.89	4.15	14.71	4.12	15.89	4.40	16.09	4.30
20	17.04	5.49	15.46	4.77	15.78	5.01	14.71	4.24
21	21.09	7.23	21.32	6.71	21.43	6.56	21.13	6.46
22	15.69	6.15	14.96	5.49	17.54	5.08	17.04	5.01
23	14.44	3.46	13.89	3.64	13.59	3.28	14.34	3.72

TABLE B-2. MEANS AND STANDARD DEVIATIONS FOR THE CATHOLIC AND
MENNONITE POPULATIONS

	Catholic Rural		Catholic Urban		Mennonite Rural		Mennonite Urban	
	means	s.d.	means	s.d.	means	s.d.	means	s.d.
1	28.11	4.57	28.28	5.01	28.19	4.65	26.92	4.98
2	25.34	5.32	24.42	5.96	19.91	6.15	20.03	7.04
3	30.88	4.20	30.84	4.60	31.08	4.22	30.74	4.13
4	36.52	4.52	36.30	5.27	39.76	5.43	39.34	6.87
5	41.07	4.01	40.74	4.38	39.92	5.60	39.18	6.71
6	31.55	4.39	32.71	4.19	30.41	3.68	30.95	3.81
7	24.45	3.56	23.66	4.00	23.51	3.98	23.08	3.32
8	27.17	3.70	27.57	4.53	31.71	4.31	30.66	4.24
9	21.72	4.28	20.86	5.32	19.90	4.71	19.37	4.60
10	15.94	3.41	16.11	4.00	17.40	3.76	16.74	4.23
11	16.54	3.38	16.49	3.97	15.98	3.78	14.87	4.42
12	15.13	3.37	14.91	3.84	17.21	3.85	16.45	3.66
13	11.94	6.33	12.55	7.47	12.70	6.05	12.61	6.83
14	10.77	4.52	10.96	5.63	12.78	4.70	12.29	6.15
15	15.06	5.89	14.43	6.12	15.83	5.16	16.05	5.66
16	17.50	4.14	17.92	4.72	15.03	4.07	15.00	4.49
17	14.90	3.72	15.12	4.86	15.56	3.77	15.47	4.94
18	13.84	3.89	12.65	4.50	15.62	4.48	14.53	4.16
19	15.95	4.27	15.61	3.98	15.54	3.62	15.34	3.98
20	15.27	4.45	14.58	4.35	16.62	4.02	15.11	3.29
21	23.51	4.97	23.34	6.12	20.23	6.39	19.03	7.01
22	15.78	4.56	15.14	4.85	17.13	4.26	17.16	5.36
23	14.22	3.88	14.15	3.68	15.68	3.29	14.21	3.75

TABLE B-3. CORRELATION MATRIX FOR THE SOUTHERN RURAL POPULATION
(N = 45)

	1	2	3	4	5	6	7	8	9	10	11	12	13	14	15	16	17	18	19	20	21	22	23
1		46	40	50	49	07	50	36	39	47	28	−11	27	22	14	36	27	18	48	06	44	12	09
2			42	31	39	10	44	35	38	38	13	−08	08	15	01	22	08	−03	30	13	33	−11	−03
3				61	60	46	58	66	32	28	31	−07	−07	09	00	00	02	−05	11	19	30	−02	17
4					81	33	58	45	35	50	53	13	35	38	25	37	36	18	04	44	47	25	33
5						40	59	57	33	36	41	01	22	23	25	36	37	08	03	37	46	08	22
6							21	42	−15	−01	12	00	−10	−06	−18	−24	−13	−24	−17	05	12	−01	05
7								63	46	54	21	18	11	04	21	35	35	18	26	33	30	18	31
8									29	29	14	19	−03	−12	23	24	24	08	29	37	24	11	24
9										71	55	20	26	34	38	60	46	33	56	29	68	35	32
10											54	29	39	42	21	59	31	23	47	29	58	29	25
11												28	41	61	29	35	27	14	40	40	60	36	52
12													27	14	46	36	54	31	27	62	01	64	52
13														77	59	46	49	40	35	62	33	52	51
14															29	28	28	16	40	46	49	29	51
15																61	78	56	33	70	26	63	49
16																	73	64	46	47	50	54	33
17																		55	26	61	24	63	40
18																			28	50	08	64	29
19																				33	56	31	45
20																					22	52	68
21																						15	33
22																							50
23																							

NOTE: Correlation coefficients are rounded to two decimal places.

	1	2	3	4	5	6	7	8	9	10	11	12	13	14	15	16	17	18	19	20	21	22	23
1		62	50	53	45	06	48	48	48	31	52	14	44	41	20	36	22	09	34	35	41	12	31
2			50	38	41	15	50	39	40	27	44	00	33	33	02	24	08	02	24	23	18	10	15
3				64	64	35	54	57	19	24	24	12	16	17	-05	07	-03	04	02	17	23	-07	06
4					80	29	64	65	33	21	39	08	40	39	11	25	13	05	10	37	31	10	29
5						32	55	68	30	13	30	-04	30	31	-06	24	04	-03	07	20	24	01	13
6							11	31	08	20	04	-02	07	-01	-09	00	-13	04	-22	-04	24	-05	02
7								51	40	13	35	12	35	39	13	39	11	-05	15	24	32	-01	25
8									42	20	38	19	31	33	03	17	02	15	05	25	16	10	24
9										23	50	18	42	37	21	42	23	15	28	28	48	18	24
10											36	39	25	24	35	22	25	39	25	23	35	37	19
11												09	50	50	28	31	20	21	33	48	38	32	40
12													22	26	32	27	28	40	25	37	02	38	36
13														70	38	45	39	18	47	52	39	38	45
14															39	34	36	16	44	48	18	32	44
15																40	74	40	42	41	24	53	47
16																	42	14	48	41	41	30	46
17																		28	41	41	20	10	45
18																			27	40	02	52	22
19																				31	17	27	33
20																					18	38	59
21																						18	26
22																							33
23																							

NOTE: Correlation coefficients are rounded to two decimal places.

	1	2	3	4	5	6	7	8	9	10	11	12	13	14	15	16	17	18	19	20	21	22	23
1		26	36	18	14	11	14	31	24	-21	-11	-08	-11	-07	-06	-05	-22	-19	03	12	01	03	-09
2			40	29	35	23	14	24	11	-05	14	-03	-10	-01	-34	-07	-28	-08	-00	11	27	-27	07
3				50	27	28	-11	24	-05	-08	-15	-02	-34	-21	-44	-21	-45	-22	-23	-16	-10	-09	-15
4					35	35	-21	24	-09	-07	-18	-14	-24	-16	-40	-12	-41	-28	-32	-13	-02	-21	-16
5						34	-11	28	-05	-30	-21	-10	-22	-17	-34	-25	-31	-35	-28	-05	07	-24	-36
6							-23	01	-03	-11	-22	-30	-34	-31	-36	-46	-45	-31	-46	-24	06	-21	-28
7								20	17	06	27	19	36	21	25	12	16	-00	24	19	20	08	21
8									21	-00	06	10	-00	05	-10	-02	-11	-07	-11	25	15	08	-10
9										22	20	36	25	16	26	26	07	31	34	37	47	23	32
10											24	31	23	12	24	34	21	39	20	27	26	38	32
11												36	49	43	23	40	39	26	46	29	43	16	47
12													45	41	28	32	30	42	42	40	08	44	43
13														65	39	51	45	46	57	43	29	34	54
14															25	38	23	31	49	31	18	11	36
15																36	55	45	29	28	15	48	24
16																	42	37	42	43	34	32	47
17																		42	44	27	17	37	38
18																			40	48	15	36	41
19																				29	21	25	49
20																					32	31	40
21																						-06	24
22																							35
23																							

NOTE: Correlation coefficients are rounded to two decimal places.

Study of Religious and Political Attitudes

TABLE B-6. CORRELATION MATRIX FOR THE CATHOLIC URBAN POPULATION
(N = 198)

	1	2	3	4	5	6	7	8	9	10	11	12	13	14	15	16	17	18	19	20	21	22	23
1		49	33	21	20	04	35	20	34	31	21	01	23	26	06	32	-03	03	22	07	34	01	03
2			30	31	22	-11	37	19	28	24	36	04	12	18	10	26	10	10	23	15	40	12	23
3				41	41	33	23	32	15	09	-01	-07	-23	-15	-25	-02	-25	-10	-13	01	12	-19	00
4					57	30	22	32	16	-03	14	-12	-11	-15	-11	-09	-18	-12	-16	-03	22	-10	-04
5						44	13	26	07	02	03	-09	-16	-19	-20	-01	-22	-06	-18	-02	10	-05	00
6							-10	20	-18	-10	-25	-08	-27	-32	-26	-23	-35	-06	-42	-13	-14	-12	-18
7								12	18	14	22	08	17	16	08	23	08	09	14	11	25	10	09
8									29	12	07	02	-06	-05	-04	10	-01	07	01	-12	29	-05	-13
9										34	39	18	37	35	19	53	23	21	39	29	50	19	25
10											19	20	38	42	23	39	20	39	28	32	27	24	30
11												04	40	38	25	47	30	09	36	15	36	22	25
12													22	28	42	24	31	30	19	40	-01	51	32
13														66	46	48	38	26	49	33	26	38	36
14															37	50	33	25	47	38	26	37	40
15																34	72	48	24	41	21	64	31
16																	33	30	45	29	39	32	25
17																		53	29	40	28	52	37
18																			16	50	23	43	43
19																				27	26	23	27
20																					11	49	52
21																						17	12
22																							45
23																							

NOTE: Correlation coefficients are rounded to two decimal places.

TABLE B-7. CORRELATION MATRIX FOR THE MENNONITE RURAL POPULATION
(N = 237)

	1	2	3	4	5	6	7	8	9	10	11	12	13	14	15	16	17	18	19	20	21	22	23
1		33	37	19	13	03	18	20	29	22	17	16	17	12	13	08	07	10	23	12	27	13	07
2			08	07	-07	-16	21	05	37	18	45	02	39	34	15	36	19	22	28	27	40	05	25
3				41	39	32	09	42	15	02	01	-02	-15	-18	-07	-15	-18	-10	02	00	09	-15	-05
4					83	19	20	48	17	-05	06	-14	-10	-14	-02	-06	07	-10	-13	08	19	-20	-02
5						24	17	46	06	-08	-01	-15	-16	-16	-08	-19	-01	-15	-19	03	07	-25	-08
6							03	28	01	-03	-07	-07	-19	-14	-09	-17	-15	-01	-17	00	-07	-07	-03
7								29	30	23	28	03	30	24	12	23	17	11	17	22	36	-00	20
8									25	09	08	01	-07	-08	13	-03	02	01	-04	16	17	-07	03
9										33	43	18	35	31	29	30	26	24	28	32	51	23	29
10											33	30	34	34	37	34	33	22	40	42	27	26	35	35
11												13	48	43	33	45	40	29	27	31	48	14	37
12													23	22	42	25	22	43	31	37	-01	45	19
13														67	41	53	37	37	43	39	49	35	37
14															38	49	32	32	41	31	39	35	33
15																43	43	41	34	42	32	48	33
16																	39	37	38	35	49	32	34
17																		40	24	46	34	26	43
18																			33	54	21	40	54
19																				27	29	39	26
20																					29	29	49
21																						14	20
22																							20
23																							

NOTE: Correlation coefficients are rounded to two decimal places.

Appendix B

	1	2	3	4	5	6	7	8	9	10	11	12	13	14	15	16	17	18	19	20	21	22	23
1		21	13	14	23	16	08	16	17	05	14	27	29	28	01	25	11	20	26	-02	04	-19	21
2			-15	-23	-19	-17	11	-04	43	27	37	23	46	31	40	41	31	-03	58	10	43	27	42
3				35	36	44	14	22	12	-11	-05	-02	-26	-02	-32	-02	-08	11	03	-27	00	-33	-10
4					88	58	15	56	24	15	-06	06	-10	02	-04	21	25	33	-19	-00	26	03	04
5						56	17	56	23	13	09	05	-03	-08	-18	24	18	35	-15	00	22	-03	-01
6							22	54	09	05	-24	-15	-36	-10	-30	-16	-08	07	-38	-27	-09	-23	-03
7								22	48	12	16	11	20	-05	16	32	35	26	-04	-07	30	01	-08
8									49	41	05	13	-03	17	08	25	29	46	-03	39	17	11	
9										53	45	30	39	38	67	62	59	48	20	66	44	25	
10											58	26	53	49	57	63	53	45	51	37	70	54	32
11												45	69	47	49	68	62	40	54	47	46	53	40
12													27	48	60	42	50	52	50	33	10	53	36
13														50	45	69	48	21	57	47	60	44	43
14															35	53	41	29	49	40	29	36	51
15																51	70	48	49	44	51	69	41
16																	66	48	65	41	77	44	35
17																		54	42	46	58	62	42
18																			26	38	37	37	15
19																				28	56	48	24
20																					31	53	16
21																						40	23
22																							47
23																							

NOTE: Correlation coefficients are rounded to two decimal places.

	1	2	3	4	5	6	7	8	9	10	11	12	13	14	15	16	17	18	19	20	21	22	23
1		71	37	35	37	12	55	55	54	56	48	33	46	36	49	23	16	33	55	36	44	-02	45
2			30	27	37	17	50	45	49	57	53	16	32	23	34	21	03	19	30	11	44	-03	28
3				50	53	51	41	42	11	21	10	33	11	-02	19	20	-01	26	03	19	40	-10	04
4					79	50	43	56	17	28	35	29	21	17	20	15	-10	04	-07	10	25	05	26
5						60	50	58	25	25	31	23	14	13	25	02	-00	15	-07	08	29	-07	29
6							37	40	08	11	03	41	00	08	23	-10	-01	06	-27	16	15	12	16
7								54	58	56	45	42	50	50	47	30	28	34	47	28	38	-05	40
8									25	31	43	27	19	26	03	01	26	17	29	34	08	39	
9										56	66	26	59	56	44	48	34	24	61	28	46	-12	44
10											55	56	51	47	53	57	29	42	39	38	48	28	38
11												26	70	61	37	58	16	17	47	30	55	-01	37
12													45	39	50	37	16	59	34	64	14	44	40
13														84	47	61	37	39	65	47	47	30	48
14															44	52	31	35	64	28	23	23	45
15																47	62	46	48	51	33	39	49
16																	51	24	40	39	45	27	16
17																		39	36	48	44	41	41
18																			42	65	29	34	57
19																				35	27	-00	45
20																					35	38	61
21																						01	33
22																							23
23																							

NOTE: Correlation coefficients are rounded to two decimal places.

TABLE B-10. CORRELATION MATRIX FOR THE MIDWESTERN URBAN POPULATION
(N = 140)

	1	2	3	4	5	6	7	8	9	10	11	12	13	14	15	16	17	18	19	20	21	22	23
1		52	56	53	51	26	38	41	19	-01	26	-12	09	15	-08	06	02	13	-05	15	32	-08	15
2			37	29	30	12	40	39	24	09	35	-08	07	23	07	07	07	07	15	08	21	-17	17
3				61	61	42	36	44	04	-22	15	-20	-14	-02	-21	-18	-11	-12	-27	-02	-32	-29	-07
4					78	37	44	56	10	-05	20	-19	-01	07	-01	03	19	03	-23	23	37	-15	09
5						36	42	59	06	-09	10	-14	-10	01	-06	-00	11	01	-25	20	35	-10	03
6							13	19	-18	-21	-03	-23	-23	-23	-14	-23	-25	-17	-02	-46	-03	13	-12	-17
7								53	32	11	30	-08	23	23	13	14	26	09	10	27	39	-04	23
8									27	06	22	-02	04	12	09	22	26	11	08	28	33	01	22
9										36	46	19	35	27	20	44	32	26	41	30	39	24	35
10											18	29	46	28	38	46	34	49	45	47	33	42	44
11												-04	45	48	13	46	39	18	38	24	34	04	41
12													12	10	38	20	25	42	27	40	-08	41	19
13														62	29	54	40	37	48	39	29	26	52
14															34	39	40	24	40	26	28	15	47
15																32	59	43	33	43	01	42	32
16																	55	36	44	42	22	33	49
17																		36	32	48	24	33	48
18																			25	66	19	52	45
19																				23	02	35	46
20																					39	36	50
21																						-02	27
22																							29
23																							

NOTE: Correlation coefficients are rounded to two decimal places.

TABLE B-11. THE ROTATED FACTOR MATRIX—SOUTHERN RURAL POPULATION
(N = 45)

	I	II	III	IV	V	VI	VII	VIII	IX	X	XI
1	.100	.366	-.244	.125	.183	.191	.124	-.809	.066	.015	.007
2	.967	.342	-.218	.059	.098	.840	.045	-.137	-.077	-.153	-.027
3	-.148	.829	-.106	-.008	.101	.216	.051	-.019	.081	.167	.282
4	.172	.715	-.278	.350	-.319	.016	-.041	-.192	.051	.109	.115
5	.329	.740	-.237	.172	-.228	.109	.139	-.147	-.133	.202	.062
6	-.176	.438	.079	.004	-.039	-.168	-.074	.016	-.102	.815	.028
7	.087	.785	-.271	-.037	.077	.048	-.210	-.222	.066	-.145	-.271
8	.203	.742	-.085	-.191	.341	.162	-.109	.013	.006	.285	-.124
9	.219	.216	-.800	.040	.202	.147	-.067	-.017	.165	-.161	.164
10	-.024	.247	-.775	.251	-.021	.158	-.290	-.194	.126	-.018	-.216
11	.067	.220	-.547	.467	.030	-.077	-.197	-.025	-.020	.050	.516
12	.362	.002	-.077	.090	.101	-.032	-.878	.120	.047	.034	.007
13	.381	-.040	-.101	.831	.045	.041	-.086	-.143	.185	.026	-.123
14	.068	-.010	-.278	.896	.059	.073	-.014	-.037	.024	-.021	.140
15	.847	.077	-.081	.234	.159	-.017	-.133	.052	.188	-.058	.061
16	.626	.065	-.571	.100	.017	.050	-.095	-.138	.297	-.076	-.186
17	.838	.129	-.191	.114	-.064	.015	-.284	-.158	.137	-.070	.015
18	.456	.028	-.122	.101	.063	-.057	-.055	-.018	.823	-.117	-.065
19	.138	-.007	-.424	.219	.778	.130	-.125	-.237	.087	-.056	-.001
20	.541	.340	-.006	.496	.167	.073	-.341	.287	.184	.011	-.059
21	.180	.184	-.764	.287	.236	.031	.203	-.086	-.145	.177	.125
22	.457	-.034	-.131	.198	.055	-.118	-.519	-.128	.524	.118	.206
23	.206	.326	-.089	.523	.402	-.321	-.353	.143	.026	-.166	.133

NOTE: Variable loadings are rounded to three decimal places.

TABLE B-12. THE ROTATED FACTOR MATRIX—SOUTHERN URBAN POPULATION
(N = 137)

	I	II	III	IV	V	VI	VII	VIII	IX	X
1	.443	-.107	-.012	.273	.620	.125	.034	-.185	-.065	.154
2	.382	.076	.011	.078	.740	.140	-.058	-.039	.002	.186
3	.739	.009	-.058	-.066	.412	-.099	.153	-.007	.224	-.037
4	.844	-.125	-.016	.100	.117	.174	-.035	-.183	.132	-.034
5	.871	.009	-.006	.062	.077	.127	-.148	-.009	.158	.008
6	.278	.147	.059	.065	-.029	-.003	-.019	.001	.874	-.043
7	.695	-.109	-.251	.238	.203	.119	.148	-.095	-.110	.121
8	.806	.143	.211	.145	.062	.147	.107	-.093	.032	-.030
9	.306	.054	.181	.742	.143	.191	.072	-.054	-.173	.191
10	.028	-.287	.329	.206	.472	.109	.470	.102	.328	-.061
11	.187	-.018	.258	.405	.476	.406	-.101	-.340	-.074	-.092
12	.066	-.089	.249	-.002	-.053	.091	.880	-.222	-.047	.139
13	.201	-.187	.085	.227	.112	.739	.018	-.240	.100	.249
14	.254	-.184	.037	.045	.146	.821	.128	-.194	-.074	-.092
15	-.026	-.815	.264	.124	.019	.181	.126	-.185	-.049	.111
16	.157	-.251	.005	.407	.009	.067	.099	-.318	.036	.678
17	.038	-.820	.143	.064	.011	.131	.048	-.199	-.093	.216
18	.026	-.148	.857	.051	.062	-.037	.176	-.149	.035	.126
19	-.048	-.239	.161	.012	.292	.348	.073	-.047	-.135	.712
20	.180	-.170	.287	.028	.148	.235	.093	-.752	-.059	.096
21	.108	-.248	-.089	.771	.176	.056	-.002	-.092	.335	.036
22	-.024	-.376	.648	.138	-.014	.282	.133	-.108	-.001	.020
23	.092	-.292	.023	.117	.038	.213	.169	-.779	.051	.128

NOTE: Variable loadings are rounded to three decimal places.

TABLE B-13. THE ROTATED FACTOR MATRIX—CATHOLIC RURAL POPULATION
(N = 82)

	I	II	III	IV	V	VI	VII	VIII	IX	X	XI
1	-.070	.252	.047	.873	.028	.078	.123	-.012	.010	-.111	-.017
2	-.075	.572	-.314	.082	.263	.273	.370	-.088	.306	.098	-.053
3	-.199	.807	.013	.189	-.115	.042	.012	-.083	-.077	-.076	-.111
4	.054	.696	-.004	.066	.069	.094	-.270	-.169	-.131	-.222	.299
5	-.087	.245	-.098	-.013	.103	.771	-.106	-.219	-.046	-.289	.004
6	-.161	.247	-.022	.017	.167	.162	-.102	-.833	-.127	.093	.139
7	.219	-.150	.049	.148	.076	-.107	.842	.037	-.016	-.182	-.026
8	-.001	.246	.069	.135	.115	.165	.219	.063	.117	-.776	-.055
9	.098	-.100	.109	.364	.566	-.147	-.068	-.086	.185	-.134	-.566
10	.009	.100	.343	-.369	.318	-.590	.009	.020	.250	-.111	-.104
11	.397	.061	.181	-.239	.447	.022	.367	.284	.011	.190	-.116
12	.392	.078	.409	-.173	-.017	.016	.057	.147	.220	-.093	-.617
13	.773	-.204	.250	-.031	.159	-.049	.177	.130	.220	.078	-.037
14	.880	-.094	-.061	-.030	.024	-.051	.049	.127	.122	-.051	-.124
15	.139	-.587	.512	.110	.127	-.132	.092	.138	.167	.015	.008
16	.367	-.019	.255	.047	.381	-.195	-.135	.576	.208	.028	.140
17	.107	-.433	.459	-.179	.154	.110	.125	.484	.140	.222	.006
18	.194	-.200	.211	-.131	.048	-.224	-.115	.133	.694	.140	-.245
19	.452	-.122	.068	.130	.167	-.083	.127	.431	.085	.298	-.447
20	.251	-.063	.172	.126	.214	.036	.067	.143	.774	-.184	-.024
21	.120	-.044	-.053	-.024	.905	.029	.115	.002	.118	-.046	-.010
22	.079	-.084	.860	.068	-.078	-.148	.006	.059	.170	-.036	-.159
23	.393	.117	.304	-.027	.212	-.222	.189	.198	.303	.407	-.141

NOTE: Variable loadings are rounded to three decimal places.

TABLE B-14. THE ROTATED FACTOR MATRIX—CATHOLIC URBAN POPULATION
(N = 198)

	I	II	III	IV	V	VI	VII	VIII	IX	X	XI
1	−.031	.165	−.248	.179	.159	.769	.045	−.074	.159	.272	−.073
2	.088	.080	.012	−.231	−.006	.797	−.048	.169	.146	.019	.312
3	−.317	.426	.309	−.160	.106	.377	.107	.132	.196	.250	−.075
4	−.028	.705	−.026	−.107	−.347	.200	−.196	.306	.152	.053	.010
5	−.110	.808	.083	−.081	−.029	.122	−.022	.093	.036	.036	.127
6	−.117	.746	.207	.221	.226	−.096	.133	−.058	−.126	−.079	−.173
7	.054	.064	−.013	−.029	.015	.210	.029	.054	.948	.074	.092
8	.101	.234	.058	.186	.136	.079	.091	.841	.041	.222	.018
9	.069	.029	−.252	−.192	−.000	.123	.046	.203	.014	.803	.125
10	.080	.003	−.415	−.231	.677	.237	.009	.184	.010	.079	.009
11	.166	.029	−.264	−.076	−.054	.142	−.069	.017	.085	.216	.811
12	.322	−.070	−.120	−.211	.001	.002	.814	.094	.037	.037	−.052
13	.275	−.069	−.819	−.072	.090	.014	.019	−.081	.076	.167	.124
14	.149	−.159	−.743	−.178	.162	.113	.135	−.058	.064	.160	.146
15	.848	−.120	−.243	−.047	−.001	.075	.177	−.037	−.007	.045	.033
16	.196	−.078	−.284	.049	.321	.115	.208	−.114	.109	.568	.455
17	.792	−.252	−.086	−.191	.055	−.017	−.004	.053	.017	.143	.144
18	.596	−.029	.015	−.371	.536	−.070	−.020	.064	.070	.129	−.055
19	.001	−.390	−.487	−.231	−.050	.195	.124	.121	−.018	.300	.224
20	.347	.043	−.177	−.649	.113	.016	.216	−.216	.067	.259	−.142
21	.327	.053	−.134	.014	.020	.326	−.331	.256	.084	.544	.103
22	.672	.046	−.224	−.231	.008	.024	.414	−.080	−.011	.010	.108
23	.222	.008	−.209	−.774	.142	.048	.112	−.070	−.015	−.003	.196

NOTE: Variable loadings are rounded to three decimal places.

TABLE B-15. THE ROTATED FACTOR MATRIX—MENNONITE RURAL POPULATION
(N = 237)

	I	II	III	IV	V	VI	VII	VIII	IX	X	XI
1	.084	.109	.124	.911	.002	.016	.087	.142	.068	.069	.019
2	.504	−.022	−.157	.346	.285	−.234	−.049	.393	−.099	−.141	−.249
3	−.143	.423	−.072	.478	−.023	.305	−.030	.050	.105	−.185	−.425
4	.003	.925	−.099	.094	.094	.018	.044	.071	−.048	.075	−.038
5	−.039	.939	−.094	.041	−.044	.091	.057	−.040	−.039	−.002	.076
6	−.098	.147	−.043	.033	.055	.935	.012	−.024	−.040	−.073	−.036
7	.218	.125	−.050	.084	.098	.013	.906	.118	.098	.065	−.034
8	−.195	.533	.125	.018	.027	.214	.338	.280	−.001	−.012	−.404
9	.191	.106	.177	.145	.117	.022	.123	.825	.142	.071	−.002
10	.147	−.012	.209	.053	.233	.009	.099	.237	.798	.044	.026
11	.474	.034	−.087	.034	.281	−.015	.003	.465	.148	.262	−.090
12	.017	−.068	.795	.082	.270	−.102	.042	.030	.062	−.112	−.041
13	.783	−.088	.210	.055	.204	−.057	.166	.114	.086	.114	.069
14	.805	−.073	.224	−.031	.127	.010	.094	.093	.187	.015	.163
15	.226	.014	.580	−.047	.184	−.012	−.008	.132	.116	.452	−.220
16	.585	−.128	.170	−.103	.185	−.094	.056	.111	.121	.320	−.385
17	.188	.064	.147	.032	.442	−.152	.046	.065	−.003	.720	.121
18	.167	−.093	.345	.015	.711	.032	−.011	.045	.174	.089	−.037
19	.394	−.123	.269	.238	.120	−.182	.041	−.095	.524	.042	−.298
20	.225	.115	.361	.030	.685	−.009	.137	.112	−.146	.103	−.118
21	.499	.093	−.043	.158	−.017	.017	.190	.419	.048	.438	−.234
22	.216	−.180	.719	.055	.038	.068	−.103	.088	.226	.181	.120
23	.162	−.034	−.028	−.012	.789	.015	.058	.114	.261	.165	.052

NOTE: Variable loadings are rounded to three decimal places.

TABLE B-16. THE ROTATED FACTOR MATRIX—MENNONITE URBAN POPULATION
(N = 38)

	I	II	III	IV	V	VI	VII	VIII	IX	X	XI
1	.066	.136	.086	.938	.031	.111	.035	.059	-.102	-.019	.009
2	.088	-.211	.358	.136	.086	.219	-.043	-.011	-.814	-.017	.019
3	-.061	.272	-.021	.022	.066	-.036	.883	.106	.036	-.155	.004
4	.077	.921	.102	.005	.023	.054	.093	.170	.137	-.044	-.121
5	.016	.925	.096	.132	.046	-.090	.157	.138	.060	.055	.094
6	-.158	.505	-.232	.074	.170	.055	.213	.650	-.003	-.223	.138
7	.083	.071	.171	.043	.929	-.100	.050	.073	-.006	-.073	.036
8	.118	.465	.191	.029	.112	.023	.042	.733	-.015	.214	-.172
9	.307	.107	.597	-.002	.417	.103	.170	.279	-.239	.107	-.193
10	.276	-.004	.745	-.066	-.066	.172	-.133	.421	.090	.002	.303
11	.340	-.041	.498	.051	.130	.233	.108	-.117	-.084	.332	.574
12	.858	-.016	.032	.251	.002	.199	.123	-.055	-.084	.144	.042
13	.056	-.082	.655	.243	.134	.294	-.197	-.228	-.125	.312	.300
14	.227	-.186	.395	.232	-.093	.666	.176	.129	.107	.284	-.098
15	.729	-.119	.391	-.097	.085	.171	-.345	-.007	-.122	-.009	.070
16	.278	.158	.792	.154	.193	.190	.045	-.102	-.071	.201	.043
17	.579	.208	.447	-.086	.330	.261	-.107	-.039	-.094	.175	.062
18	.660	.207	.311	.138	.197	-.058	.091	.246	.265	.182	-.076
19	.397	-.256	.663	.188	-.226	.018	.221	-.116	-.356	.060	.042
20	.288	-.013	.234	-.063	-.081	.066	-.189	.067	.023	.853	.081
21	.097	.196	.899	-.111	.131	.014	-.079	.085	-.184	.049	-.050
22	.618	.007	.298	-.349	-.065	.268	-.233	.055	-.197	.255	.169
23	.233	.082	.125	.044	-.030	.852	-.116	-.004	-.238	-.028	.116

NOTE: Variable loadings are rounded to three decimal places.

TABLE B-17. THE ROTATED FACTOR MATRIX—MIDWESTERN RURAL POPULATION
(N = 37)

	I	II	III	IV	V	VI	VII	VIII	IX	X	XI
1	.039	.245	.272	.269	-.104	.753	.157	-.056	.083	.106	.156
2	-.104	.161	.001	.150	.016	.892	.030	-.203	-.010	-.093	.079
3	-.059	.407	.149	-.048	-.001	.160	.799	-.190	.083	-.201	.078
4	-.156	.928	.025	.097	.071	.076	.106	-.039	.013	-.056	.091
5	.034	.857	.038	.038	-.076	.199	.110	-.062	.070	-.257	.085
6	.023	.459	.103	-.113	.023	.037	.169	-.045	-.092	-.826	.071
7	-.150	.291	.128	.424	-.293	.313	.162	.022	.238	-.298	.473
8	.042	.513	.243	.079	.065	.310	.047	-.135	-.093	-.063	.682
9	-.265	.048	.127	.553	-.244	.382	-.146	-.186	.404	-.204	.044
10	-.649	.109	.261	.260	-.145	.500	-.030	-.086	-.084	-.083	.122
11	-.334	.263	.063	.629	.067	.318	-.169	-.397	.091	.017	-.036
12	-.427	.130	.640	.247	.058	.048	.185	.184	-.224	-.310	.221
13	-.130	.073	.254	.860	-.078	.130	.038	-.242	-.170	-.005	.051
14	-.117	.089	.146	.914	-.111	.078	-.049	.056	-.105	.023	.053
15	-.195	.168	.352	.284	-.638	.328	.047	.094	-.180	-.163	-.079
16	-.668	.033	.099	.465	-.302	.007	.175	-.274	-.097	.141	-.123
17	-.091	-.084	.265	.175	-.867	-.054	-.046	-.269	-.132	.066	.033
18	-.021	-.007	.813	.171	-.160	.144	.202	-.009	-.093	.024	.036
19	-.009	-.201	.324	.682	-.237	.312	.101	.093	.230	.202	.138
20	-.193	.042	.844	.141	-.170	-.007	-.005	-.210	-.093	-.048	.053
21	-.136	.131	.156	.187	-.224	.267	.160	-.816	.067	-.043	.095
22	-.139	-.071	.272	.094	-.222	-.044	-.094	.029	-.878	-.107	.018
23	.174	.278	.683	.314	-.218	.213	-.331	-.112	.029	-.055	.014

NOTE: Variable loadings are rounded to three decimal places.

Study of Religious and Political Attitudes   [269]

TABLE B-18. THE ROTATED FACTOR MATRIX—MIDWESTERN URBAN POPULATION
(N = 140)

	I	II	III	IV	V	VI	VII	VIII	IX	X	XI
1	.162	.688	−.019	.042	−.178	.079	.086	.065	−.043	.471	−.070
2	.079	.274	.044	.040	.065	.138	.027	.009	.095	.866	.180
3	.028	.755	−.062	.035	−.176	.042	−.165	.213	.179	.191	.085
4	−.007	.859	.124	.083	.150	.028	.084	.127	.092	−.003	.094
5	−.097	.884	.068	.062	.077	−.027	.051	.068	.025	−.007	.139
6	−.107	.308	.129	−.032	−.110	−.058	−.011	.855	−.045	.050	.057
7	.196	.360	.020	.150	.104	.107	.059	.067	.035	.152	.780
8	−.108	.622	.073	−.064	.107	.181	.219	−.076	−.085	.113	.512
9	.085	.063	−.195	.328	.023	.742	.034	−.161	−.203	.112	.227
10	.148	−.133	.007	.577	.179	.054	.383	−.229	−.455	.157	−.008
11	.424	.107	.077	−.005	.140	.713	.171	.088	.124	.223	.011
12	−.012	−.107	−.846	−.051	.165	.058	.199	−.174	−.192	−.051	−.028
13	.758	−.053	.026	.194	.072	.187	.307	−.153	−.163	−.059	.053
14	.857	.059	−.039	.045	.248	.129	.077	−.054	−.019	.094	.047
15	.168	−.093	−.252	.072	.813	−.053	.116	−.097	−.249	.126	.076
16	.211	.035	.141	.049	.280	.531	.470	−.261	−.215	−.075	−.098
17	.205	.104	−.030	.023	.745	.310	.324	−.095	−.045	−.107	.079
18	.129	−.008	−.375	.179	.178	.024	.628	.163	−.372	.123	−.071
19	.365	−.239	−.057	−.070	.057	.312	.185	−.489	−.358	.216	.181
20	.101	.157	−.357	.294	.257	.067	.703	.034	−.081	−.036	.113
21	.202	.345	.015	.749	−.018	.258	.155	.095	.127	−.031	.147
22	.092	−.083	−.230	−.007	.204	.103	.179	.029	−.838	−.161	−.032
23	.405	.018	−.003	−.000	.088	.190	.696	−.150	−.084	.089	.155

NOTE: Variable loadings are rounded to three decimal places.

APPENDIX C

Analysis of Variance Summary Tables for the Study of Professors

TABLE C-1. THE ANALYSIS OF CHURCH ORIENTATION ATTITUDE DIFFERENCES AMONG COLLEGE PROFESSORS

Source of Variation	Sum of Squares	df	Mean Square	F Ratio
A	117.613	1	117.613	NS
B	412.535	1	412.535	9.56**
C	53.901	1	53.901	NS
D	1304.113	1	1304.113	30.23**
E	158.044	2	79.022	NS
AB	18.368	1	18.368	NS
AC	9.568	1	9.568	NS
AD	4.835	1	4.835	NS
AE	11.633	2	5.817	NS
BC	2.813	1	2.813	NS
BD	10.035	1	10.035	NS
BE	86.811	2	43.406	NS
CD	25.313	1	25.313	NS
CE	69.211	2	34.606	NS
DE	70.233	2	35.117	NS
ABC	0.168	1	0.168	NS
ABD	43.512	1	43.512	NS
ABE	139.244	2	69.622	NS
ACD	86.113	1	86.113	NS
ACE	57.144	2	28.572	NS
ADE	119.878	2	59.939	NS
BCD	3.901	1	3.901	NS
BCE	4.433	2	2.217	NS
BDE	366.744	2	183.372	4.25*
CDE	145.200	2	76.200	NS
ABCD	16.501	1	16.501	NS
ABCE	43.678	2	21.839	NS
ABDE	162.300	2	81.150	NS
ACDE	20.233	2	10.117	NS
BCDE	142.811	2	71.406	NS
ABCDE	160.311	2	80.156	NS
Residual	28426.267	659#	43.135	
Total	32293.464	719		

NOTE: A = Region; B = Type of College; C = Size of College Faculty; D = Rank of Professor; E = Discipline.
* P < .05
** P < .01
# 672 — 13 (correction)

TABLE C-2. THE ANALYSIS OF RITUALISM ATTITUDE DIFFERENCES AMONG
COLLEGE PROFESSORS

Source of Variation	Sum of Squares	df	Mean Square	F Ratio
A	14.168	1	14.168	NS
B	560.035	1	560.035	9.32**
C	13.068	1	13.068	NS
D	362.668	1	362.668	6.03*
E	3581.575	2	1790.788	29.79**
AB	109.668	1	109.668	NS
AC	26.068	1	26.068	NS
AD	127.512	1	127.512	NS
AE	92.803	2	46.401	NS
BC	.035	1	.035	NS
BD	15.901	1	15.901	NS
BE	69.919	2	34.960	NS
CD	8.668	1	8.668	NS
CE	439.653	2	219.826	3.66*
DE	101.219	2	50.610	NS
ABC	.501	1	.501	NS
ABD	117.613	1	117.613	NS
ABE	91.136	2	45.568	NS
ACD	27.613	1	27.613	NS
ACE	34.603	2	17.301	NS
ADE	21.258	2	10.629	NS
BCD	1.013	1	1.013	NS
BCE	87.553	2	43.776	NS
BDE	51.319	2	25.660	NS
CDE	74.519	2	37.260	NS
ABCD	47.535	1	47.535	NS
ABCE	16.469	2	8.235	NS
ABDE	80.058	2	40.029	NS
ACDE	25.258	2	12.629	NS
BCDE	107.508	2	53.754	NS
ABCDE	61.769	2	30.885	NS
Residual	39618.800	659#	60.120	
Total	45987.485	719		

NOTE: A = Region; B = Type of College; C = Size of College Faculty; D = Rank of Professor; E = Discipline.
  * P < .05
 ** P < .01
 # 672 — 13 (correction)

Source of Variation	Sum of Squares	df	Mean Square	F Ratio
A	67.835	1	67.835	NS
B	197.401	1	197.401	5.05*
C	30.013	1	30.013	NS
D	567.113	1	567.113	14.52**
E	414.603	2	207.301	5.31*
AB	.113	1	.113	NS
AC	.068	1	.068	NS
AD	14.735	1	14.735	NS
AE	5.169	2	2.585	NS
BC	1.013	1	1.013	NS
BD	28.401	1	28.401	NS
BE	93.803	2	46.901	NS
CD	4.835	1	4.835	NS
CE	.558	2	.279	NS
DE	204.925	2	102.463	NS
ABC	1.013	1	1.013	NS
ABD	3.613	1	3.613	NS
ABE	431.258	2	215.629	5.52*
ACD	105.035	1	105.035	NS
ACE	119.669	2	59.835	NS
ADE	40.536	2	20.268	NS
BCD	27.613	1	27.613	NS
BCE	.925	2	.463	NS
BDE	103.669	2	51.835	NS
CDE	61.969	2	30.985	NS
ABCD	31.668	1	31.668	NS
ABCE	53.725	2	26.863	NS
ABDE	66.658	2	33.329	NS
ACDE	57.769	2	28.885	NS
BCDE	126.058	2	63.029	NS
ABCDE	151.636	2	75.818	NS
Residual	25738.400	659#	39.057	
Total	28751.799	719		

NOTE: A = Region; B = Type of College; C = Size of College Faculty; D = Rank of Professor; E = Discipline.

* P < .05
** P < .01
# 672 — 13 (correction)

TABLE C-4. THE ANALYSIS OF FUNDAMENTALISTIC ATTITUDE DIFFERENCES AMONG
COLLEGE PROFESSORS

Source of Variation	Sum of Squares	df	Mean Square	F Ratio
A	189.113	1	189.113	NS
B	4094.568	1	4094.568	45.68**
C	1078.001	1	1078.001	12.03**
D	368.368	1	368.368	4.11*
E	3614.858	2	1807.429	20.17**
AB	144.901	1	144.901	NS
AC	93.168	1	93.168	NS
AD	.401	1	.401	NS
AE	5.025	2	2.513	NS
BC	43.512	1	43.512	NS
BD	6.235	1	6.235	NS
BE	28.419	2	14.210	NS
CD	3.901	1	3.901	NS
CE	68.969	2	34.485	NS
DE	314.636	2	157.318	NS
ABC	20.335	1	20.335	NS
ABD	37.813	1	37.813	NS
ABE	126.719	2	63.360	NS
ACD	64.201	1	64.201	NS
ACE	10.003	2	5.001	NS
ADE	214.669	2	107.335	NS
BCD	137.813	1	137.813	NS
BCE	138.775	2	69.388	NS
BDE	781.119	2	390.560	4.36*
CDE	25.203	2	12.601	NS
ABCD	167.235	1	167.235	NS
ABCE	259.719	2	129.860	NS
ABDE	298.908	2	149.454	NS
ACDE	137.303	2	68.651	NS
BCDE	65.108	2	32.554	NS
ABCDE	196.386	2	98.193	NS
Residual	59064.800	659#	89.628	
Total	71800.184	719		

NOTE: A = Region; B = Type of College; C = Size of College Faculty; D = Rank of Professor; E = Discipline.

* P < .05
** P < .01
# 672 − 13 (correction)

TABLE C-5. THE ANALYSIS OF THEISM ATTITUDE DIFFERENCES AMONG COLLEGE PROFESSORS

Source of Variation	Sum of Squares	df	Mean Square	F Ratio
A	435.556	1	435.556	NS
B	3735.556	1	3735.556	31.02**
C	1411.200	1	1411.200	11.72**
D	259.200	1	259.200	NS
E	4609.102	2	2304.551	19.13**
AB	810.689	1	810.689	6.73*
AC	41.089	1	41.089	NS
AD	13.889	1	13.889	NS
AE	68.469	2	34.235	NS
BC	28.800	1	28.800	NS
BD	.800	1	.800	NS
BE	121.586	2	69.793	NS
CD	53.356	1	53.356	NS
CE	155.475	2	77.738	NS
DE	768.025	2	384.013	3.19*
ABC	8.022	1	8.022	NS
ABD	8.022	1	8.022	NS
ABE	221.686	2	110.843	NS
ACD	91.022	1	91.022	NS
ACE	53.019	2	26.510	NS
ADE	250.936	2	125.468	NS
BCD	115.200	1	115.200	NS
BCE	293.258	2	146.629	NS
BDE	811.508	2	405.754	3.37*
CDE	118.686	2	59.343	NS
ABCD	226.689	1	226.689	NS
ABCE	155.603	2	77.801	NS
ABDE	882.553	2	441.276	3.66*
ACDE	252.419	2	126.210	NS
BCDE	178.758	2	89.379	NS
ABCDE	161.536	2	80.768	NS
Residual	79371.600	659#	120.442	
Total	95713.309	719		

NOTE: A = Region; B = Type of College; C = Size of College Faculty; D = Rank of Professor; E = Discipline.
* P < .05
** P < .01
# 672 — 13 (correction)

TABLE C-6. The Analysis of Idealism Attitude Differences Among College Professors

Source of Variation	Sum of Squares	df	Mean Square	F Ratio
A	3.472	1	3.472	NS
B	91.022	1	91.022	NS
C	.089	1	.089	NS
D	154.939	1	154.939	6.20*
E	134.653	2	67.326	NS
AB	5.000	1	5.000	NS
AC	.089	1	.089	NS
AD	4.672	1	4.672	NS
AE	61.553	2	30.776	NS
BC	70.939	1	70.939	NS
BD	83.689	1	82.689	NS
BE	60.169	2	30.085	NS
CD	80.000	1	80.000	NS
CE	15.069	2	7.535	NS
DE	22.919	2	11.460	NS
ABC	.050	1	.050	NS
ABD	77.356	1	77.356	NS
ABE	12.058	2	6.029	NS
ACD	57.800	1	57.800	NS
ACE	24.536	2	12.268	NS
ADE	119.253	2	59.626	NS
BCD	38.272	1	38.272	NS
BCE	6.286	2	3.143	NS
BDE	33.303	2	16.651	NS
CDE	50.925	2	25.462	NS
ABCD	22.050	1	22.050	NS
ABCE	74.408	2	37.204	NS
ABDE	61.803	2	30.901	NS
ACDE	3.558	2	1.779	NS
BCDE	28.253	2	14.126	NS
ABCDE	28.808	2	14.404	NS
Residual	16472.400	659#	24.996	
Total	17899.394	719		

NOTE: A = Region; B = Type of College; C = Size of College Faculty; D = Rank of Professor; E = Discipline.

* P < .05

672 — 13 (correction)

Source of Variation	Sum of Squares	df	Mean Square	F Ratio
A	211.250	1	211.250	7.93**
B	601.339	1	601.339	22.59**
C	28.800	1	28.800	NS
D	.672	1	.672	NS
E	1814.186	2	907.093	34.07**
AB	101.250	1	101.250	NS
AC	.800	1	.800	NS
AD	12.272	1	12.272	NS
AE	19.658	2	9.829	NS
BC	.022	1	.022	NS
BD	14.450	1	14.450	NS
BE	21.536	2	10.768	NS
CD	3.200	1	3.200	NS
CE	11.608	2	5.804	NS
DE	365.753	2	182.876	6.87**
ABC	2.222	1	2.222	NS
ABD	19.339	1	19.339	NS
ABE	45.175	2	22.588	NS
ACD	53.356	1	53.356	NS
ACE	123.325	2	61.663	NS
ADE	2.836	2	1.418	NS
BCD	2.689	1	2.689	NS
BCE	59.303	2	29.651	NS
BDE	174.358	2	87.179	3.27*
CDE	37.508	2	18.754	NS
ABCD	18.689	1	18.689	NS
ABCE	26.719	2	13.360	NS
ABDE	227.919	2	113.960	4.28*
ACDE	89.036	2	44.518	NS
BCDE	57.103	2	28.551	NS
ABCDE	14.019	2	7.010	NS
Residual	17546.267	659#	26.626	
Total	21716.659	719		

NOTE: A = Region; B = Type of College; C = Size of College Faculty; D = Rank of Professor; E = Discipline.
* P < .05
** P < .01
# 672 — 13 (correction)

TABLE C-8. THE ANALYSIS OF MYSTICISM ATTITUDE DIFFERENCES AMONG
COLLEGE PROFESSORS

Source of Variation	Sum of Squares	df	Mean Square	F Ratio
A	102.756	1	102.756	NS
B	105.800	1	105.800	NS
C	54.450	1	54.450	NS
D	341.689	1	341.689	8.90**
E	2828.219	2	1414.110	36.83**
AB	140.450	1	140.450	NS
AC	64.800	1	64.800	NS
AD	6.806	1	6.806	NS
AE	92.019	2	46.010	NS
BC	16.200	1	16.200	NS
BD	.450	1	.450	NS
BE	62.775	2	31.388	NS
CD	2.689	1	2.689	NS
CE	95.208	2	47.604	NS
DE	103.419	2	51.710	NS
ABC	8.450	1	8.450	NS
ABD	25.689	1	25.689	NS
ABE	114.008	2	57.004	NS
ACD	2.939	1	2.939	NS
ACE	167.608	2	83.804	NS
ADE	61.053	2	30.526	NS
BCD	28.006	1	28.006	NS
BCE	90.508	2	45.254	NS
BDE	161.275	2	80.638	NS
CDE	18.586	2	9.293	NS
ABCD	2.689	1	2.689	NS
ABCE	175.608	2	87.804	NS
ABDE	385.053	2	192.526	5.01**
ACDE	52.619	2	26.310	NS
BCDE	18.453	2	9.226	NS
ABCDE	51.053	2	25.526	NS
Residual	25304.667	659#	38.399	**
Total	30685.994	719		

NOTE: A = Region; B = Type of College; C = Size of College Faculty; D = Rank of Professor; E = Discipline.

* P < .05
** P < .01
# 672 — 13 (correction)

Table C-9. Summary of Findings of College Professor Study

Source of Variation	Church Orientation	Ritualism	Altruism	Fundamentalism	Theism	Idealism	Superstition	Mysticism
A							**	
B	**	**	*	**	**		**	
C				**	**			
D	**	*	**	*		*		**
E		**	*	**	**		**	**
AB					**			
AC								
AD								
AE								
BC								
BD								
BE								
CD								
CE		*						
DE					*		*	
ABC								
ABD								
ABE			*					
ACD								
ACE								
ADE								
BCD								
BCE								
BDE	*			*	*		*	
CDE								
ABCD								
ABCE								
ABDE					*		*	*
ACDE								
BCDE								
ABCDE								

Note: A = Region; B = Type of College; C = Size of College Faculty; D = Rank of Professor; E = Discipline.
* Significant at .05 level.
** Significant at .01 level.

APPENDIX D

Analysis of Variance Summary Tables for the Two Studies of Socioeconomic Status and Religious Attitudes

TABLE D-1. THE ANALYSIS OF RELIGIOUS ATTITUDE DIFFERENCES AMONG THE SOCIAL CLASSES
(as measured by Warner's ISC)

Source of Variation	Sum of Squares	df	Mean Square	F Ratio
	Church Orientation			
Between groups	271.49	4	67.87	1.78
Within groups	4003.38	105	38.13	
Total	4274.87	109		
	Ritualism			
Between groups	1043.97	4	260.99	4.93**
Within groups	5555.13	105	52.91	
Total	6599.10	109		
	Altruism			
Between groups	153.00	4	38.25	1.555
Within groups	2582.45	105	24.59	
Total	2735.45	109		
	Fundamentalism			
Between groups	294.99	4	73.75	2.29
Within groups	3378.73	105	32.18	
Total	3673.72	109		
	Theism			
Between groups	77.19	4	19.30	.596
Within groups	3400.27	105	32.38	
Total	3477.46	109		
	Idealism			
Between groups	56.37	4	11.27	.357
Within groups	3280.68	105	31.55	
Total	3337.05	109		
	Superstition			
Between groups	315.84	4	78.96	3.998**
Within groups	2073.76	105	19.75	
Total	2389.60	109		
	Mysticism			
Between groups	458.17	4	114.54	4.59**
Within groups	2620.09	105	24.95	
Total	3078.26	109		

** P < .01

TABLE D-2. THE ANALYSIS OF RELIGIOUS ATTITUDE DIFFERENCES AMONG OCCUPATION GROUPS

Source of Variation	Sum of Squares	df	Mean Square	F Ratio
Church Orientation				
Between groups	223.28	6	37.21	1.216
Within groups	3150.94	103	30.59	
Total	3374.22	109		
Ritualism				
Between groups	1071.62	6	178.60	3.61**
Within groups	5089.73	103	49.41	
Total	6161.35	109		
Altruism				
Between groups	291.08	6	48.51	2.044
Within groups	2444.37	103	23.73	
Total	2735.45	109		
Fundamentalism				
Between groups	354.30	6	59.05	1.83
Within groups	3319.42	103	32.23	
Total	3673.72	109		
Theism				
Between groups	142.96	6	23.83	.736
Within groups	3334.50	103	32.37	
Total	3477.46	109		
Idealism				
Between groups	65.76	6	10.96	.497
Within groups	2271.29	103	22.05	
Total	2337.05	109		
Superstition				
Between groups	430.69	6	71.78	3.74**
Within groups	1974.30	103	19.17	
Total	2404.99	109		
Mysticism				
Between groups	754.20	6	125.70	5.559**
Within groups	2328.89	103	22.61	
Total	3083.09	109		

** $P < .01$

TABLE D-3. THE ANALYSIS OF RELIGIOUS ATTITUDE DIFFERENCES AMONG DWELLING AREAS

Source of Variation	Sum of Squares	df	Mean Square	F Ratio
	Church Orientation			
Between groups	342.21	5	68.44	.544
Within groups	13093.34	104	125.90	
Total	13435.55	109		
	Ritualism			
Between groups	895.37	5	179.07	3.537**
Within groups	5265.98	104	50.63	
Total	6161.35	109		
	Altruism			
Between groups	287.44	5	57.49	2.44*
Within groups	2448.01	104	23.54	
Total	2735.45	109		
	Fundamentalism			
Between groups	452.61	5	90.52	2.92*
Within groups	3221.11	104	30.97	
Total	3673.72	109		
	Theism			
Between groups	75.85	5	15.17	.464
Within groups	3401.61	104	32.71	
Total	3477.46	109		
	Idealism			
Between groups	184.74	5	36.95	1.79
Within groups	2152.31	104	20.70	
Total	2337.05	109		
	Superstition			
Between groups	249.09	5	49.82	2.42*
Within groups	2140.51	104	20.58	
Total	2389.60	109		
	Mysticism			
Between groups	363.26	5	72.65	2.78*
Within groups	2715.00	104	26.11	
Total	3078.26	109		

* P < .05
** P < .01

TABLE D-4. THE ANALYSIS OF RELIGIOUS ATTITUDE DIFFERENCES AMONG HOUSE TYPE GROUPS

Source of Variation	Sum of Squares	df	Mean Square	F Ratio
	Church Orientation			
Between groups	368.55	5	73.71	2.55*
Within groups	3005.67	104	28.90	
Total	3374.22	109		
	Ritualism			
Between groups	935.12	5	187.02	3.72**
Within groups	5226.88	104	50.26	
Total	6162.00	109		
	Altruism			
Between groups	320.82	5	64.16	2.76*
Within groups	2414.63	104	23.22	
Total	2735.45	109		
	Fundamentalism			
Between groups	306.73	5	61.35	1.895
Within groups	3366.99	104	32.37	
Total	3673.72	109		
	Theism			
Between groups	122.41	5	24.48	.759
Within groups	3355.05	104	32.26	
Total	3477.46	109		
	Idealism			
Between groups	81.14	5	16.23	.748
Within groups	2255.91	104	21.69	
Total	2337.05	109		
	Superstition			
Between groups	244.62	5	48.92	2.37*
Within groups	2144.98	104	20.62	
Total	2389.60	109		
	Mysticism			
Between groups	474.44	5	94.89	3.79**
Within groups	2603.82	104	25.03	
Total	3078.26	109		

* $P < .05$
** $P < .01$

Source of Variation	Sum of Squares	df	Mean Square	F Ratio
	Church Orientation			
Between groups	201.54	6	33.59	1.10
Within groups	3144.32	103	30.53	
Total	3345.86	109		
	Ritualism			
Between groups	885.03	6	147.51	2.88*
Within groups	5276.32	103	51.23	
Total	6161.35	109		
	Altruism			
Between groups	95.50	6	15.92	.621
Within groups	2639.95	103	25.63	
Total	2735.45	109		
	Fundamentalism			
Between groups	291.00	6	48.50	1.48
Within groups	3382.72	103	32.84	
Total	3673.72	109		
	Theism			
Between groups	68.98	6	11.50	.348
Within groups	3408.48	103	33.09	
Total	3477.46	109		
	Idealism			
Between groups	18.81	6	3.14	.139
Within groups	2318.24	103	22.51	
Total	2337.05	109		
	Superstition			
Between groups	401.68	6	66.95	3.469**
Within groups	1987.92	103	19.30	
Total	2389.60	109		
	Mysticism			
Between groups	429.56	6	71.59	2.78*
Within groups	2648.70	103	25.72	
Total	3078.26	109		

* $P < .05$
** $P < .01$

TABLE D-6. THE ANALYSIS OF CHURCH ORIENTATION ATTITUDE DIFFERENCES

Source	Sum of Squares	Degrees of Freedom	Mean Squared	F Ratio
Denomination	29.678	2	14.839	.43
Involvement	384.271	1	384.271	11.21**
Class	530.678	2	265.339	7.74**
Denomination-class	143.855	4	35.964	1.05
Denomination-involvement	356.146	2	178.073	5.20**
Class-involvement	122.879	2	61.439	1.79
Denomination-involvement-class	223.454	4	55.864	1.63
Within groups	5553.102	162	34.278	
Total	7344.063			

* P < .05
** P < .01

TABLE D-7. THE ANALYSIS OF RITUALISTIC ATTITUDE DIFFERENCES

Source	Sum of Squares	Degrees of Freedom	Mean Squared	F Ratio
Denomination	2814.812	2	1407.406	21.78**
Involvement	712.022	1	712.022	11.02**
Class	625.878	2	312.939	4.84**
Denomination-class	327.988	4	81.997	1.27
Denomination-involvement	364.011	2	182.006	2.82
Class-involvement	175.544	2	87.772	1.36
Denomination-involvement-class	215.523	4	53.881	.83
Within groups	10468.200	162	64.619	
Total	15703.978			

** P < .01

TABLE D-8. THE ANALYSIS OF ALTRUISTIC ATTITUDE DIFFERENCES

Source	Sum of Squares	Degrees of Freedom	Mean Squared	F Ratio
Denomination	21.377	2	10.689	.34
Involvement	672.801	1	672.801	21.46**
Class	203.078	2	101.539	3.24*
Denomination-class	14.355	4	3.589	.11
Denomination-involvement	38.801	2	19.401	.62
Class-involvement	75.432	2	37.716	1.20
Denomination-involvement-class	62.466	4	15.614	.50
Within groups	5078.602	162	31.349	
Total	6166.912			

* P < .05
** P < .01

TABLE D-9. THE ANALYSIS OF FUNDAMENTALISTIC ATTITUDE DIFFERENCES

Source	Sum of Squares	Degrees of Freedom	Mean Squared	F Ratio
Denomination	551.633	2	275.817	6.85**
Involvement	1301.421	1	1301.421	32.32**
Class	1064.099	2	532.049	13.21**
Denomination-class	143.967	4	35.992	.89
Denomination-involvement	9.078	2	4.539	.11
Class-involvement	98.078	2	49.039	1.22
Denomination-involvement-class	111.724	4	27.931	.69
Within groups	6522.801	162	40.264	
Total	9802.801			

** P < .01

TABLE D-10. THE ANALYSIS OF THEISTIC ATTITUDE DIFFERENCES

Source	Sum of Squares	Degrees of Freedom	Mean Squared	F Ratio
Denomination	1040.178	2	520.089	10.54**
Involvement	1400.021	1	1400.021	28.36**
Class	946.678	2	473.339	9.59**
Denomination-class	264.189	4	66.047	1.34
Denomination-involvement	62.047	2	31.024	.63
Class-involvement	66.879	2	33.439	.68
Denomination-involvement-class	97.854	4	24.464	.50
Within groups	7996.400	162	49.360	
Total	11874.246			

** P < .01

TABLE D-11. THE ANALYSIS OF IDEALISTIC ATTITUDE DIFFERENCES

Source	Sum of Squares	Degrees of Freedom	Mean Squared	F Ratio
Denomination	98.209	2	49.105	1.33
Involvement	604.998	1	604.998	16.43*
Class	202.178	2	101.089	2.75
Denomination-class	32.357	4	8.089	.22
Denomination-involvement	50.637	2	25.319	.69
Class-involvement	61.734	2	30.867	.84
Denomination-involvement-class	127.532	4	31.883	.87
Within groups	5965.000	162	36.821	
Total	7142.645			

** P < .01

TABLE D-12. THE ANALYSIS OF SUPERSTITIOUS ATTITUDE DIFFERENCES

Source	Sum of Squares	Degrees of Freedom	Mean Squared	F Ratio
Denomination	35.677	2	17.839	.79
Involvement	128.355	1	128.355	5.69*
Class	673.410	2	336.705	4.92**
Denomination-class	74.891	4	18.723	.83
Denomination-involvement	313.079	2	156.539	6.94**
Class-involvement	173.479	2	86.470	3.84*
Denomination-involvement-class	103.087	4	25.772	1.14
Within groups	3655.601	162	22.565	
Total	5157.578			

* P < .05
** P < .01

TABLE D-13. THE ANALYSIS OF MYSTICAL ATTITUDE DIFFERENCES

Source	Sum of Squares	Degrees of Freedom	Mean Squared	F Ratio
Denomination	137.076	2	68.538	2.31
Involvement	70.938	1	70.938	2.40
Class	993.377	2	496.689	16.76**
Denomination-class	307.758	4	76.190	2.57*
Denomination-involvement	132.746	2	66.373	2.24
Class-involvement	77.646	2	38.823	1.31
Denomination-involvement-class	53.619	4	13.405	.45
Within groups	4801.701	162	29.640	
Total	6574.861			

* P < .05
** P < .01

Socioeconomic Status and Religious Attitudes [287]

TABLE D-14. MEAN RELIGIOSITY SCORES OF CHURCH MEMBERS BY DENOMINATION, LEVEL OF ACTIVITY, AND SOCIAL CLASS

	Church Orientation	Ritualism	Altruism	Fundamentalism	Theism	Idealism	Superstition	Mysticism
Baptist								
Active members								
Upper-middle class	25.9	17.9	33.8	39.3	39.7	32.7	20.9	30.7
Lower-middle class	32.2	18.4	34.2	39.7	41.1	32.0	24.1	31.0
Lower class	31.7	18.9	37.1	42.7	44.6	35.4	23.4	34.6
Inactive members								
Upper-middle class	30.7	23.3	30.1	33.1	32.6	28.6	24.4	31.6
Lower-middle class	27.4	12.1	28.7	33.4	35.4	27.8	26.9	31.1
Lower class	34.5	19.0	31.9	38.6	37.6	29.2	31.3	36.8
Catholic								
Active members								
Upper-middle class	32.7	29.9	32.9	35.3	38.8	31.8	25.0	30.7
Lower-middle class	29.9	29.4	33.7	38.0	41.8	32.5	23.0	29.9
Lower class	36.9	35.7	35.7	38.9	42.8	36.6	28.1	38.3
Inactive members								
Upper-middle class	25.6	21.6	31.6	28.0	31.2	30.4	21.1	26.2
Lower-middle class	25.9	21.9	30.8	34.1	41.6	32.8	22.8	27.6
Lower class	30.9	27.2	32.1	35.8	38.8	30.9	27.1	36.0
Methodist								
Active members								
Upper-middle class	30.3	23.6	32.8	31.7	35.0	30.4	24.1	32.7
Lower-middle class	32.2	21.1	34.8	39.3	35.8	33.7	20.2	30.0
Lower class	32.0	22.9	34.7	38.5	39.8	34.5	24.9	31.5
Inactive members								
Upper-middle class	28.2	21.0	30.8	27.1	28.0	29.1	21.5	27.2
Lower-middle class	25.3	15.1	26.7	29.2	28.7	26.8	24.9	29.7
Lower class	29.0	20.8	32.2	35.7	35.3	31.0	28.9	31.9

APPENDIX E

1. **Questionnaire used in Study of Arrogation-Derogation and Religiosity**
2. **Example of Arrogated Summary**
3. **Example of Derogated Summary**

1. QUESTIONNAIRE USED IN STUDY OF ARROGATION-DEROGATION AND RELIGIOSITY

THIS IS AN ANONYMOUS QUESTIONNAIRE—DO NOT SIGN YOUR NAME

Directions: Select 5 or 6 of your fellow students *in this class* (their names can be found on distributed sheet) and rate each of them in turn on the rating forms below and on the next pages. Do not rate yourself (if you do so your protocol will be invalidated).

Name of the student being rated_____

1. This student appears to be wasting the professor's time in this class.
   __Obviously; __Probably; __Can't Say; __Apparently Not; __Definitely Not
2. This person seems to be an interested student and an able contributor to the class.
   __Most Certainly; __Apparently; __Can't Say; __Probably Not; __Definitely Not
3. I find that this person contributes little of any value to this class.
   __Very True; __Apparently; __Can't Say; __False; __Definitely False
4. I would like to have another class with this person.
   __Certainly; __Perhaps; __I Don't Care; __Prefer Not To; __Definitely Not
5. This person is apparently interested in an education and in things intellectual.
   __Definitely True; __Probably; __Can't Say; __Probably Not; __Definitely Not
6. This person's interests are in something other than education and worthwhile pursuits.
   __Most True; __Apparently True; __Can't Say; __Apparently False; __False
7. This person either has (a) no ideas, or (b) no ideas of value.
   __Sad but True; __Probably True; __Can't Say; __Apparently False; __False
8. Check the appropriate responses:
   __I would like to know this person better.
   __I know this person and like him or her.
   __I like this student very much.
   __I don't know much about this student.
   __What I know about this student makes me dislike him or her.
   __I'm inclined to dislike this person.
   __I dislike this person intensely.
   __I hate this person's guts.
9. I find this person:
   __most charming
   __pleasant
   __tolerable
   __innocuous
   __unpleasant

—distasteful

—intolerable

10. I welcome this person's association and presence.

—Definitely Not; —Preferably Not; —Can't Say; —True; —Definitely True

THESE ARE PRIVATE RATINGS—KEEP THEM THAT WAY

2. ARROGATED SUMMARY
A Summary of Your Fellow Students' Appraisal of You

(John Jones), you were rated or appraised by (9) of your fellow students. Following is a summary of their opinions or ratings of you. You can, by inspecting the responses below, see how these students rated you, or what they think of you. Each mark is a fellow student who made that particular comment in regard to you. THUS, IN RESPONSE TO THESE STATEMENTS *REGARDING YOU* YOUR FELLOW STUDENTS MADE THESE COMMENTS.

1. This student (YOU) appears to be wasting the professor's time in this class.
   Of the 9 of your fellow students who rated you on this statement,

   0 said YOU "Obviously WERE."

   0 said YOU "Probably WERE."

   0 couldn't or wouldn't say.

   2 said YOU "Apparently were NOT."

   7 said YOU "Definitely Were NOT."

2. This person (YOU) seems to be an interested student and an able contributor to the class.
   Of the 9 of your fellow students who rated you on this statement,

   6 said YOU "Most Certainly WERE."

   3 said YOU "Apparently WERE."

   0 couldn't or wouldn't say.

   0 said YOU "Probably Were NOT."

   0 said YOU "Definitely Were NOT."

3. I find that this person (YOU) contributes little of any value to this class.
   Of the 9 of your fellow students who rated you on this statement,

   0 said of YOU that "This was Very TRUE."

   0 said of YOU that "This was Apparently TRUE."

   0 couldn't or wouldn't say.

   4 said of YOU that "This was FALSE."

   5 said of YOU that "This was Definitely FALSE."

4. I would like to have another class with this person (YOU).
   Of the 9 of your fellow students who rated you on this statement,

   9 said of YOU that "They Certainly WOULD."

   0 said of YOU that "They Perhaps WOULD."

   0 didn't care.

   0 said of YOU that "They Preferred NOT TO."

   0 said of YOU that "They Definitely DID NOT WANT TO."

5. This person (YOU) is apparently interested in an education and in things intellectual.
   Of the 9 of your fellow students who rated you on this statement,

   8 said that this is "Definitely TRUE OF YOU."

   1 said that this is "probably TRUE OF YOU."

   0 couldn't or wouldn't say.

   0 said that this is "Probably NOT TRUE OF YOU."

   0 said that this is "Definitely NOT TRUE OF YOU."

6. This person's interests (YOURS) are in something other than education and worthwhile pursuits.
   Of the 9 of your fellow students who rated you on this statement,

0 said that "This was MOST TRUE OF YOU."
0 said that "This Was APPARENTLY TRUE OF YOU."
0 couldn't or wouldn't say.
1 said that "This was APPARENTLY NOT TRUE OF YOU."
8 said that "This was NOT TRUE OF YOU."

7. This person (YOU) has (a) no ideas, or (b) no ideas of value.
   Of the 9 of your fellow students who rated you on this statement,
   0 said that "This was Sad but TRUE OF YOU."
   0 said that "This was APPARENTLY TRUE OF YOU."
   0 couldn't or wouldn't say.
   4 said that "This was Apparently NOT TRUE OF YOU."
   5 said that "This was NOT TRUE OF YOU."

8. Of the 9 of your fellow students who rated you on this statement,
   2 checked "I would like to know this person (YOU) better."
   4 checked "I know this person (YOU) and like him or her."
   3 checked "I like this student (YOU) very much."
   0 checked "I don't know much about this student (YOU)."
   0 checked "What I know about this student (YOU) makes me dislike him or her (YOU)."
   0 checked "I'm inclined to dislike this person (YOU)."
   0 checked "I dislike this person (YOU) intensely."
   0 checked "I hate this person's (YOUR) guts."

9. Of the 9 of your fellow students who rated you on this statement,
   4 checked "I find this person (YOU) most charming."
   5 checked "I find this person (YOU) pleasant."
   0 checked "I find this person (YOU) tolerable."
   0 checked "I find this person (YOU) innocuous."
   0 checked "I find this person (YOU) unpleasant."
   0 checked "I find this person (YOU) distasteful."
   0 checked "I find this person (YOU) intolerable."

10. I welcome this person's association and presence (YOURS).
    Of the 9 of your fellow students who rated you on this statement,
    0 said "Definitely NOT."
    0 said "Preferably NOT."
    0 couldn't or wouldn't say.
    6 said "TRUE."
    3 said "Definitely TRUE."

THESE ARE PRIVATE RATINGS—KEEP THEM THAT WAY

3. DEROGATED SUMMARY
A SUMMARY OF YOUR FELLOW STUDENTS' APPRAISAL OF YOU

(Mary Smith), you were rated or appraised by (9) of your fellow students. Following is a summary of their opinions or ratings of you. You can, by inspecting the responses below, see how these students rated you, or what they think of you. Each mark is a fellow student who made that particular comment in regard to you. THUS, IN RESPONSE TO THESE STATEMENTS *REGARDING YOU* YOUR FELLOW STUDENTS MADE THESE COMMENTS.

1. This student (YOU) appears to be wasting the professor's time in this class.
   Of the 9 of your fellow students who rated you on this statement,
   1 said YOU "Obviously WERE."
   5 said YOU "Probably WERE."
   3 couldn't or wouldn't say.
   0 said YOU "Apparently Were NOT."
   0 said YOU "Definitely Were NOT."

2. This person (YOU) seems to be an interested student and an able contributor to the class.
Of the 9 of your fellow students who rated you on this statement,
0 said YOU "Most Certainly WERE."
0 said YOU "Apparently WERE."
1 couldn't or wouldn't say.
6 said YOU "Probably Were NOT."
2 said YOU "Definitely Were NOT."

3. I find that this person (YOU) contributes little of any value to this class.
Of the 9 of your fellow students who rated you on this statement,
8 said of YOU that "This Was Very TRUE."
1 said of YOU that "This was Apparently TRUE."
0 couldn't or wouldn't say.
0 said of YOU that "This Was FALSE."
0 said of YOU that "This was Definitely FALSE."

4. I would like to have another class with this person (YOU).
Of the 9 of your fellow students who rated you on this statement,
0 said of YOU that "They Certainly WOULD."
0 said of YOU that "They Perhaps WOULD."
1 didn't care
5 said of YOU that "They Preferred NOT TO."
3 said of YOU that "They Definitely DID NOT WANT TO."

5. This person (YOU) is apparently interested in an education and in things intellectual.
Of the 9 of your fellow students who rated you on this statement,
0 said that this is "Definitely TRUE OF YOU."
0 said that this is "Probably TRUE OF YOU."
2 couldn't or wouldn't say.
7 said that this is "Probably NOT TRUE OF YOU."
0 said that this is "Definitely NOT TRUE OF YOU."

6. This person's interests (YOURS) are in something other than education and worthwhile pursuits.
Of the 9 of your fellow students who rated you on this statement,
2 said that "This Was MOST TRUE OF YOU."
5 said that "This Was Apparently TRUE OF YOU."
2 couldn't or wouldn't say.
0 said that "This Was Apparently NOT TRUE OF YOU."
0 said that "This Was NOT TRUE OF YOU."

7. This person (YOU) has (a) no ideas, or (b) no ideas of value.
Of the 9 of your fellow students who rated you on this statement,
3 said that "This was Sad but TRUE OF YOU."
6 said that "This Was Apparently TRUE OF YOU."
0 couldn't or wouldn't say.
0 said that "This was Apparently NOT TRUE OF YOU."
0 said that "This was NOT TRUE OF YOU."

8. Of the 9 of your fellow students who rated you on this statement,
0 checked "I would like to know this person (YOU) better."
0 checked "I know this person (YOU) and like him or her."
0 checked "I like this student (YOU) very much."
1 checked "I don't know much about this student (YOU)."
5 checked "What I know about this student (YOU) makes me dislike him or her (YOU)."
3 checked "I'm inclined to dislike this person (YOU)."
0 checked "I dislike this person (YOU) intensely."
0 checked "I hate this person's (YOUR) guts."

9. Of the 9 of your fellow students who rated you on this statement,
    0 checked "I find this person (YOU) most charming."
    0 checked "I find this person (YOU) pleasant."
    3 checked "I find this person (YOU) tolerable."
    1 checked "I find this person (YOU) innocuous."
    3 checked "I find this person (YOU) unpleasant."
    2 checked "I find this person (YOU) distasteful."
    0 checked "I find this person (YOU) intolerable."
10. I welcome this person's association and presence (YOURS).
    Of the 9 of your fellow students who rated you on this statement,
    2 said "Definitely NOT."
    5 said "Preferably NOT."
    2 couldn't or wouldn't say.
    0 said "TRUE."
    0 said "Definitely TRUE."

THESE ARE PRIVATE RATINGS—KEEP THEM THAT WAY

Correlation Matrices of
Religious Attitude Scales in
Three Adult Populations

TABLE F-1. MATRIX OF INTERCORRELATIONS OF THE EIGHT RELIGIOUS ATTITUDE SCALES IN THE CLERGYMAN POPULATION

	Church Orientation	Ritual-ism	Altru-ism	Funda-mentalism	Theism	Idealism	Supersti-tion	Mysticism
Church orientation		.32	.54	.42	.41	.38	.35	.47
Ritualism			.17	.12	.18	.14	.22	.24
Altruism				.31	.30	.55	.24	.51
Fundamentalism					.90	.13	.52	.43
Theism						.13	.51	.46
Idealism							.09	.38
Superstition								.44
Mysticism								

TABLE F-2. MATRIX OF INTERCORRELATIONS OF THE EIGHT RELIGIOUS ATTITUDE SCALES IN THE PROFESSOR POPULATION

	Church Orientation	Ritual-ism	Altru-ism	Funda-mentalism	Theism	Idealism	Supersti-tion	Mysticism
Church orientation		.44	.67	.61	.56	.31	.40	.52
Ritualism			.30	.32	.32	.07	.34	.36
Altruism				.59	.58	.52	.40	.60
Fundamentalism					.89	.34	.56	.64
Theism						.34	.58	.67
Idealism							.17	.37
Superstition								.56
Mysticism								

TABLE F-3. MATRIX OF INTERCORRELATIONS OF THE EIGHT RELIGIOUS ATTITUDE SCALES IN THE METHODIST POPULATION

	Church Orientation	Ritual-ism	Altru-ism	Funda-mentalism	Theism	Idealism	Supersti-tion	Mysticism
Church orientation		.49	.58	.36	.37	.27	.24	.56
Ritualism			.18	.09	.03	-.05	.24	.17
Altruism				.61	.62	.49	.26	.65
Fundamentalism					.84	.29	.23	.50
Theism						.35	.23	.58
Idealism							.02	.36
Superstition								.41
Mysticism								

BIBLIOGRAPHY

Adinarayan, S. P., and Rajamanickam, M. 1962. A study of student attitudes toward religion, the spiritual and the supernatural. *Journal of Social Psychology* 57:105–11.

Adorno, T. W. et al. 1950. *The Authoritarian Personality.* New York: Harper.

Allen, Edmund E., and Hites, Robert W. 1961. Factors in religious attitudes of older adolescents. *Journal of Social Psychology* 55:265–73.

Allinsmith, Wesley, and Allinsmith, Beverly. 1948. Religious affiliation and politico-economic attitude: a study of eight major religious groups. *Public Opinion Quarterly* 12:377–89.

Allport, G. W.; Gillespie, J. M.; and Young, J. 1948. The religion of the post-war college student. *Journal of Psychology* 25:3–33.

Allport, G. W., and Vernon, P. E. 1931. A test for personal values. *Journal of Abnormal and Social Psychology* 26:231–48.

Anastasi, A. 1954. *Psychological testing.* New York: Macmillan.

Anders, Sarah. 1955. Religious behavior of church families. *Marriage and Family Living* 17:54–57.

Anderson, C. H. 1968. Religious communality among academics. *Journal for the Scientific Study of Religion* 7:87–96.

Argyle, M. 1958. *Religious behavior.* London: Routledge & Kegan Paul.

Arsenian, Seth. 1943. Change in evaluative attitudes during four years of college. *Journal of Applied Psychology* 27:338–49.

Asch, S. E. 1952. Effect of group pressure upon the modification and distortion of judgments. In *Readings in social psychology,* ed. G. E. Swanson, T. M. Newcomb, and E. L. Hartley. New York: Holt, Rinehart & Winston.

Bahr, H. A.; Bartel, L. F.; and Chadwick, B. A. 1971. Orthodoxy, activism, and the salience of religion. *Journal for the Scientific Study of Religion* 10:185–91.

Bain, Read. 1927. Religious attitudes of college students. *American Journal of Sociology* 32:762–70.

Barron, F. 1953. An ego-strength scale which predicts response to psychotherapy. *Journal of Consulting Psychology* 17:327–33.

Bell, Wendell. 1957. Anomie, social isolation, and the class structure. *Sociometry,* 20:105–16.

Berelson, B., and Steiner, G. A. 1964. Religious institutions. In *Human be-*

havior: an inventory of scientific findings, pp. 384–86. New York: Harcourt, Brace & World.

Blum, Barbara S., and Mann, John H. 1960. The effect of religious membership on religious prejudice. *Journal of Social Psychology* 52:97–101.

Bock, D. C., and Warner, N. C. 1972. Religious belief as a factor in obedience to destructive commands. *Review of Religious Research* 13:185–91.

Bohrnstedt, George W.; Borgatta, E. F.; and Evans, Robert R. 1968. Religious affiliation, religiosity and MMPI scores. *Journal for the Scientific Study of Religion* 7:255–58.

Boisen, A. T. 1955. *Religion in crisis and custom.* New York: Harper.

Brewer, E. D. 1962. Religion and the churches. In *The southern Appalachian region: a survey,* ed. Thomas R. Ford. Lexington: University of Kentucky Press.

Broen, William E., Jr. 1955. Personality correlates of certain religious attitudes. *Journal of Consulting Psychology* 19:64.

———. 1957. A factor-analytic study of religious attitudes. *Journal of Abnormal and Social Psychology* 54:176–79.

Brown, D. G., and Lowe, W. L. 1951. Religious beliefs and personality characteristics of college students. *Journal of Social Psychology* 33:103–29.

Brown, D. R., and Bystryn, D. 1956. College environment, personality, and social ideology of three ethnic groups. *Journal of Social Psychology* 44:279–88.

Brown, L. B. 1962. A study of religious belief. *British Journal of Psychology* 53:259–72.

Buegel, H. F. 1960. Comparison of SCAT scores of high school juniors in parochial and public schools. *Psychological Reports* 7:497–98.

Bultena, Louis. 1949. Church membership and church attendance in Madison, Wisconsin. *American Sociological Review* 14:384–89.

Burchinal, Lee G. 1959. Some social status criteria and church membership and church attendance. *Journal of Social Psychology* 49:53–64.

Burtt, H. E., and Falkenberg, D. R. 1941. The influence of majority and expert opinion on religious attitudes. *Journal of Social Psychology* 14:269–78.

Carney, Richard E., and McKeachie, Wilbert J. 1963. Religion, sex, social class, probability of success, and student personality. *Journal for the Scientific Study of Religion* 3:32–42.

Centers, R. 1949. *The psychology of social classes.* Princeton: Princeton University Press.

Chilton, Roland J. 1969. A review and comparison of simple statistical tests for scalogram analysis. *American Sociological Review* 34:238–45.

Christie, Richard, and Geis, F. L. 1970. *Studies in Machiavellianism.* New York: Academic.

Clayton, Richard R. 1971. 5-D or 1. *Journal for the Scientific Study of Religion* 10:37–40.

Cohn, Werner. 1962. Is religion universal? Problems of definition. *Journal for the Scientific Study of Religion* 2:25–33.

Cronbach, L. J. 1960. *Essentials of psychological testing*. 2nd ed. New York: Harper & Row.

Dahlstrom, W. Grant, and Welsh, G. S. 1960. *An MMPI handbook*. Minneapolis: University of Minnesota Press.

Dean, Dwight G. 1961. Alienation: its meaning and measurement. *American Sociological Review* 26:753–58.

————. 1968. Anomie, powerlessness, and religious participation. *Journal for the Scientific Study of Religion* 7:252–54.

Dean, Dwight G., and Reeves, Jon A. 1962. Anomie: a comparison of a Catholic and a Protestant sample. *Sociometry* 25:209–12.

Demerath, N. J., III. 1965. *Social class in American Protestantism*. Chicago: Rand McNally.

Demerath, N. J., III, and Hammond, Phillip E. 1969. *Religion in social context: tradition and transition*. New York: Random House.

Dreger, R. M. 1952. Some personality correlates of religious attitudes as determined by projective techniques. *Psychological Monographs* 66: No. 3 (whole No. 335).

Dudycha, George. 1933. The religious beliefs of college students. *Journal of Applied Psychology* 17:585–603.

Dynes, Russell R. 1954a. Church-sect typology: an empirical study. Ph.D. dissertation, Ohio State University.

————. 1954b. Toward the sociology of religion. *Sociology and Social Research* 38:227–32.

————. 1955. Church-sect typology and socio-economic status. *American Sociological Review* 20:555–60.

Edwards, Allen L. 1957a. *The social desirability variable in personality assessment and research*. New York: Dryden Press.

————. 1957b. *Techniques of attitude scale construction*. New York: Appleton-Century-Crofts.

Eitzen, D. Stanley, and Maranell, Gary M. 1968. The political party affiliation of college professors. *Social Forces* 47:145–53.

Elkind, David, and Elkind, Sally. 1962. Varieties of religious experience in young adolescents. *Journal for the Scientific Study of Religion* 2:102–12.

Eysenck, H. J. 1947. *Dimensions of personality*. London: Routledge & Kegan Paul.

————. 1954. *Psychology of politics*. London: Routledge & Kegan Paul.

Faulkner, J. E., and DeJong, G. F. 1966. Religiosity in 5-D: an empirical analysis. *Social Forces* 45:246–54.

Ferguson, Leonard W. 1944. Socio-psychological correlates of the primary attitude scales: I. religionism; II. humanitarianism. *Journal of Social Psychology* 19:81–98.

Fichter, Joseph. 1954. *Social relations in the urban parish*. Chicago: University of Chicago Press.

Finner, Stephen L. 1970. Religious membership and religious preference: equal indicators of religiosity? *Journal for the Scientific Study of Religion* 9:273–79.

Ford, Thomas R. 1960. Status, residence and fundamentalist religious beliefs in the southern Appalachians. *Social Forces* 39:41–48.

Fordyce, W. E. 1956. Social desirability in the MMPI. *Journal of Consulting Psychology* 20:171–75.

Francesco, E. 1962. A pervasive value: conventional religiosity. *Journal of Social Psychology* 57:467–70.

Frenkel-Brunswick, Else. 1949. Intolerance of ambiguity as an emotional and perceptual personality variable. *Journal of Personality* 18:108–43.

Funk, R. A. 1956. Religious attitudes and manifest anxiety in a college population. *American Psychologist* 2:375.

Gaustad, Edwin S. 1962. *Historical atlas of religion in America.* New York: Harper & Row.

Gilliland, A. R. 1940. The attitude of college students toward God and the church. *Journal of Social Psychology* 11:11–18.

————. 1953. Changes in religious beliefs of college students. *Journal of Social Psychology* 37:113–16.

Gillin, John. 1955. National and regional cultural values in the United States. *Social Forces* 34:107–13.

Gladstone, Roy, and Gupta, G. C. 1963. A cross-cultural study of the behavioral aspects of the concept of religion. *Journal of Social Psychology* 60:203–13.

Glock, Charles Y. 1959a. Differential commitment of religion: some sources and consequences. Paper presented at the American Sociological Association annual meeting in Chicago, Ill., Sept. 3–5, 1959.

————. 1959b. The religious revival in America. In *Religion and the face of America: Papers of the Conference . . . Nov. 28, 29, and 30, 1958,* ed. Jane Zahn. Berkeley: University of California Extension.

————. 1962. On the study of religious commitment. Research supplement, *Religious Education,* July-August, pp. 98–110.

Glock, Charles Y., and Stark, Rodney. 1965. *Religion and society in tension.* Chicago: Rand McNally.

————. 1966. *Christian beliefs and anti-Semitism.* New York: Harper & Row.

Goldman-Eisler, F. 1953. Breastfeeding and character formation. In C. Kluckholm, et al., *Personality in nature, society and culture,* pp. 146–84. New York: Knopf.

Goldschmidt, Walter R. 1944. Class denominationalism in rural California churches. *American Journal of Sociology* 49:348–55.

Gordon, Milton M. 1963. *Social class in American sociology.* New York: McGraw-Hill.

Gorer, Geoffrey. 1955. *Exploring English character.* New York: Criterion Books.

Gorsuch, R. L., and McFarland, S. G. 1972. Single vs. multiple-item scales for measuring religious values. *Journal for the Scientific Study of Religion* 11:53–64.

Gragg, Donald B. 1942. Religious attitudes of denominational college students. *Journal of Social Psychology* 15:245–54.

Gray, David B. 1970. Measuring attitudes toward the church. *Journal for the Scientific Study of Religion* 9:293–97.

Hadden, Jeffrey K. 1963. An analysis of some factors associated with religion and political affiliation in a college population. *Journal for the Scientific Study of Religion* 2:209–16.

Haimes, Peter, and Hetherington, Mavis. 1964. Attitudes of the clergy toward behavior problems of children. *Journal of Social Psychology* 62:329–34.

Hanawalt, Nelson G. 1963. Feelings of security and of self-esteem in relation to religious beliefs. *Journal of Social Psychology* 59:347–53.

Harmon, Harry H. 1967. *Modern factor analysis.* 2nd ed. Chicago: University of Chicago Press.

Havens, Joseph. 1963. The changing climate of research on the college student and his religion. *Journal for the Scientific Study of Religion* 3:52–69.

Hoffman, M. L. 1953. Some psychodynamic factors in compulsive conformity. *Journal of Abnormal and Social Psychology* 48:383–93.

Horst, Paul. 1965. *Factor analysis of data matrices.* New York: Holt, Rinehart & Winston.

Hoult, Thomas Ford. 1958. *The sociology of religion.* New York: Holt-Dryden.

Hovland, C. I.; James, I. L.; and Kelly, H. H. 1953. *Communication and persuasion.* New Haven: Yale University Press.

Howells, T. H. 1928. A comparative study of those who accept as against those who reject religious authority. *University of Iowa Studies in Character,* vol. 2, no. 2.

Hunt, R. A., and King, Morton. 1971. The intrinsic-extrinsic concept: a review and evaluation. *Journal for the Scientific Study of Religion* 10:399–56.

Iisager, Holger. 1949. Factors influencing the formation and change of political and religious attitudes. *Journal of Social Psychology* 29:253–65.

James, William. 1902. *The varieties of religious experience.* New York: Modern Library.

Johnson, Benton. 1962. Ascetic Protestantism and political preference. *Public Opinion Quarterly* 16:35–46.

———. 1964. Ascetic Protestantism and political preference in the deep South. *American Journal of Sociology* 69:359–66.

———. 1966. Theology and party preference among Protestant clergymen. *American Sociological Review* 31:200–208.

———. 1967. Theology and the position of pastors on public issues. *American Sociological Review* 32:433–42.

Katz, D., and Allport, F. H. 1931. *Students' attitudes.* Syracuse, N.Y.: Craftsman Press.

Keedy, T. C., Jr. 1958. Anomie and religious orthodoxy. *Sociology and Social Research* 43:34–37.

Kemp, C. Gratton. 1964. Self-perception in relation to open-closed belief systems. *Journal of General Psychology* 70:341–44.

Key, V. O., Jr. 1949. *Southern politics in state and nation.* New York: Knopf.

Kimber, J. A. Morris. 1947. Interests and personality traits of Bible institute students. *Journal of Social Psychology* 26:225–33.

King, Morton. 1967. Measuring the religious variable. *Journal for the Scientific Study of Religion* 6:173–85.

King, Morton, and Hunt, Richard A. 1969. Measuring the religious variable: amended findings. *Journal for the Scientific Study of Religion* 8:321–23.

Kirkpatrick, C. 1949. Religion and humanitarianism: a study of institutional implications. *Psychological Monographs* 43:1–23.

Klausner, Samuel Z. 1961. Images of man: an empirical enquiry. *Journal for the Scientific Study of Religion* 1:61–73.

Kluckhohn, C., et al. 1953. *Personality in nature, society, and culture.* New York: Knopf.

Kolb, William L. 1953. Values, positivism and the functional theory of religion: the growth of a moral dilemma. *Social Forces* 31:305–11.

Kosa, John, and Schommer, Cyril O., S.J. 1961. Religious participation, religious knowledge, and scholastic aptitude: an empirical study. *Journal for the Scientific Study of Religion* 1:88–97.

Lawson. E. D., and Stagner, R. 1954. The Ferguson religionism scale: a study of validation. *Journal of Social Psychology* 39:245–56.

Lazerwitz, Bernard. 1961. A comparison of major United States religious groups. *Journal of the American Statistical Association* 56:568–79.

————. 1962. Membership in voluntary associations and frequency of church attendance. *Journal for the Scientific Study of Religion* 2:74–84.

————. 1964. Religion and social structure in the United States. In *Religion, culture and society,* ed. Louis Schneider. New York: Wiley.

Lenski, Gerhard. 1953. Social correlates of religious interest. *American Sociological Review* 18:533–44.

Lesser, G. S. 1959. Religion and the defense responses in children's fantasy. *Journal of Projective Techniques* 23:64–68.

Leuba, James H. 1916. *The belief in God and immortality, a psychological, anthropological, and statistical study.* Boston: Sherman, French.

————. 1934. Religious beliefs of American scientists. *Harper's* 169:291–300.

————. 1950. *The reformation of the churches.* Boston: Beacon Press.

Likert, R. 1932. A technique for the measurement of attitudes. *Archives of Psychology,* no. 140.

Lindenthal, J. J.; Myers, J. K.; Pepper, M. P.; and Stern, M. S. 1970. Mental status and religious behavior. *Journal for the Scientific Study of Religion* 9:143–49.

Lindquist, E. F. 1953. *Design and analysis of experiments in psychology and education.* Boston: Houghton.

Liu, William T. 1961. The community reference system, religiosity, and race attitudes. *Social Forces* 39:324–28.

London, Perry; Schulman, B. E.; and Black, M. S. 1964. Religion, guilt, and ethical standards. *Journal of Social Psychology* 63:145–61.

Lowe, Warner. 1954. Group beliefs and socio-cultural factors in religious delusions. *Journal of Social Psychology* 40:267–74.

McKenna, Sister Helen Veronica, S.S.J. 1961. Religious attitudes and personality traits. *Journal of Social Psychology* 54:379–88.

McKinney, John C. 1954. Constructive typology and social research. In J. T. Doby et al., eds. *An introduction to social research.* Harrisburg, Pa.: Stackpole.

————. 1966. *Constructive typology and social theory.* New York: Appleton-Century-Crofts.

Maranell, Gary M. 1962. The dimensions of religiosity: studies of religious attitudes. *Proceedings of the Southwestern Sociological Society* 11:122–30.

————. 1967. An examination of some religious and political attitude correlates of bigotry. *Social Forces* 45:356–62.

————. 1968a. Regional patterns of fundamentalistic attitude configurations. *Kansas Journal of Sociology* 4:159–74.

————. 1968b. A factor analytic study of some selected religious attitudes. *Sociology and Social Research* 52:430–37.

————. 1974. *Scaling: a source book for behavioral scientists.* Chicago: Aldine.

Maranell, Gary M., and Eitzen, D. Stanley. 1970. The effect of discipline, region, and rank on the political attitudes of college professors. *Sociological Quarterly* 11:112–18.

Maranell, Gary M., and Razak, W. Nevell. 1970. A comparative study of the factor structure among professors and clergymen. *Journal for the Scientific Study of Religion* 9:137–41.

Martin, Carol, and Nichols, Robert C. 1962. Personality and religious belief. *Journal of Social Psychology* 56:3–8.

Meier, Dorothy L., and Bell, Wendell. 1959. Anomia and differential access to the achievement of life goals. *American Sociological Review* 24:189–202.

Menzel, Herbert. 1953. A new coefficient for scalogram analysis. *Public Opinion Quarterly* 17:268–80.

Moberg, David O. 1956. Religious activities and personal adjustment in old age. *Journal of Social Psychology* 43:261–67.

Mull, Helen K. 1947. A comparison of religious thinking of freshmen and seniors in a liberal arts college. *Journal of Social Psychology* 26:121–23.

Myers, Goerge C. 1962. Patterns of church distribution and movement. *Social Forces* 40:354–63.

Navran, L. A. 1954. A rationally derived MMPI scale to measure dependence. *Journal of Consulting Psychology* 18:192.

Nettler, G. 1957. A measure of alienation. *American Sociological Review* 22:670–77.

Newcomb, T. M., and Svehla, G. 1937. Intra-family relationships in attitude. *Sociometry* 1:180–205.

Obenhaus, Victor, and Schroeder, W. 1963. Church affiliation and attitudes toward selected public questions in a typical midwest county *Rural Sociology* 28:35–47.

O'Reilly, C. T. 1958. Religious practice and personal adjustment of older people. *Sociology and Social Research* 42:119–21.

Ostow, Mortimer. 1958. The nature of religious controls. *American Psychologist* 13:571–74.

Pope, Liston. 1948. Religion and the class structure. *The Annals of the American Academy of Political and Social Science* 256:84–91.

Putney, S., and Middleton, R. 1961a. Dimensions and correlates of religious ideologies. *Social Forces* 39:285–90.

———. 1961b. Rebellion, conformity, and parental religious ideologies. *Sociometry* 24:125–35.

———. 1962. Religion, normative standards, and behavior. *Sociometry* 25:141–52.

Ringer, B. B., and Glock, Charles Y. 1954–55. The political role of the church as defined by its parishioners. *Public Opinion Quarterly* 18:337–47.

Roberts, A. H., and Rokeach, M. 1956. Anomie, authoritarianism, and prejudice: a replication. *American Journal of Sociology* 61:355–58.

Robinson, John P.; Rusk, J. G.; and Head, K. B. 1968. *Measures of political attitudes*. Ann Arbor, Mich.: Institute for Social Research.

Rokeach, M. 1960. *The open and closed mind*. New York: Basic Books.

———. 1969. H. Paul Douglas lectures for 1969: Part I, Value systems in religion. *Review of Religious Research* 11:3–39.

Ross, M. G. 1950. *Religious beliefs of youth*. New York: Association Press.

Rossiter, C. 1962. *Conservatism in America*. 2nd ed. New York: Knopf & Random House.

Rosten, Leo. 1955. *A guide to the religions of America*. New York: Simon & Schuster.

Ruesch, J., et al. 1948. *Duodenal ulcer: a socio-psychological study of naval personnel and civilians*. Berkeley: University of California Press.

Rummel, R. J. 1970. *Applied factor analysis*. Evanston, Ill.: Northwestern University Press.

Salisbury, W. Seward. 1962. Religiosity, regional sub-culture, and social behavior. *Journal for the Scientific Study of Religion* 2:94–112.

Sappenfield, Bert R. 1942. The attitudes and attitude estimates of Catholic, Protestant, and Jewish students. *Journal of Social Psychology* 16:173–97.

Schneider, Louis, ed. 1964. *Religion, culture and society*. New York: Wiley.

Schuessler, Karl F. 1961. A note on statistical significance of scalogram. *Sociometry* 24:312–18.

Seeman, Melvin. 1959. On the meaning of alienation. *American Sociological Review* 24:783–91.

Selltiz, C., et al. 1959. *Research methods in social relations.* New York: Holt, Rinehart & Winston.

Sherif, M. 1952. Group influence upon the formation of norms and attitudes. In G. E. Swanson, T. M. Newcomb, and E. L. Hartley, *Readings in social psychology.* New York: Holt, Rinehart & Winston.

Shils, E. A. 1954. Authoritarianism: "right" and "left." In *Studies in the scope and method of the authoritarian personality,* ed. R. Christie and M. Jahoda. Glencoe, Ill.: Free Press.

Siegel, S. 1956. *Non-parametric statistics: for the behavorial sciences.* New York: McGraw-Hill.

Siegman, Aron Wolfe. 1961. An empirical investigation of the psychoanalytic theory of religious behavior. *Journal for the Scientific Study of Religion* 1:74–78.

Sinclair, R. D. 1928. A comparative study of those who report the experience of the Divine Presence and those who do not. *University of Iowa Studies in Character,* vol. 2, no. 3.

Solomon, Philip, et al., eds. 1961. *Sensory deprivation.* Cambridge, Mass.: Harvard University Press.

Spoerl, D. T. 1951. Some aspects of prejudice as affected by religion and education. *Journal of Social Psychology* 33:69–76.

————. 1952. The values of the post-war college student. *Journal of Social Psychology* 35:217–25.

Srole, L. 1956. Social integration and certain corollaries: an exploratory study. *American Sociological Review* 21:709–16.

Stark, Rodney. 1963. On the incompatibility of religion and science: a survey of American graduate students. *Journal for the Scientific Study of Religion* 3:3–20.

————. 1971. Psychopathology and religious commitment. *Review of Religious Research* 12:165–76.

Stouffer, S. A., et al. 1950. *Measurement and prediction.* Princeton: Princeton University Press.

Swanson, G. E.; Newcomb, T. M.; and Hartley, E. L., eds. 1952. *Readings in social psychology.* Rev. ed. New York: Holt, Rinehart & Winston.

Sward, Keith. 1931. Temperament and religious experience. *Journal of Social Psychology* 2:374–96.

Swindell, D. H., and L'Abate, L. 1970. Religiosity, dogmatism, and repression-sensitization. *Journal for the Scientific Study of Religion* 9:249–51.

Symington, T. A. 1935. *Religious liberals and conservatives.* New York: Teachers College, Columbia University.

Taylor, Janet A. 1953. A personality scale of manifest anxiety. *Journal of Abnormal and Social Psychology* 48:285–90.

Telford, C. W. 1950. A study of religious attitudes. *Journal of Social Psychology* 31:217–30.

Terman, L. M., and Miles, C. C. 1936. *Sex and personality.* New York: McGraw-Hill.

Thurstone, L. L. 1947. *Multiple-factor analysis.* Chicago: University of Chicago Press.

Thurstone, L. L., and Chave, E. J. 1929. *The measurement of attitude.* Chicago: University of Chicago Press.

Tuttle, Harold S. 1942. Religion as motivation. *Journal of Social Psychology* 15:255–64.

Vernon, Glenn. 1955. An inquiry into the scalability of church orthodoxy. *Sociology and Social Research* 39:324–27.

————. 1962. *Sociology of religion.* New York: McGraw-Hill.

Warn, L. J. 1958. A comparative investigation of dependency in epilepsy, paraplegia, and tuberculosis. Ph.D. dissertation, University of California at Los Angeles.

Warner, W. L., et al. 1949. *Social class in America.* New York: Harper.

Welford, A. T. 1947. Is religious behavior dependent upon affect or frustration? *Journal of Abnormal and Social Psychology* 42:310–19.

Welsh, G. S. 1952. A measurement of general maladjustment on the MMPI. Paper presented at the San Francisco Bay Area Clinical Psychological Association Meeting, February, 1952.

West, James. 1945. *Plainville U.S.A.* New York: Columbia University Press.

Williams, J. Paul. 1962. The nature of religion. *Journal for the Scientific Study of Religion* 2:3–14.

Williamson, Rene de Visme. 1962. Conservatism and liberalism in American Protestantism. *Annals of American Academy of Political and Social Science* 344:76–84.

Wilson, W. Cody. 1960. Extrinsic religious values and prejudice. *Journal of Abnormal and Social Psychology* 60:286–88.

Wilson, Warner, and Kawamura, W. 1967. Rigidity, adjustment and social responsibility as possible correlates of religiousness: a test of three points of view. *Journal for the Scientific Study of Religion* 6:279–80.

Wilson, Warner, and Miller, H. L. 1968. Fear, anxiety and religiousness. *Journal for the Scientific Study of Religion* 7: 111.

Winter, Gibson. 1962. Methodological reflection on "The religious factor." *Journal for the Scientific Study of Religion* 2:53–63.

Yinger. J. Milton. 1958. Areas for research in the sociology of religion. *Sociology and Social Research* 42:466–72.

————. 1957. *Religion, society and the individual.* New York: Macmillan.

Zimmerman, Franklin K. 1934. Religion: a conservative social force. *Journal of Abnormal and Social Psychology* 28:473–74.

INDEX

accretion-mobility, 127, 129–31, 133–34, 136, 137, 139–40, 147

A.C.E. *See* American Council of Education Psychological Examination for College Freshmen

adequacy of item sampling, 29

Adinarayan, S. P., 295

adjustment, personality. *See* personality adjustment

Adorno, T. W., 22, 85, 90, 295

Adventist, Seventh-Day. *See* Seventh-Day Adventist

age: altruism and, 52; church orientation and, 50; factor, 128, 130–31, 133, 137, 139, 143, 147, 151; fundamentalism and, 56; idealism and, 59; mysticism and, 63; superstition and, 62; theism and, 59; total religiosity and, 48

Alabama, 41, 124

alienation, 9, 167, 228–32

Allen, E. E., 5, 295

Allinsmith, B., 295

Allinsmith, W., 295

Allport, F. H., 299

Allport, G. W., 233, 295

Allport-Vernon scale of values, 5

Almquist, Elizabeth, 169

altruism: adjustment and, 215–21; alienation and, 230, 232; arrogation and, 186–87; definition, 10, 16; denominational differences of clergymen in, 51–53; derogation and, 186–87; factor analysis, 115, 240–41; in-

volvement, religious, and, 172–73; items, 16–17; other religion scales and, 224–27; perceptual rigidity and, 198; personality adjustment and, 215–21; political attitudes and, 98–106; professors, 138–42; relations between dimensions, 26–28; rigidity, perceptual, and 198; scholastic aptitude and, 206–10; sex and, 234–35; socioeconomic status and, 161, 165–68, 172–73; suggestibility and, 193; summary of findings, 246–47; *t* values, 16–17

ambivalence regarding religion, 4

ambivalence, religious, 222

American Council of Education Psychological Examination for College Freshmen, 8, 205

analysis of variance, 45–66; 73, 125–26, 129–57, 159–78

anarchistic attitudes, 77, 88–89, 98–108

Anastasi, A., 29, 295

Anderson, C. H., 123, 295

Anders, Sarah, 295

anti-black attitudes, 77, 89–90, 98–108

anti-Semitic attitudes, 77, 90, 98–108

anxiety, manifest, 211, 213, 216, 218, 219

Argyle, M., 75, 203, 233, 295

Arkansas, 41, 124

arrogation, social, 179–90, 201–2

Arsenian, S., 295

Asch, S., 180, 191–93, 295

attitude crystallization, 71

authoritarian attitudes, 77, 85, 98–108, 200–1
autokinetic effect, 192

Bahr, H. A., 295
Bain, Read, 295
Baptist, 34, 35, 43, 46, 51, 53, 56, 62, 66, 67, 73, 74, 163, 169, 171–75, 178
Barron, F., 213, 295
Bartel, L. F., 295
Beisecker, Analee, 191
Bell, W., 229, 295, 301
Berelson, B., 295
Bible, 10, 17, 32
bigotry factor, 117–18
bigotry, issues of, 76–77
Black, M. S., 301
Blum, B. S., 296
Bock, D. C., 296
Bohrnstedt, G., 211, 296
Boisen, A. T., 15, 296
Borgatta, E., 211, 296
Brewer, E. D., 5, 296
Broen, W. E., Jr., 211, 296
Brown, D. G., 191, 194, 224, 296
Brown, D. R., 296
Brown, L. B., 5, 296
Buegel, H. F., 296
Bultena, L., 296
Burchinal, L. G., 296
Burns, Analee. See Beisecker
Burtt, H. E., 296
business, attitudes toward, 77, 83, 98–108
Bystryn, B., 296

California, 41, 42
Carney, R. E., 296
Catholics, 13, 34, 35, 42, 46, 48, 51, 53, 56, 59, 62, 66, 71, 73–75, 93, 94, 99–101, 110–113, 118, 162, 163, 169, 171, 173–78, 204, 229
Centers, Richard, 75, 296
Chadwick, B. A., 295
Chave, E. J., 5, 15, 17, 222, 304
Chicago, 42

Chilton, R. J., 97, 296
chi-square, 185–90, 196–201
Christian church, 13
Christianity, 16; general factor, 109–12
Christie, Richard, 21, 88, 296
church activity. See involvement, religious
Church of Christ, 43–46, 51, 53, 56, 59, 67, 68, 74, 163
church orientation: adjustment and, 215–21; alienation and, 230; arrogation and, 185; definition, 10, 13–14; denominational differences of clergymen in, 48–50; derogation and, 185; factor analysis, 113, 239–41; involvement, religious, and, 170–71; items, 14–15; other religion scales and, 224–27; perceptual rigidity and, 197; personality adjustment and, 215–21; political attitudes and, 98–106; professors', 129–36; relations between dimensions, 26–28; rigidity, perceptual, and, 197; scholastic aptitude and, 206–10; sex and, 234–35; socioeconomic status and, 161, 166, 168, 170–71; suggestibility and, 193; summary of findings, 243–44; t values 14–15
civil liberties attitudes, 77, 87, 94, 95, 98–108
Clayton, R. R., 296
clergymen, 39–74
cluster analysis of denominations, 66–73
cluster analysis of political dimensions, 94–96
coefficient of concordance, 107
Cohn, W., 296
college type. See type of college
conceptual analysis, 6, 76
Connecticut, 41
conservatism, 98, 102, 103, 106–9
conservative-orthodox cluster, 67–69, 74
consistency, scale, 30–31
construct validity, 33

and, 193; summary of findings, 252–53; *t* values, 23

nationalism, 76–77
Navran, L. A., 213, 301
Nebraska, 41, 124
Nettler, G., 228, 302
Newcomb, T. M., 233, 295, 302
New England states, 41, 48, 49, 55, 56, 58, 59, 64, 74, 244
New Hampshire, 41
New York, 124
Nichols, R. C., 301
Nielson, George, 194
noetic quality, 22
normlessness, 9, 228, 229
North Carolina, 41, 124
North Dakota, 41, 124

Obenhaus, V., 5, 302
occupation, 160, 161, 164
Ohio, 42, 124
Oklahoma, 42
Oregon, 41
O'Reilly, C. T., 302
orthodoxy, religious, 4, 8, 222–27
Ostow, M., 302

Pacific Coast states, 41, 42, 48, 53, 58, 59, 244
passivity, 23
patriotism: attitudes of, 77, 84–85, 98–108, 200–1; factor, 117
Pennsylvania, 124
Pepper, M. P., 300
perceptual rigidity. *See* rigidity, perceptual
personality adjustment, 211–21
political conservatism, 75–122
Pope, L., 302
powerlessness, 9, 228–29
prejudice. *See* anti-black attitudes; anti-Semitic attitudes
Presbyterian, 42, 43, 46, 48, 51, 53, 56, 59, 62, 70, 74, 163
private colleges and universities. *See* type of college

professors, rank of. *See* rank of professors
promotion selection, 127, 129–31, 147
Protestants, 75
Putney, S., 4, 5, 8, 222, 223, 224, 227, 302

Rajamanickam, M., 295
rank of professors, 125, 129, 131, 136–38, 143, 145, 148–53, 155, 157
Razak, W. N., 301
Reeves, J. A., 228–29, 297
region, 124, 140, 142, 148, 149, 151, 153, 155, 157. *See also* midwestern states; New England states; Pacific Coast states; southern states
relations between dimensions, 26–28
reliability, 29–32
religion: definition of, 3–5; dimensions of, 5; importance of, *see* importance of religion
religious ambivalence. *See* ambivalence, religious
religious fanaticism. *See* fanaticism, religious
religious involvement. *See* involvement, religious
religious orthodoxy. *See* orthodoxy, religious
reproducibility, coefficient of, 97–106
response set, 24
responses to threat, 76–77
restoration, attitudes involving, 76, 80–81, 98–108
Rhode Island, 41
Ricardo, David, 83
rigidity, perceptual, 179, 194–202
Ringer, B. B., 75, 302
ritualism: adjustment and, 215–21; alienation and, 230; arrogation and, 185–86; definition, 10, 15; denominational differences of clergymen in, 51; derogation, 185–86; factor analysis, 239, 241; involvement, religious, and, 171–72; items, 15–16; other re-

ligion scales and, 224–27; perceptual rigidity and, 197–98; personality adjustment and, 215–21; political attitudes and, 98–106; professors, 136–38; relations between dimensions, 26–28; rigidity, perceptual and, 197–98; scholastic aptitude and, 206–10; sex and, 234–35; socioeconomic status and, 161, 162, 164–68, 171–72; suggestibility and, 193–94; summary of findings, 245–46; *t* values, 15–16

Roberts, A. H., 228, 302
Robinson, John P., 24, 29, 78, 302
Rokeach, M., 211, 228, 302
Rossiter, Clinton, 76, 105, 302
Ross, M. G., 233, 302
Rosten, Leo, 45, 302
Ruesch, J., 213, 302
Ruhe, Christopher, 91
Rummel, R. J., 237, 302
rural-urban continuum, 40, 92–93, 96–105, 107, 109–22, 169
Rusk, J. G., 302

Salisbury, W. S., 5, 302
sampling, item, 29
Sappenfield, B. R., 302
scalability, coefficient of, 97–106
scale consistency, 30–31
scale of alienation. *See* alienation
Schneider, L., 302
scholastic aptitude, 203–10
Schommer, C. O., 203–4, 300
School and College Ability Test, 205
Schroeder, W., 5, 302
Schuessler, K. F., 97, 302
Schulman, B. E., 301
scorer reliability, 29
Seeman, M., 228–30, 303
selection factors. *See* initial selection factor; accretion-mobility; promotion selection
self-estrangement, 228
Selltiz, M., 29, 303
Seventh-Day Adventist, 43, 46, 51, 53, 56, 59, 62, 66, 67, 74

sex, 233–35
Sherif, M., 180, 191, 303
shift factors. *See* discipline shift; milieu shift
Shils, E. A., 85, 303
Siegel, S., 303
Siegman, A. W., 303
Simmons, G., 77
Sinclair, R. D., 191, 303
size of college, 125, 143, 147, 155, 157
Smith, Adam, 83
social arrogation. *See* arrogation, social
social class, 159–78
social derogation. *See* derogation, social
social desirability, 8, 214, 216, 218, 219
social isolation. *See* alienation
socialization factor, 128–31, 133–34, 136, 137, 139, 140, 143, 147, 149
socioeconomic status. *See* social class
Solomon, P., 180, 303
source of income, 160
South Carolina, 41, 124
South Dakota, 41, 124
southern states, 41, 48, 53, 56, 58, 59, 66, 73, 93, 98–99, 102–3, 110, 114, 117, 118, 121, 124, 140, 142, 148–51, 155, 159–69, 205–8, 215–16, 219–21, 224–27, 234, 244
Spearman rank correlation, 31
Spoerl, D. T., 233, 303
Srole, L., 228–30, 303
stability. *See* reliability
Stagner, R., 300
standard scores, 66
Stark, R., 3, 4, 6, 123, 158, 211, 212, 215, 298, 303
state colleges and universities. *See* type of college
states' rights, attitudes concerning, 76, 79–80, 98–108
states' rights–restorationism factor, 121
Steiner, G. A., 295
Stern, M. S., 300
Stouffer, S. A., 303